I0729656

WE ATE THE ACID
JOE ROBERTS

First published in the United States of America
in 2018 by Anthology Editions, LLC
87 Guernsey Street
Brooklyn, NY 11222

anthologyeditions.com
Copyright © 2018 by Anthology Editions, LLC

Editors: Mark Iosifescu and Jesse Pollock

Design: Bryan Cipolla
Design Assistant: Alexandra Tults
Images courtesy of Joe Roberts

Additional images courtesy of: BBQLA,
Ben Chasny, Roger Gastman, Fred Guerrero,
Guerrero Gallery, GX1000, Chris Hafner,
Forest Haiss, Jack Hanley Gallery, Marlborough
Contemporary, Dennis McGrath, Matt McGrath,
Hamilton Morris, Reyes Projects, Jeremy Shockley
Shrine Gallery, David Southcombe, Jonnine
and Conrad Standish, Will Welch
Additional photography: Louis Horne, Dennis McGrath,
Ángel Villanueva, John Vogler, Ariel Zambelich

First Edition / Fourth Printing
ARC 060
Printed in China

ISBN: 978-1-944860-19-6
Library of Congress Control Number
2018953525

61)A3HT3TA3W

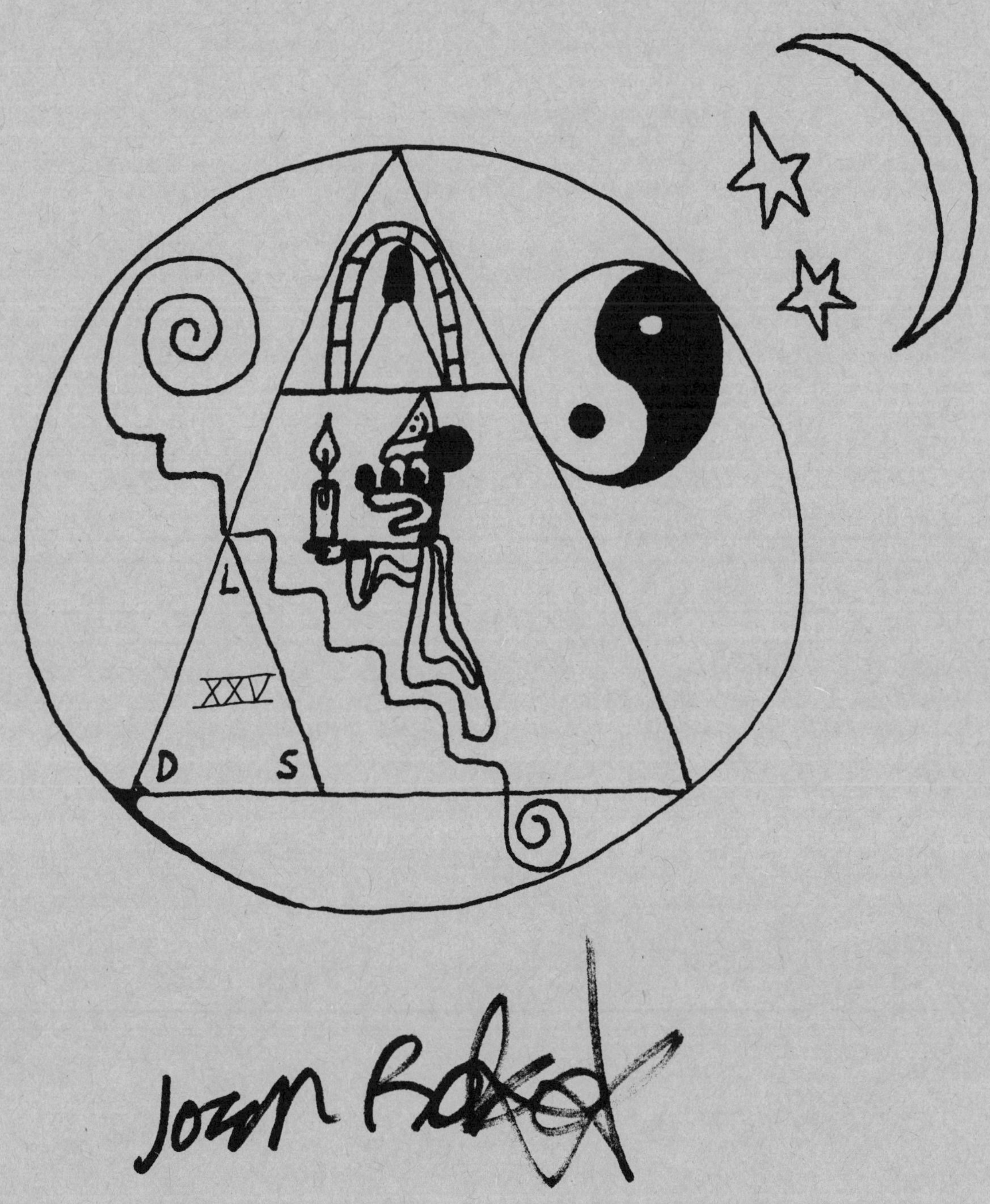

It could be argued that psychedelic drug users are the most alienated of all drug-using people in the United States. There is no other class of drugs that has been met with categorical prohibition, no other class that is more feared, and no other class for which that fear seems less warranted. It follows that those who have used psychedelics and value what they've experienced want to document and describe it, because doing so effectively might allow the experience to be communicated to others, who then might just understand what all this is about and maybe we'd all feel less alone.

But how can such an experience be understood or communicated? Scientists have tried explaining in their own way, and have spent a century refining and revising an evolving model of how psychedelics do what they do. We know that when LSD is ingested, it migrates through the blood and partitions into the brain, where it binds to extracellular sites on cortical 5-HT2A receptors, initiating an arachidonic acid-mediated intracellular signaling cascade that increases resting-state functional connectivity in the default mode network; and we also know that this seems to say very little about the experience of being a conscious human on LSD.

And so we turn to art, hoping that something of the experience can be captured there. The artistic history of psychedelics extends back several thousand years further than the history of psychedelics in the lab. There are cave paintings of mushrooms, peyote effigies, cactus temples, Huichol yarn paintings, and Shipibo pottery. They remain popular representations of these substances, despite the fact that we typically have almost no understanding of why they were made or what they really mean. Our tendency is to avert our eyes, looking to the dim confusions of the past to avoid the glaring confusion of the present.

Describing them spiritually hasn't been much easier. When psychedelics were introduced, the first generation of adherents looked to the East. This tendency could be seen in the Hinduism of Ram Dass, in Timothy Leary's fixation on *The Tibetan Book of the Dead*, in the Zen Buddhism of Alan Watts, and in the immense popularity of Ravi Shankar's ragas—in order to "be here now," it seemed one had to be somewhere else in the past. This Easternization of the psychedelic experience was so pervasive that it led some cultural historians to conclude that we'd wasted a unique opportunity, afforded by psychedelics, to create a purely Western mysticism. I don't agree with this. While the first counterculture may have failed to create a new mystical tradition out of whole cloth, these cultural historians failed to recognize a mysticism that had emerged through a patchwork construction.

Yes, a purely Western mysticism did emerge. It is a disorganized and distracted mysticism, crafted by teenagers raised in a culture of computers and cartoons and the tawdry vestiges of major religions. It is a mysticism forged in the wake of the Controlled Substances Act of 1971, where every psychedelic revelation is necessarily met by the paranoid, incredulous rebuttal, "And this is a crime?" Where transcendence is achieved not in a secluded Himalayan lamasery but in basements and bodegas and cemeteries or forests an hour's drive from the city. (Burning Man is not an example of this mysticism.)

It is a mysticism found in earmarked copies of *TiHKAL* and unfinished *Dune* paperbacks; where the cave paintings of the ancient religions became clumsily spray-painted mushrooms along the train tracks, the sacred gardens now located in fish tanks surreptitiously hidden under beds and in closets, with the ever-present fear that the helicopter you hear in the distance is coming to take you away for ordering the wrong kind of spores from the back pages of a magazine that specializes in pornographic depictions of flowering cannabis plants. A mysticism of Bigfoot and witches, ninjas and Nibiru, cops and Kokopelli, and the transient succor provided by loaves of sprouted grain bread. A mysticism colored by the half-forgotten spiritual pretensions of our forefathers and the trip reports and extraction teks of the pre-corporate Internet. With more people using more psychedelics now than at any other time in history, it is probably the greatest of all psychedelic mystical traditions, yet few claim or address it.

This is the mysticism of Joe Roberts.

The way you
choose to explore
it is
the way you
choose to explore
it.

make sure you
take notes

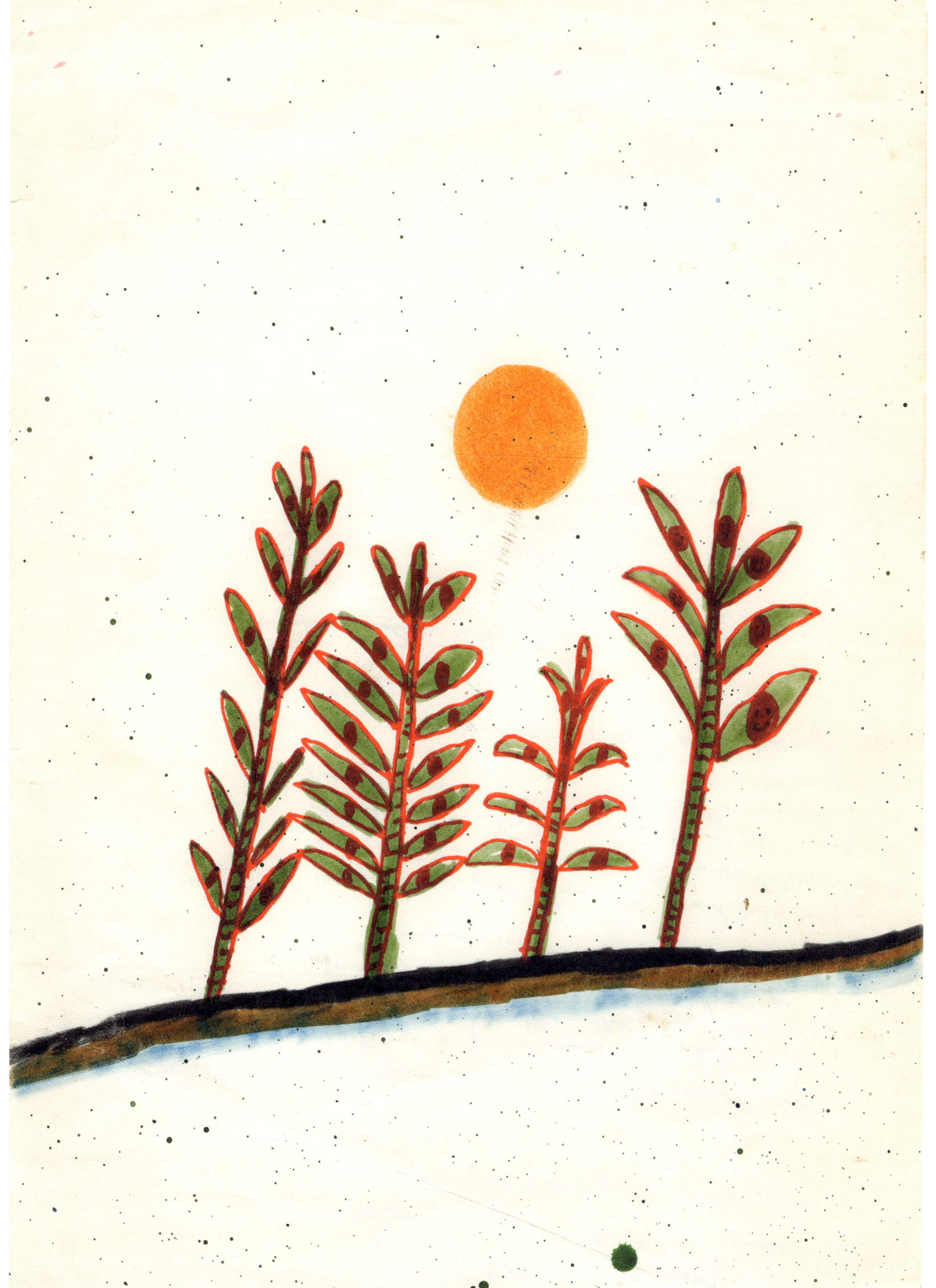

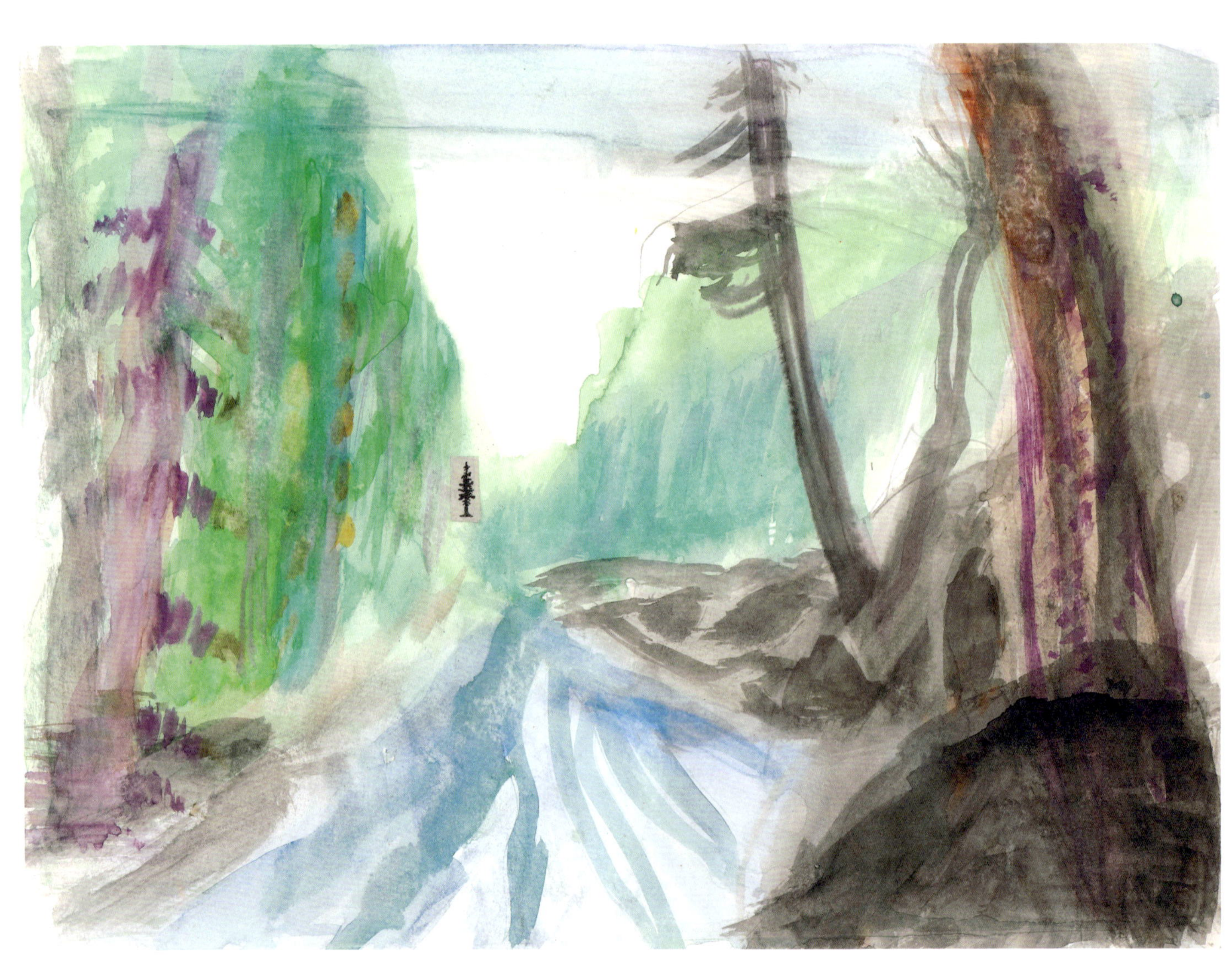

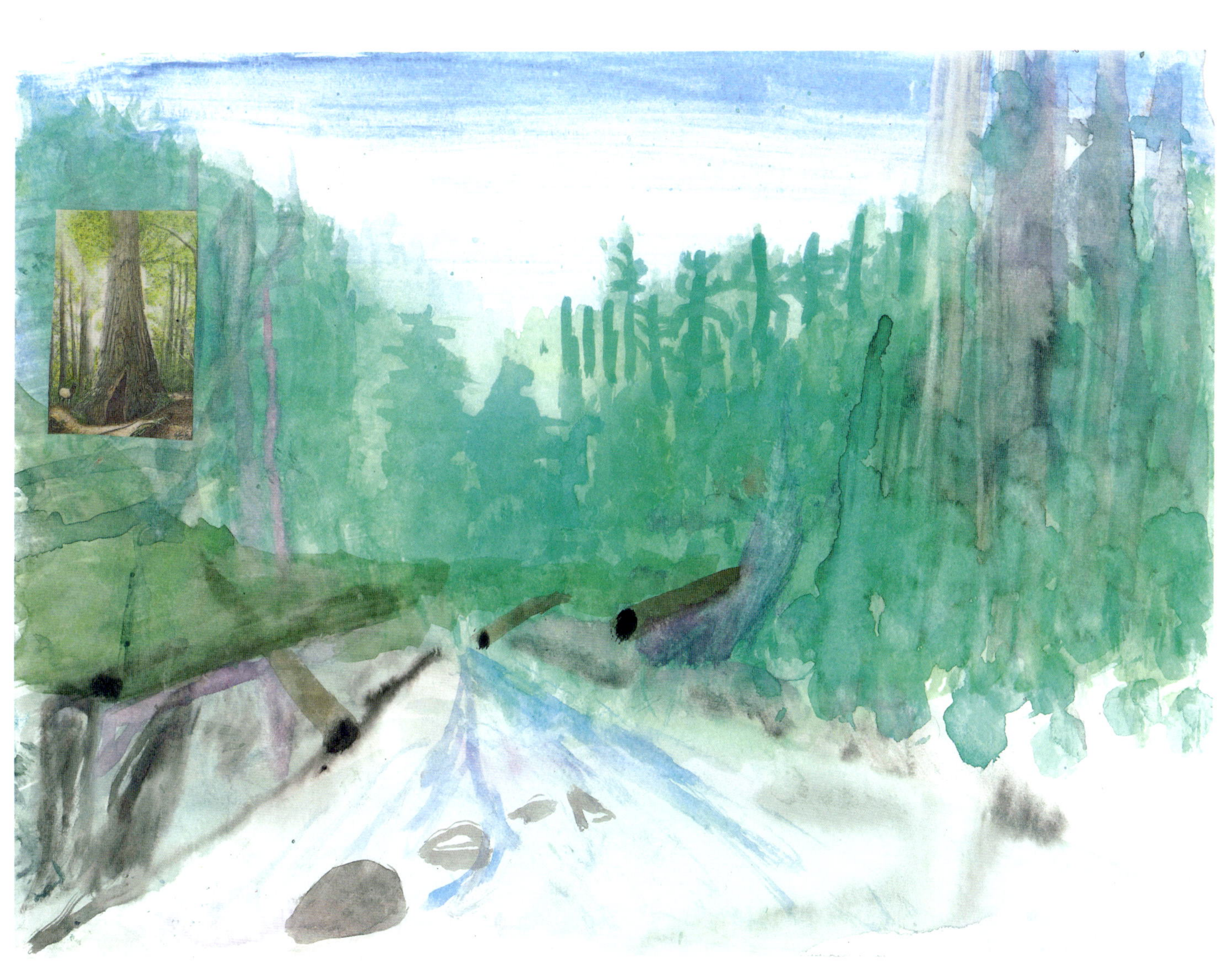

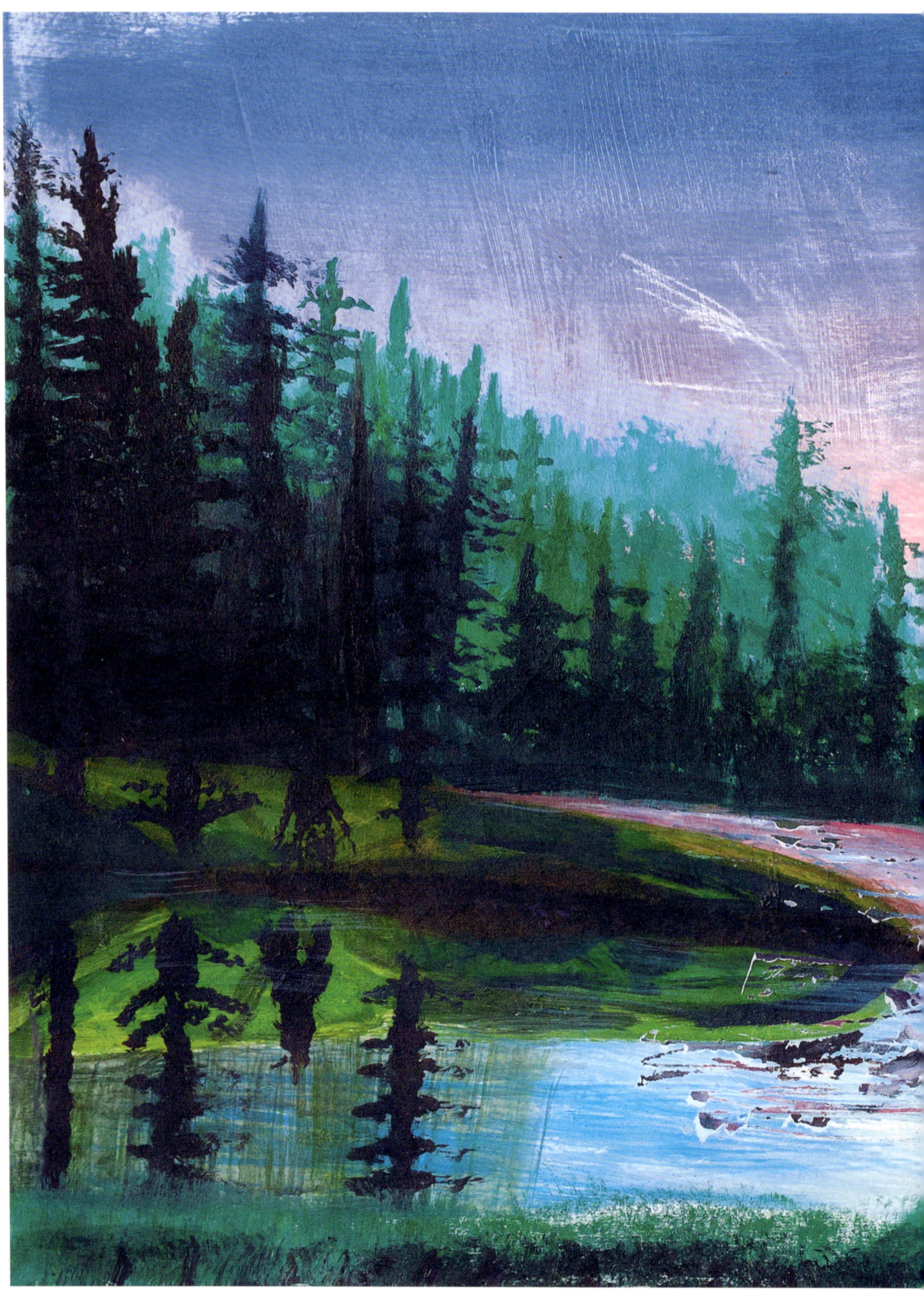

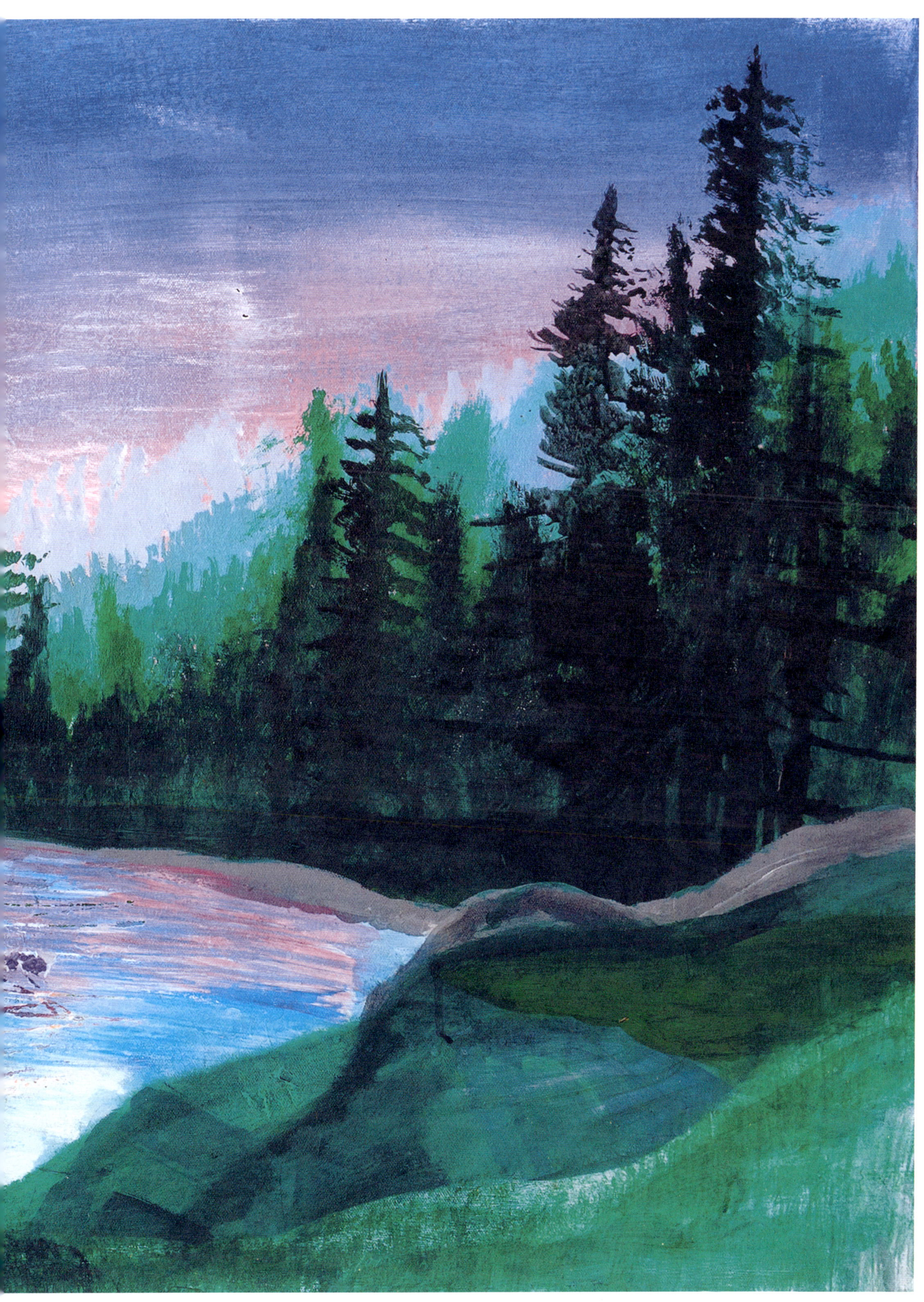

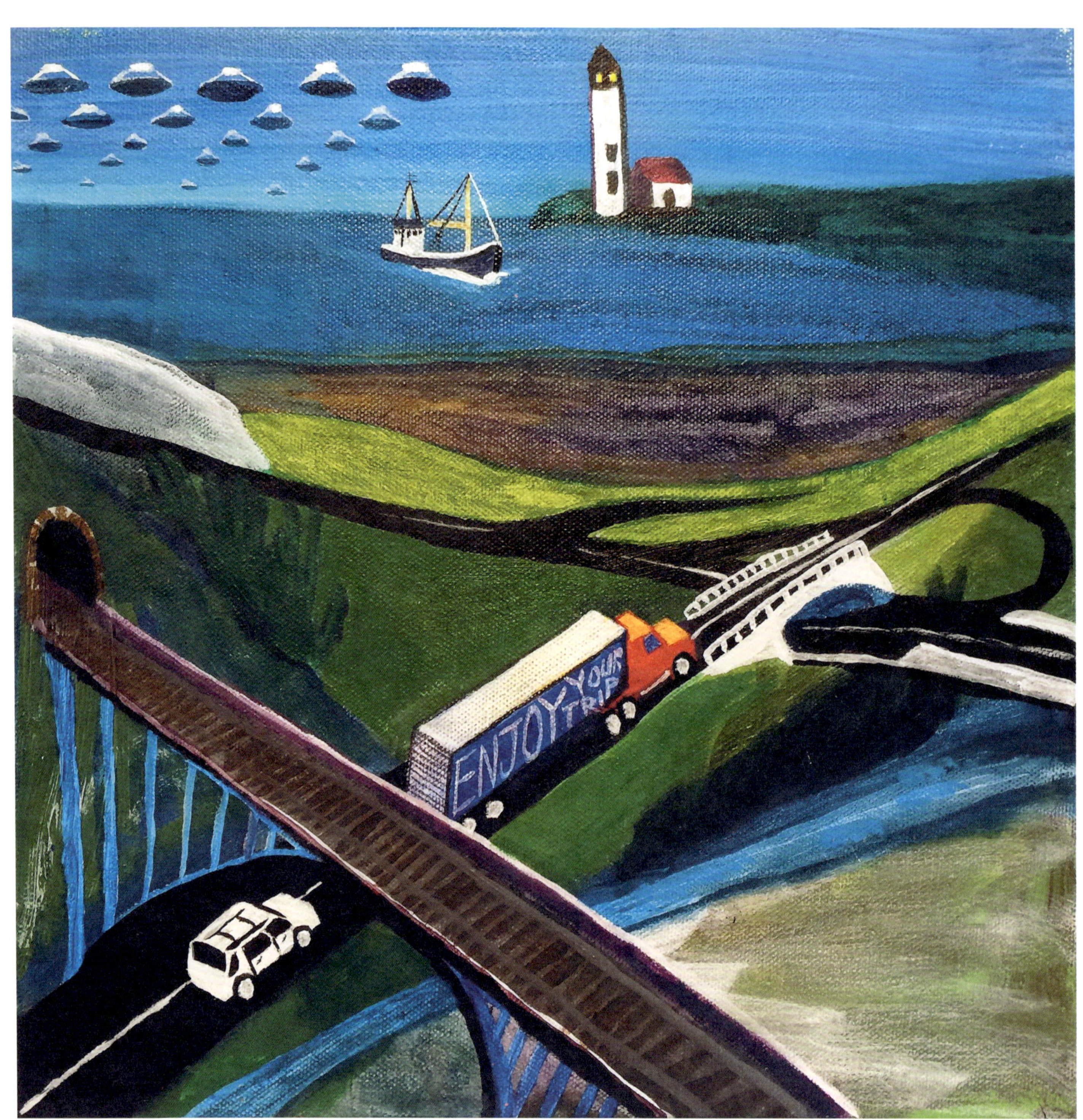
ENJOY YOUR TRIP

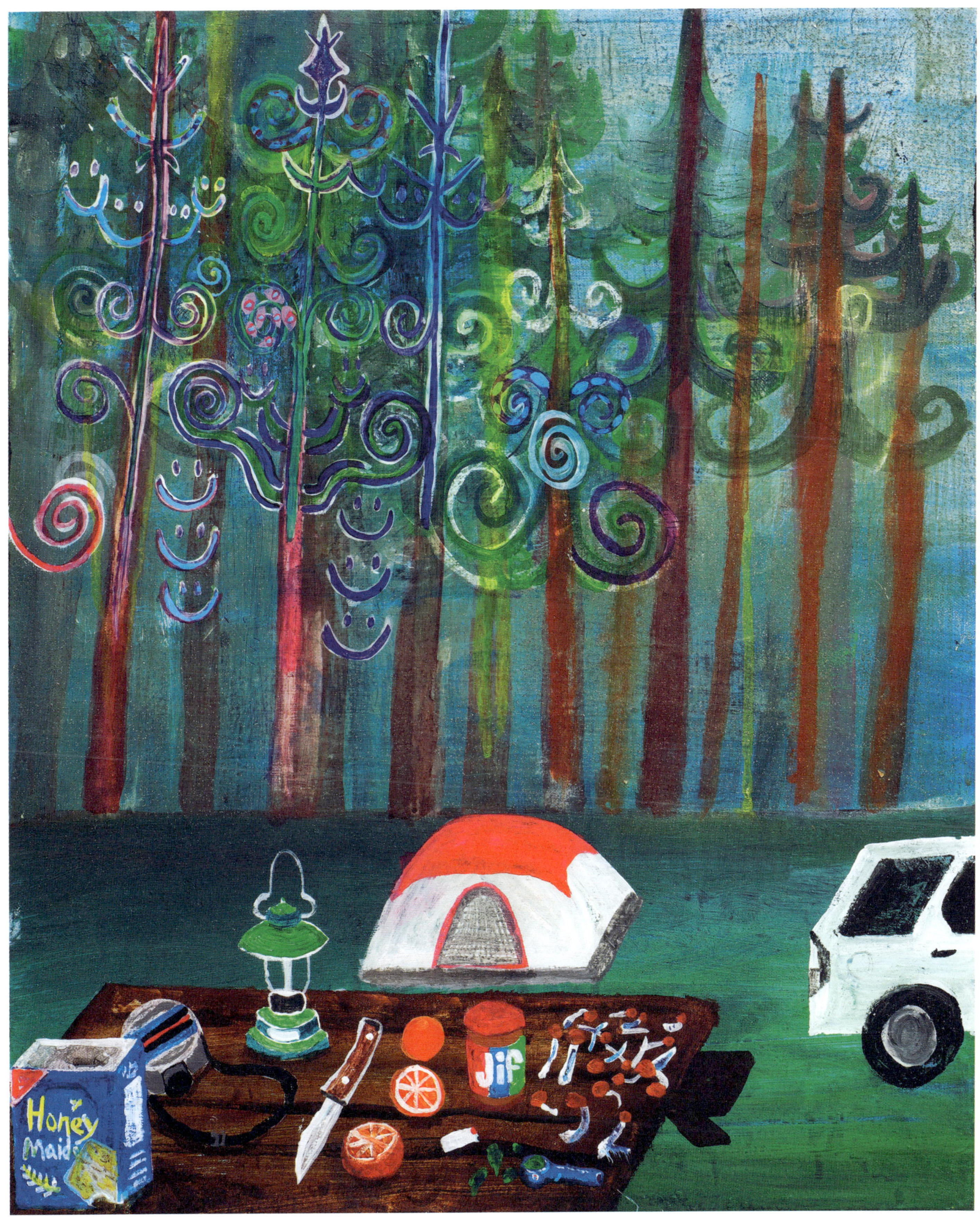

Honey
Maid
Jif

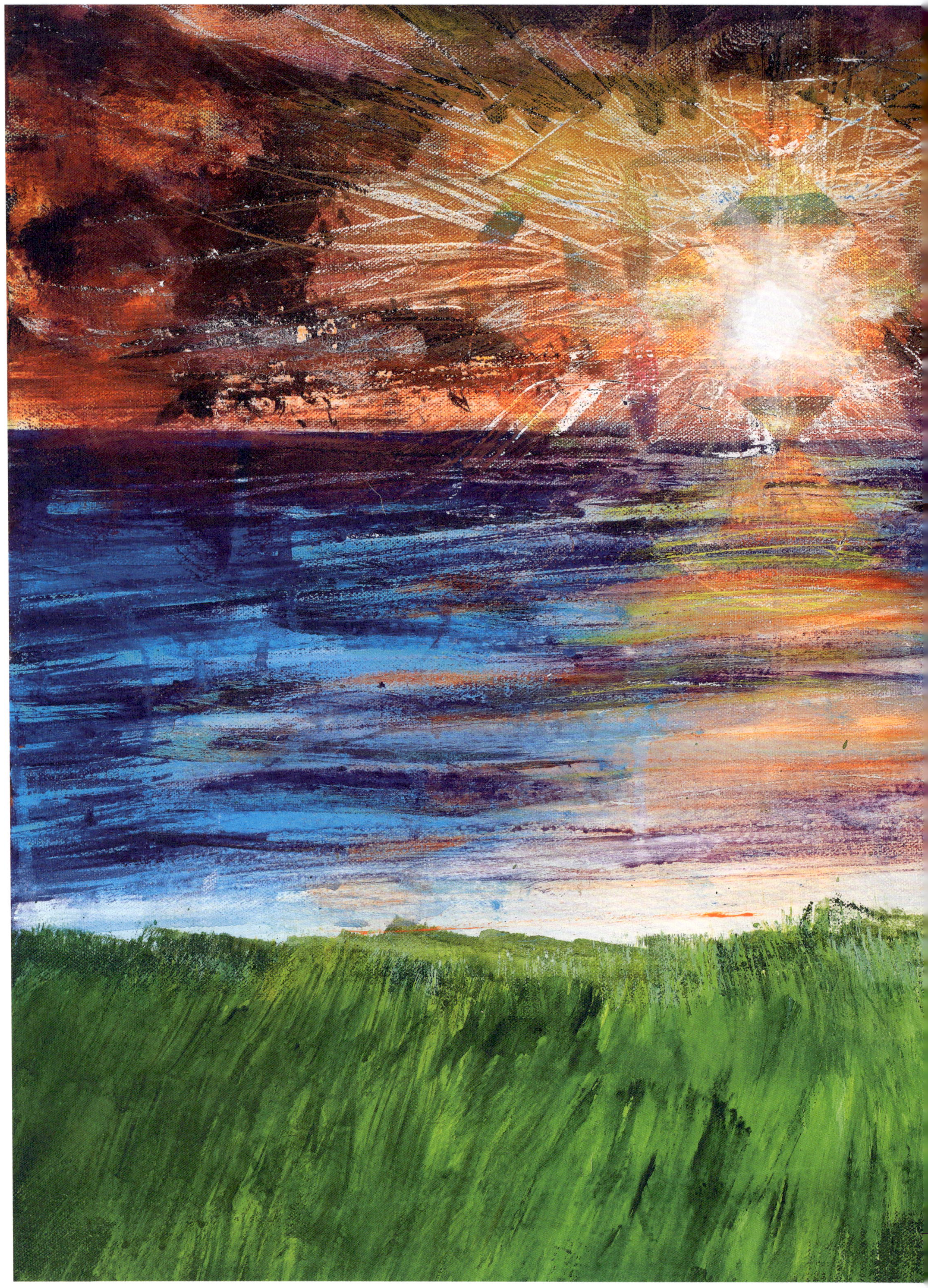

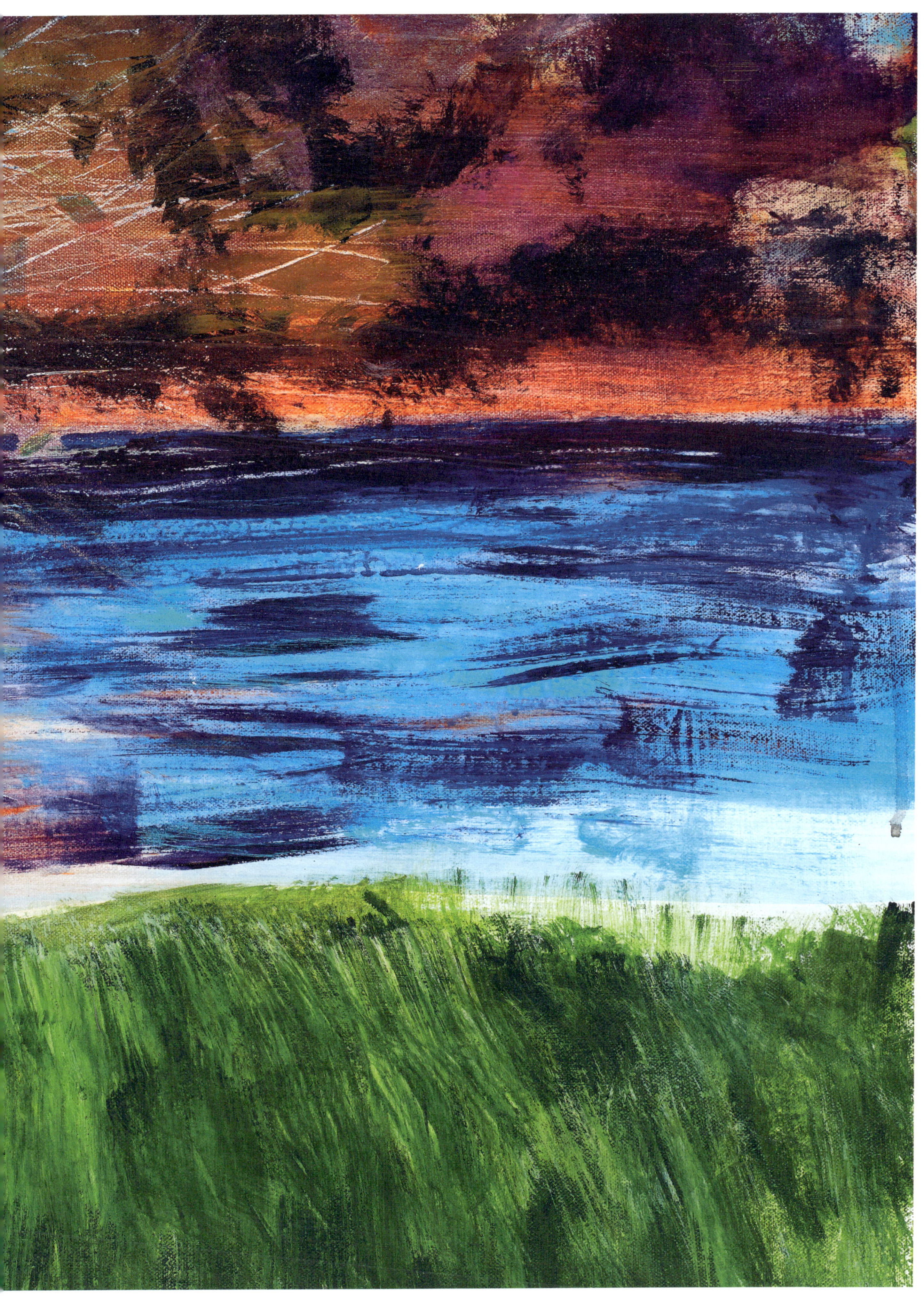

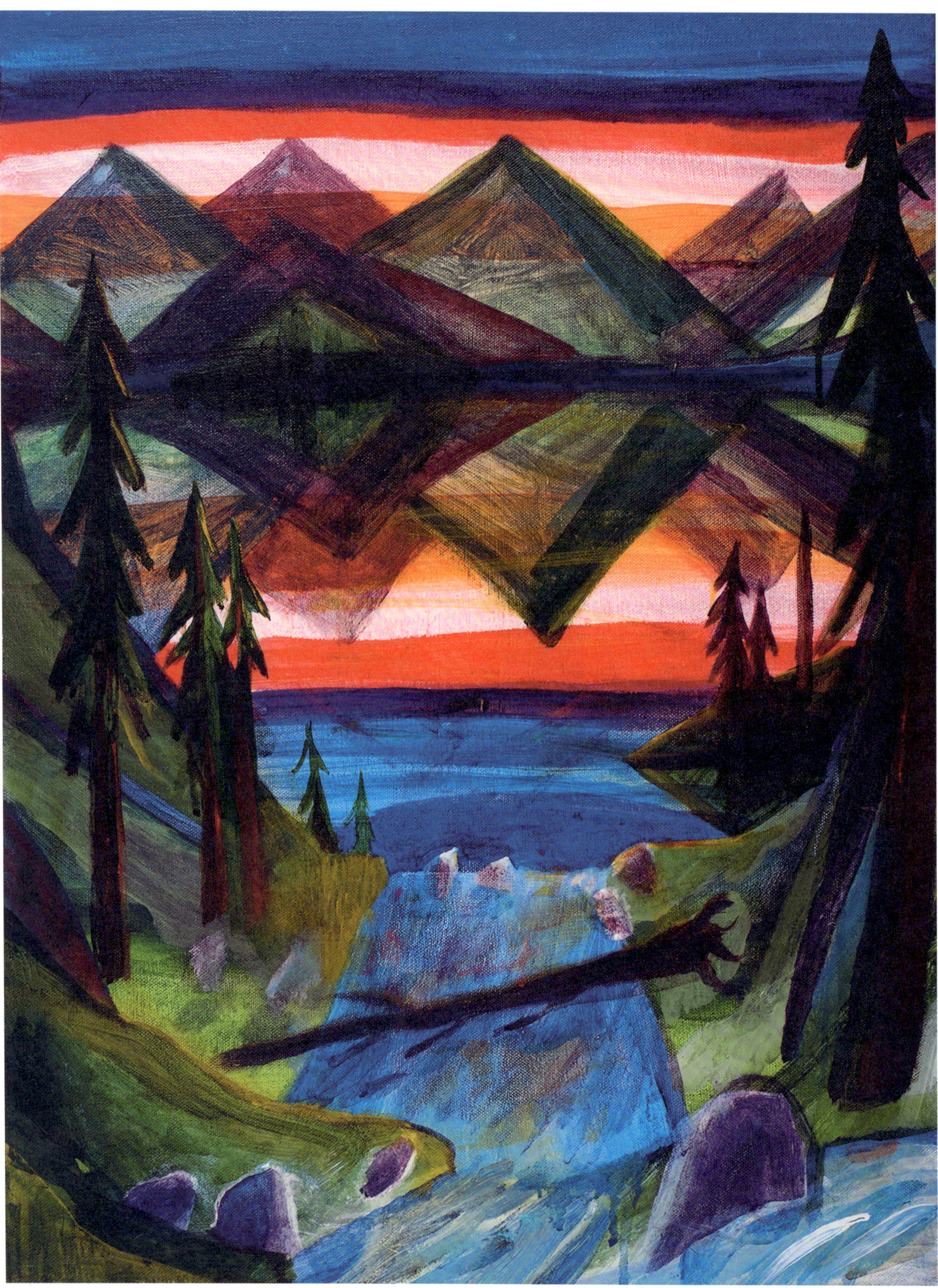

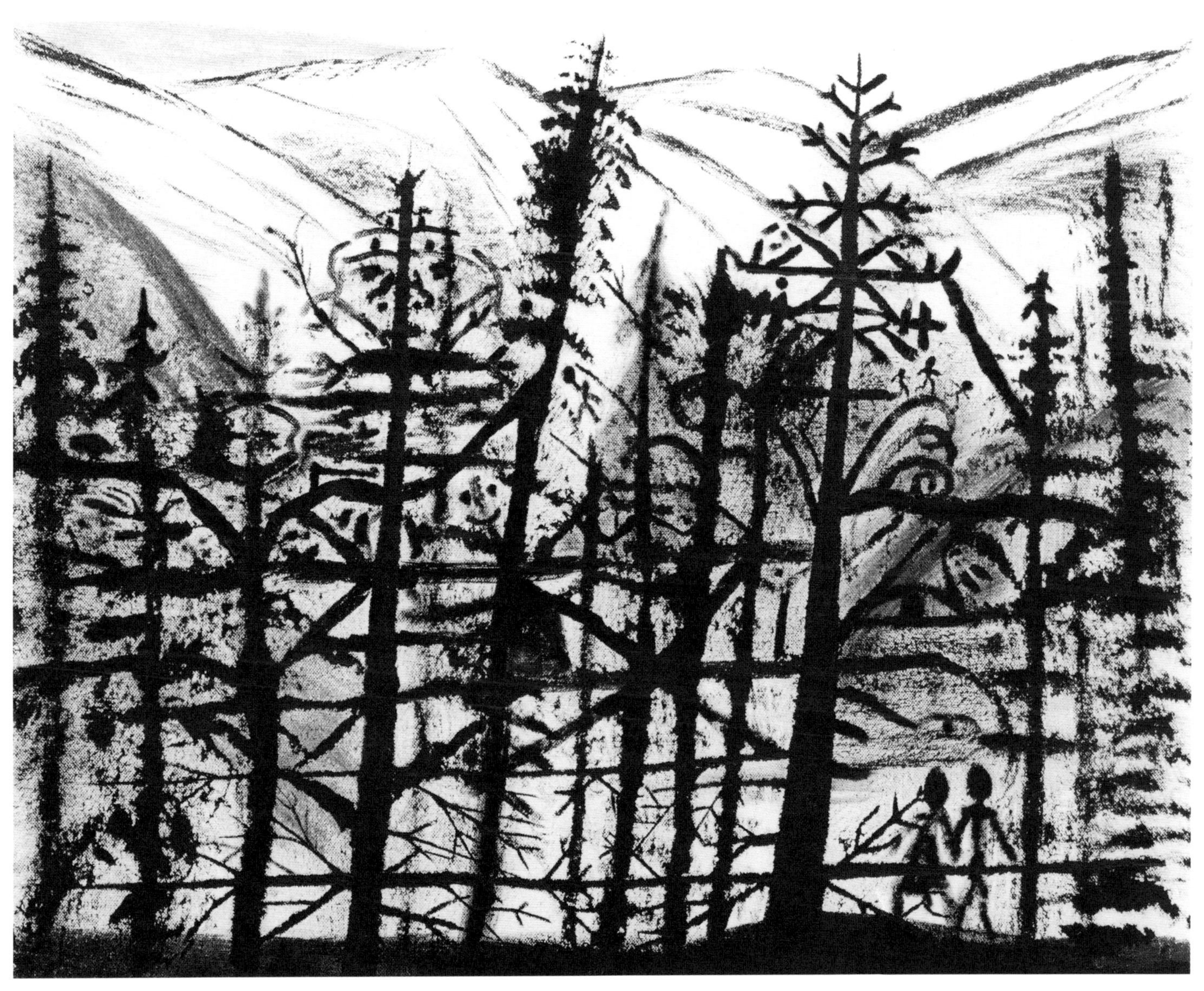

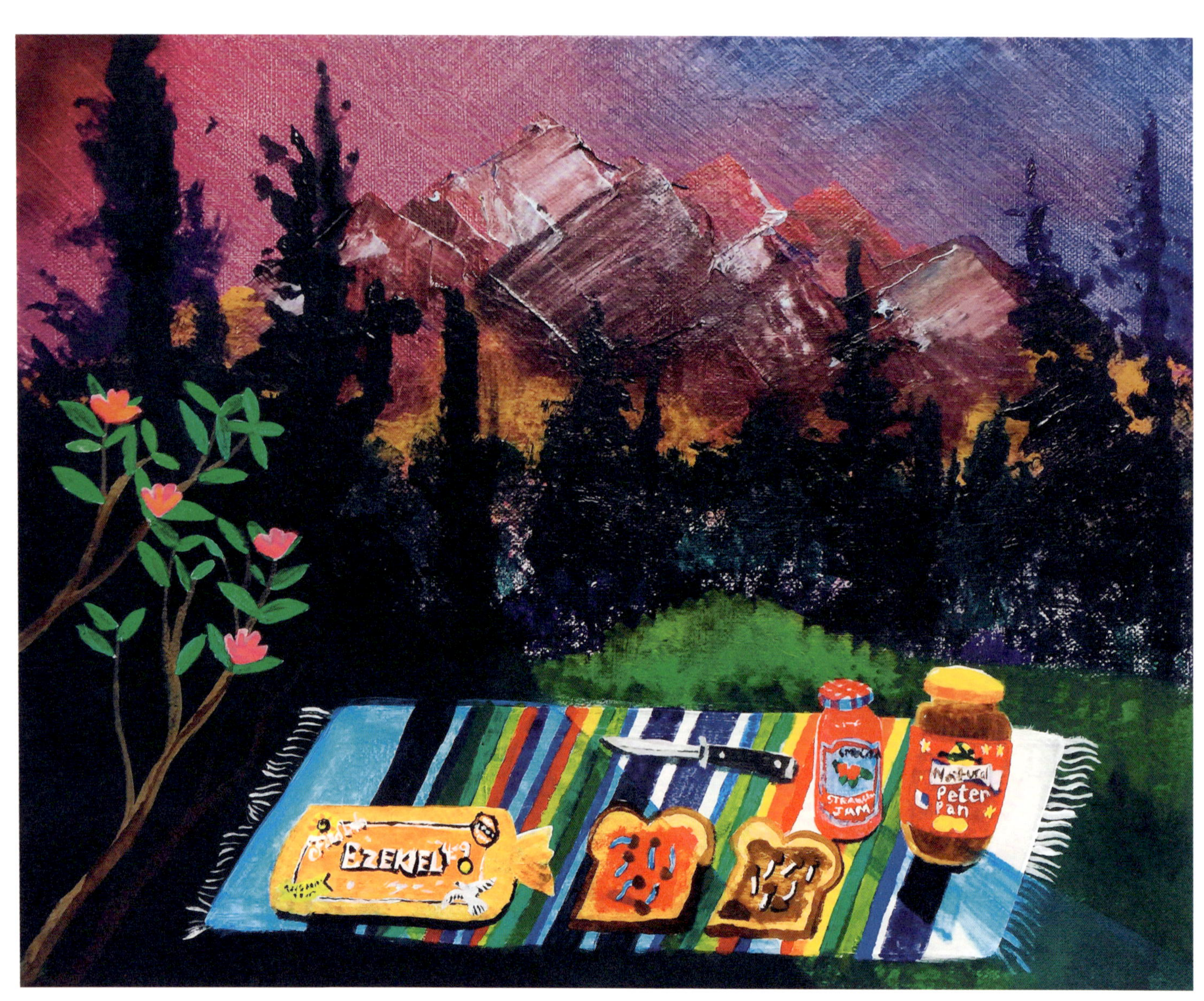
EZEKIEL 4:9
STRAWBERRY JAM
Natural
Peter Pan

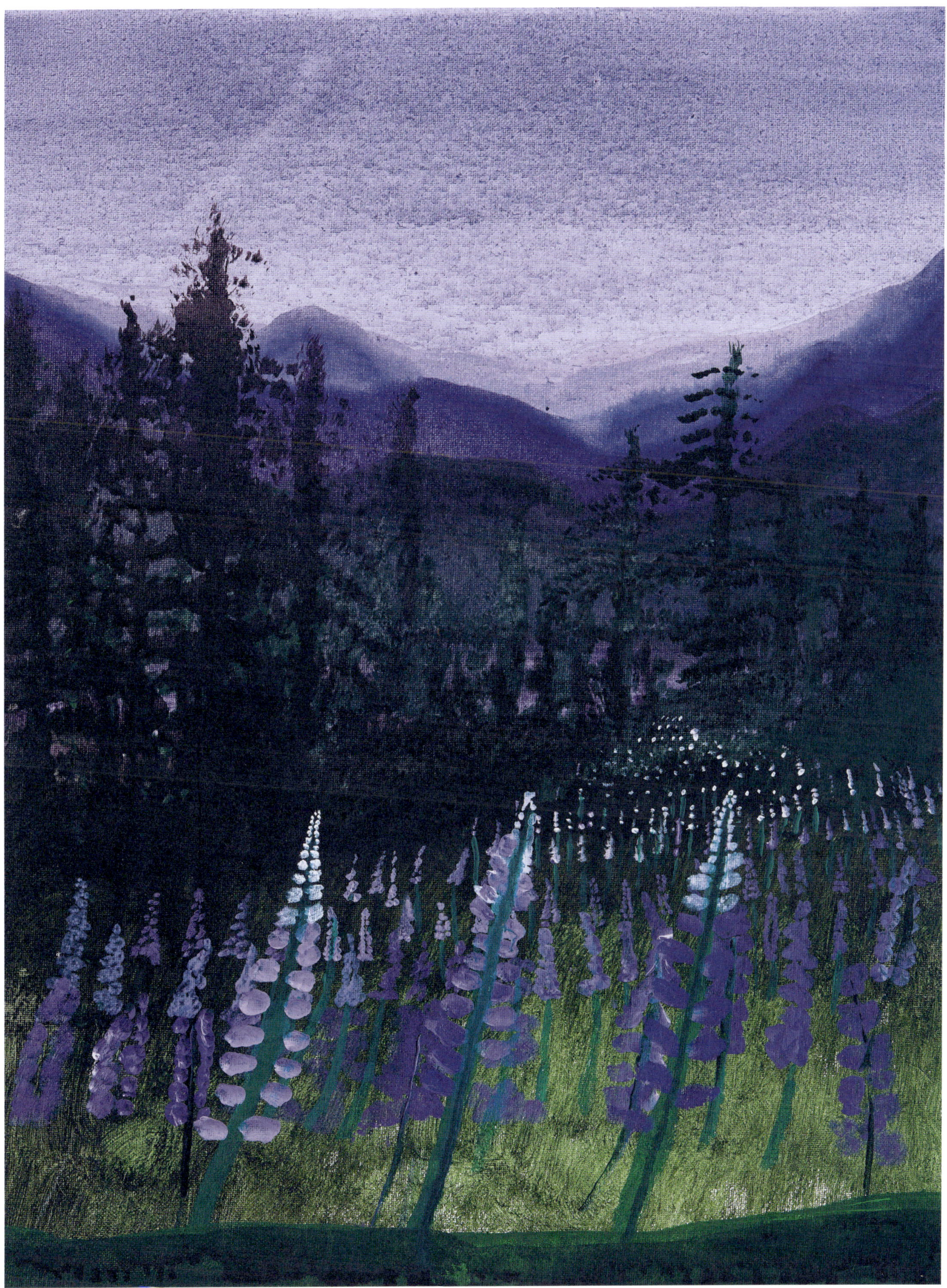

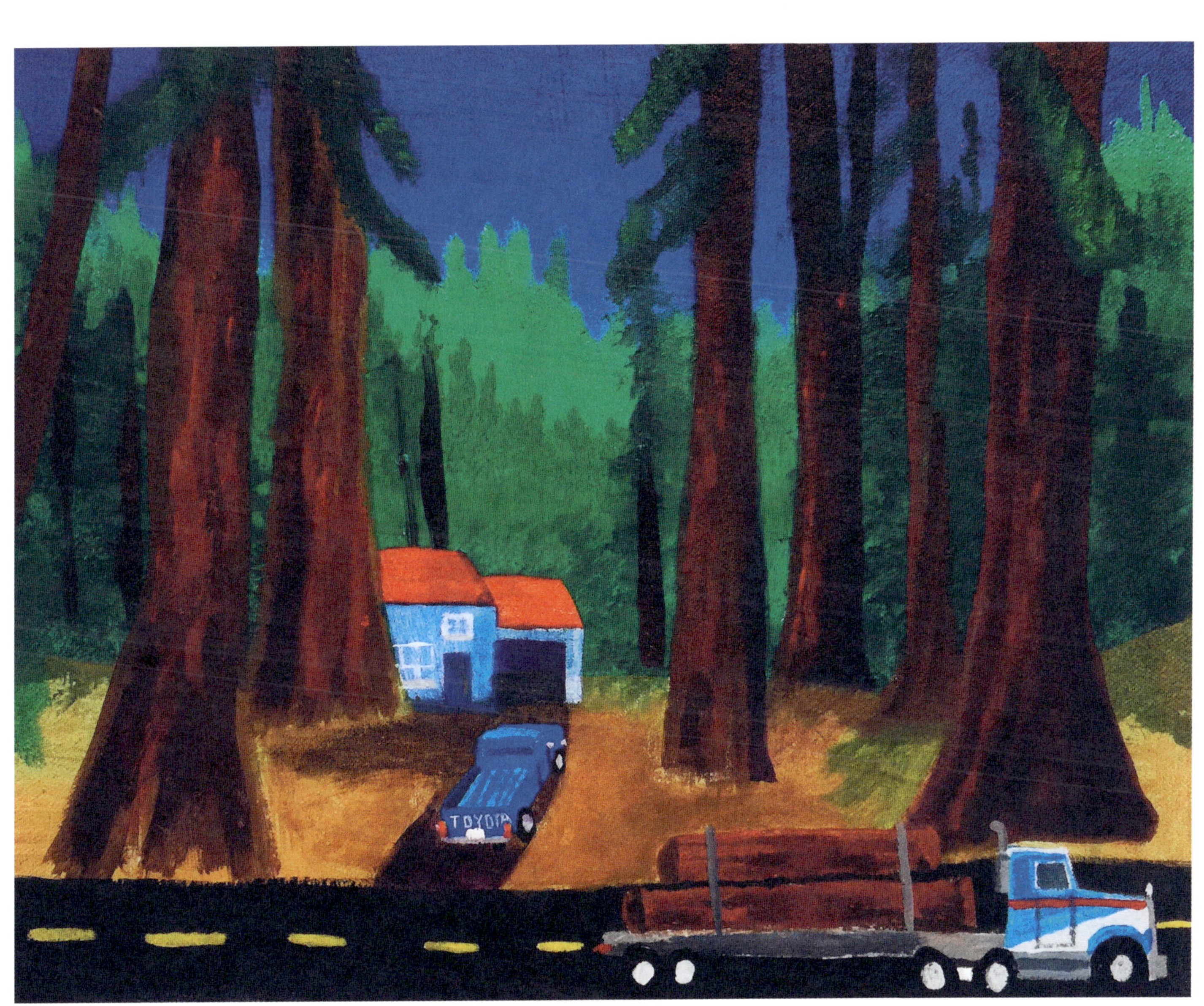

TOYOTA

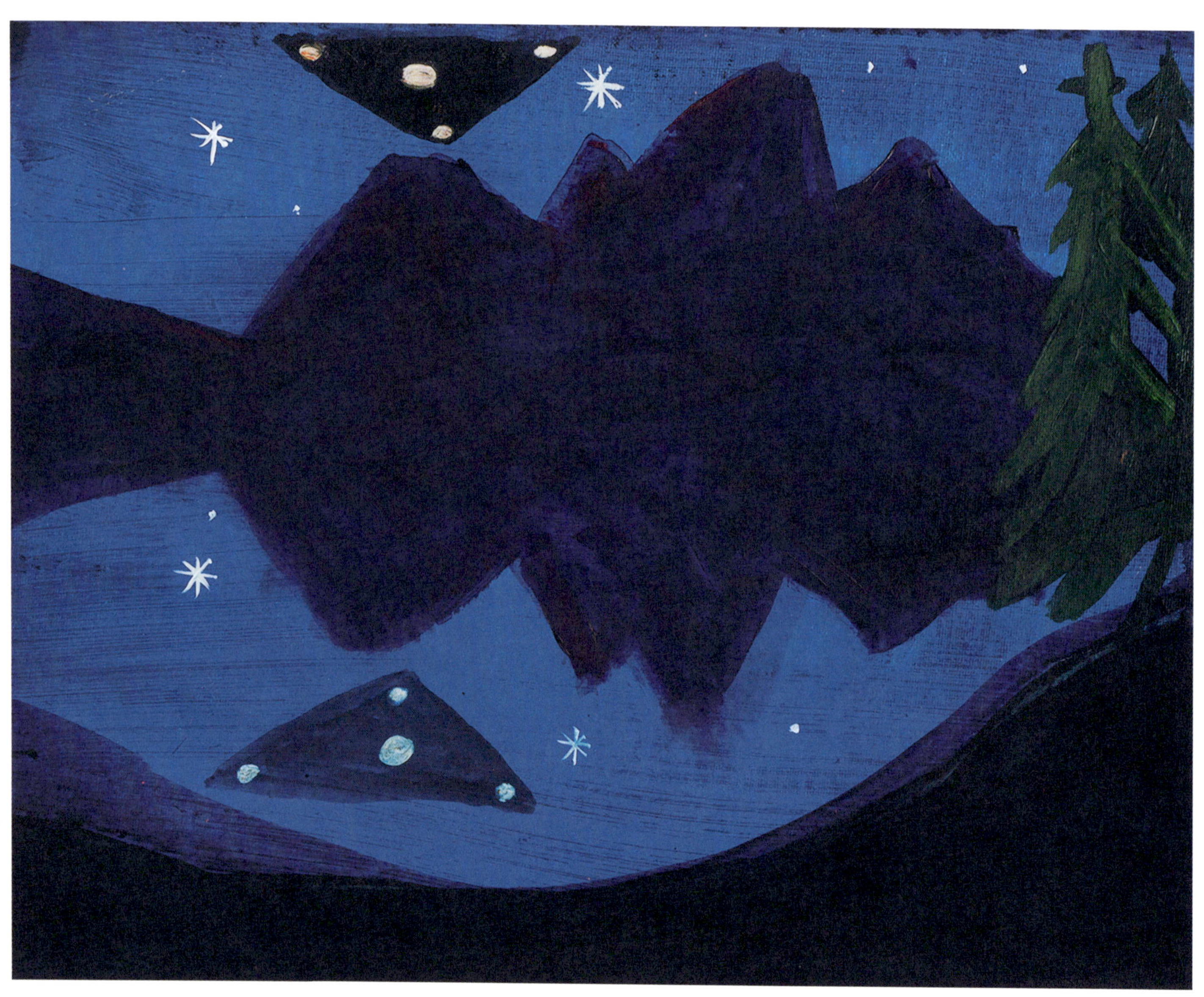

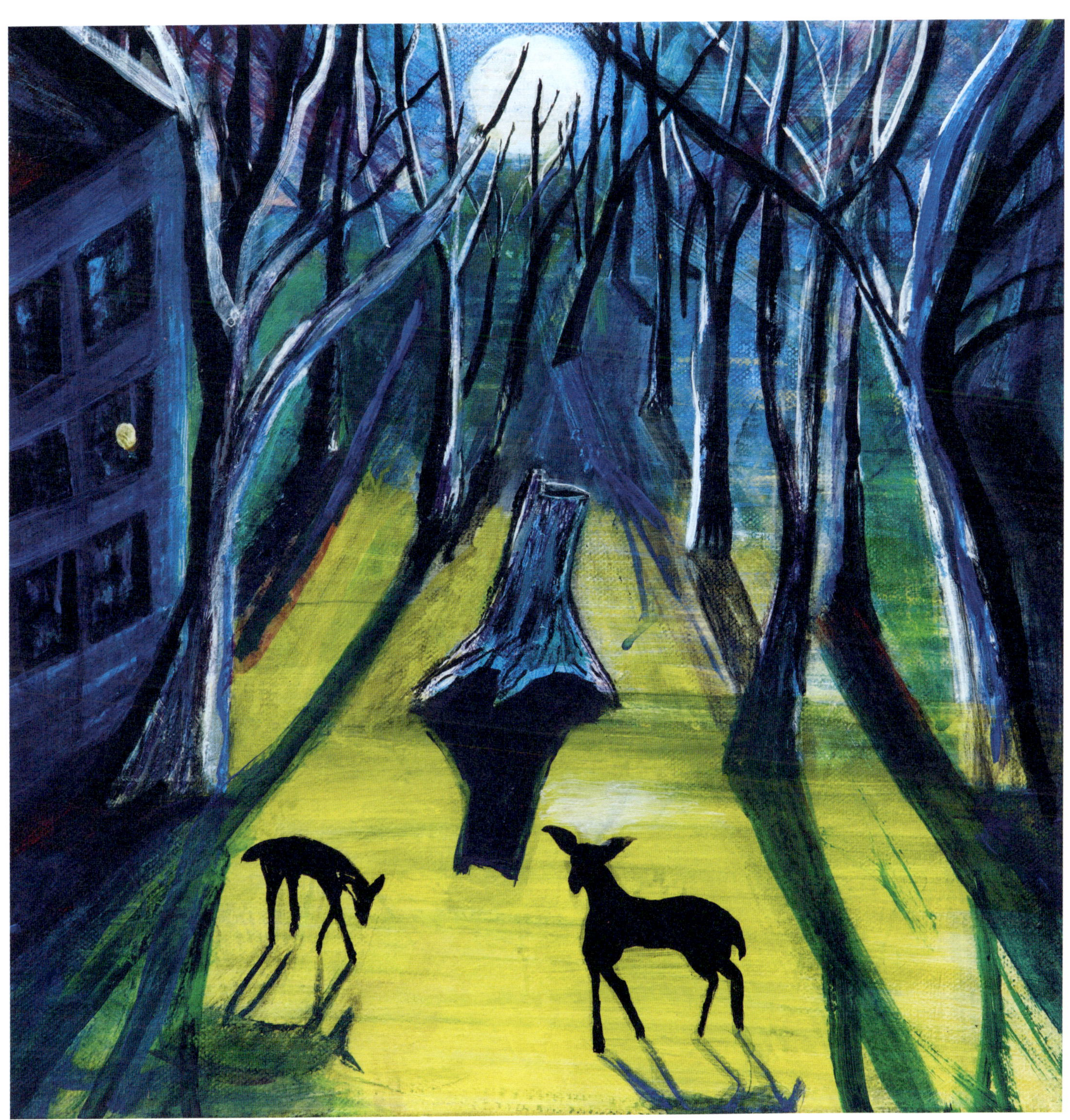

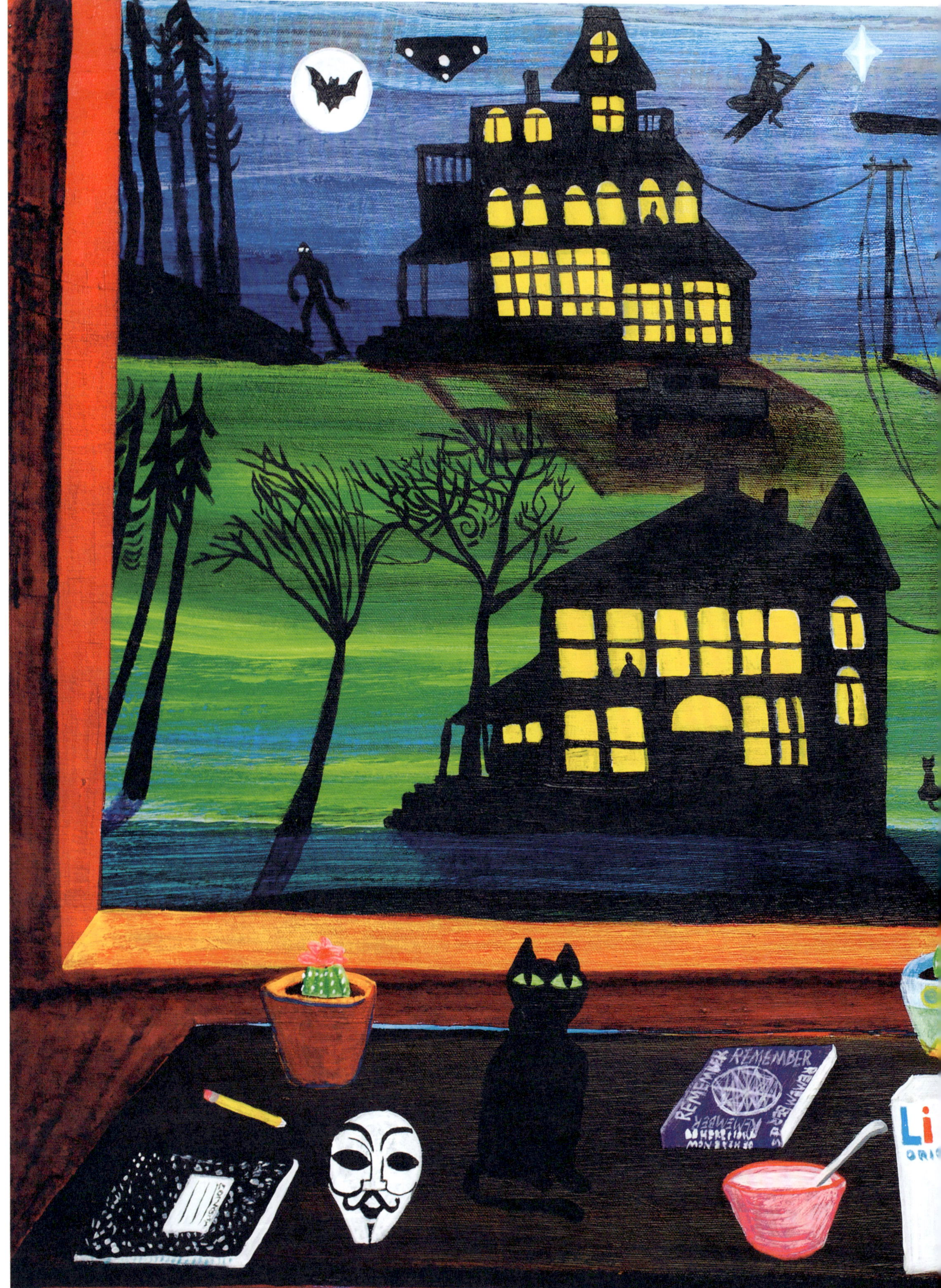

REMEMBER REMEMBER
REMEMBER
REMEMBER
REMEMBER
BE HERE NOW
Li
ORIG

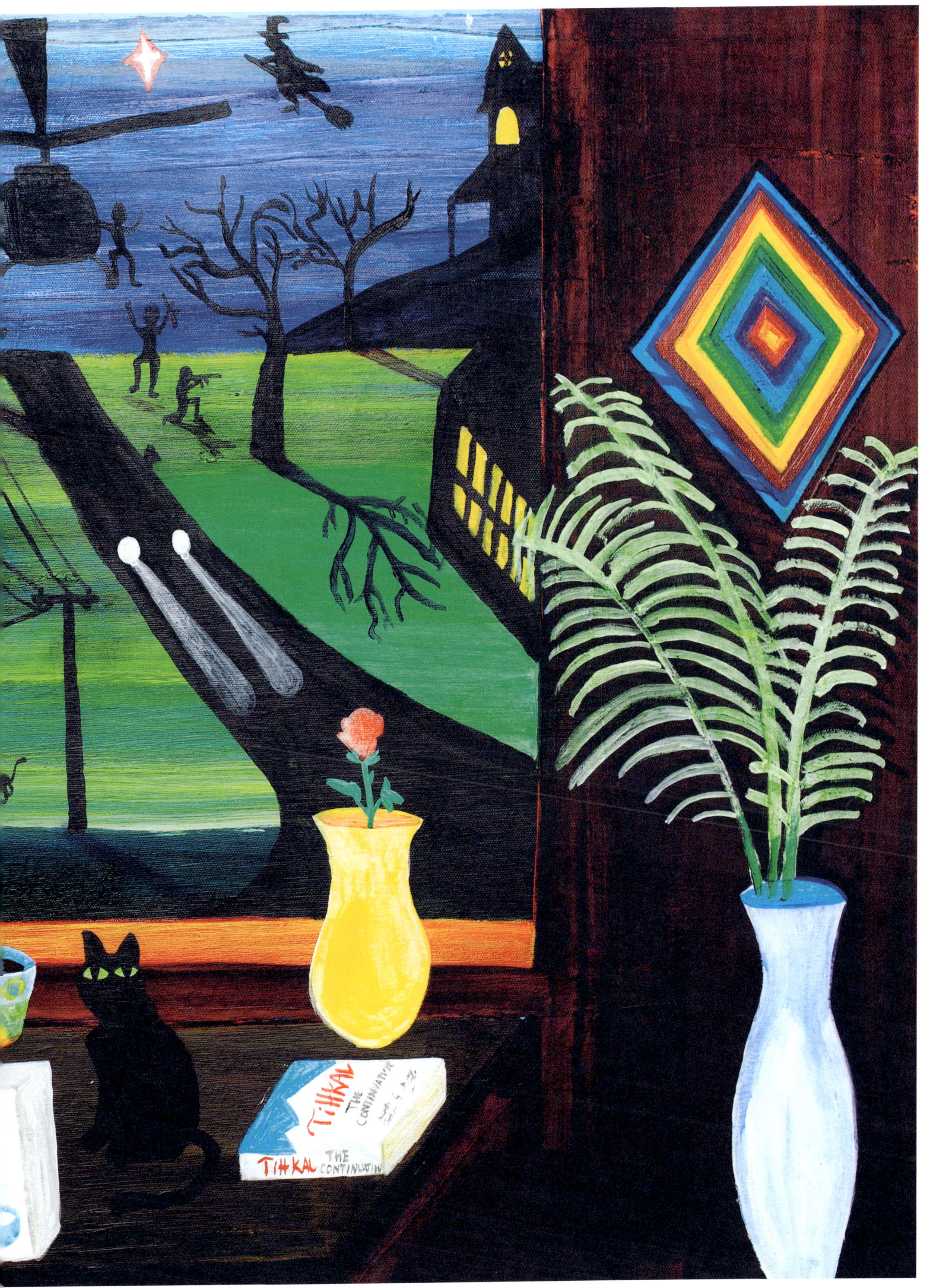
TiHKAL
THE
CONTINUATION
TiHKAL THE CONTINUATION

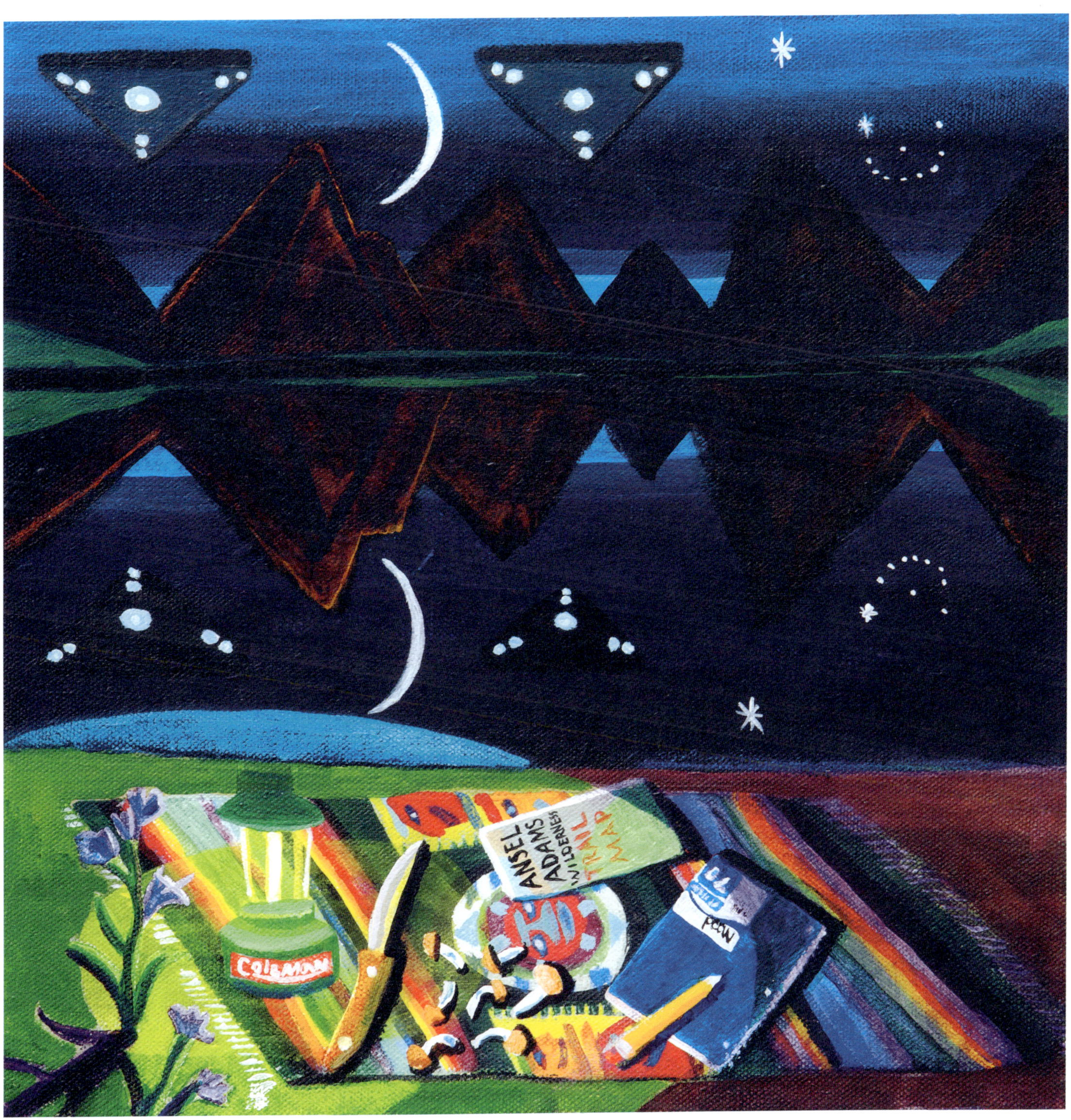
Coleman
ANSEL ADAMS WILDERNESS
TRAIL MAP
M&M

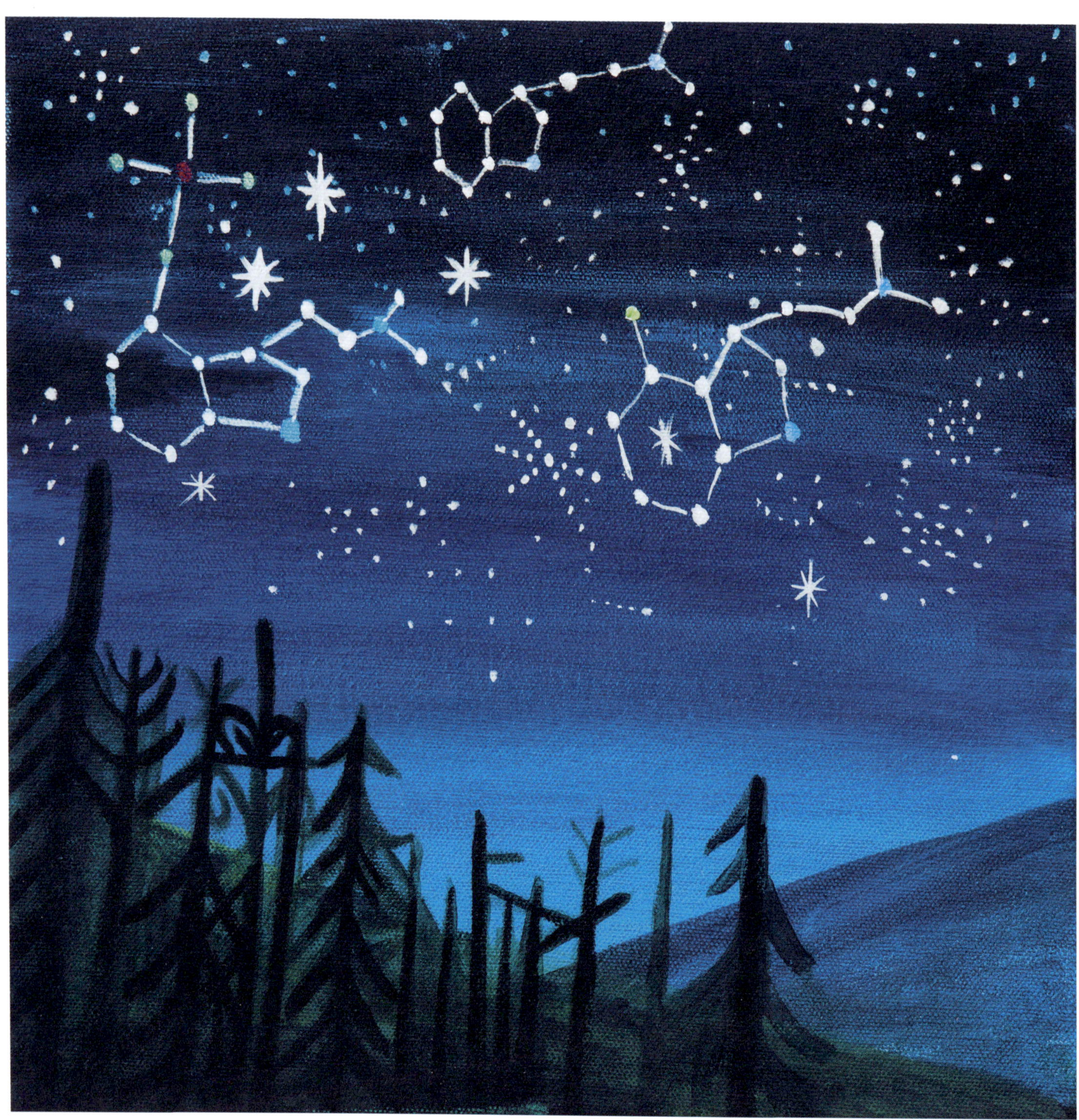

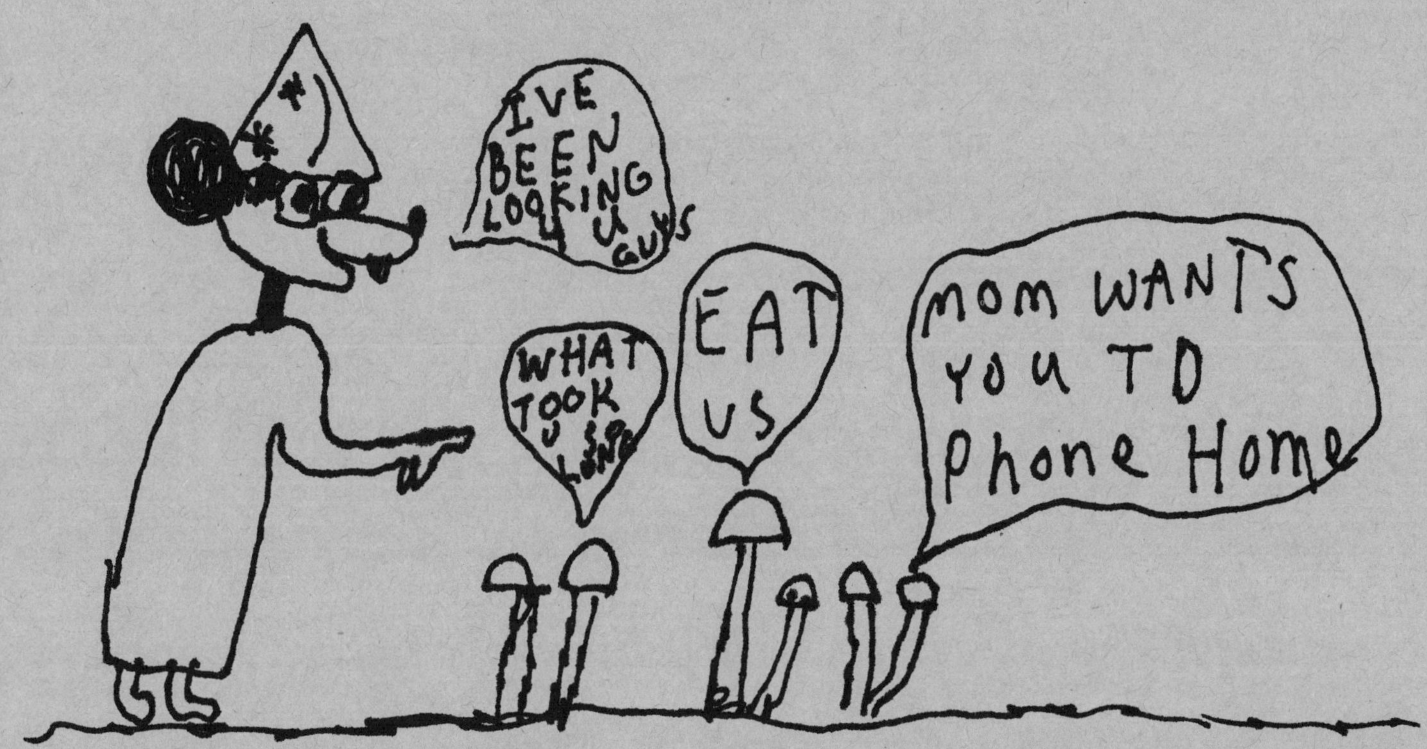

I'VE BEEN LOOKING U GUYS
WHAT TOOK U SO LONG
EAT US
MOM WANTS YOU TO PHONE HOME

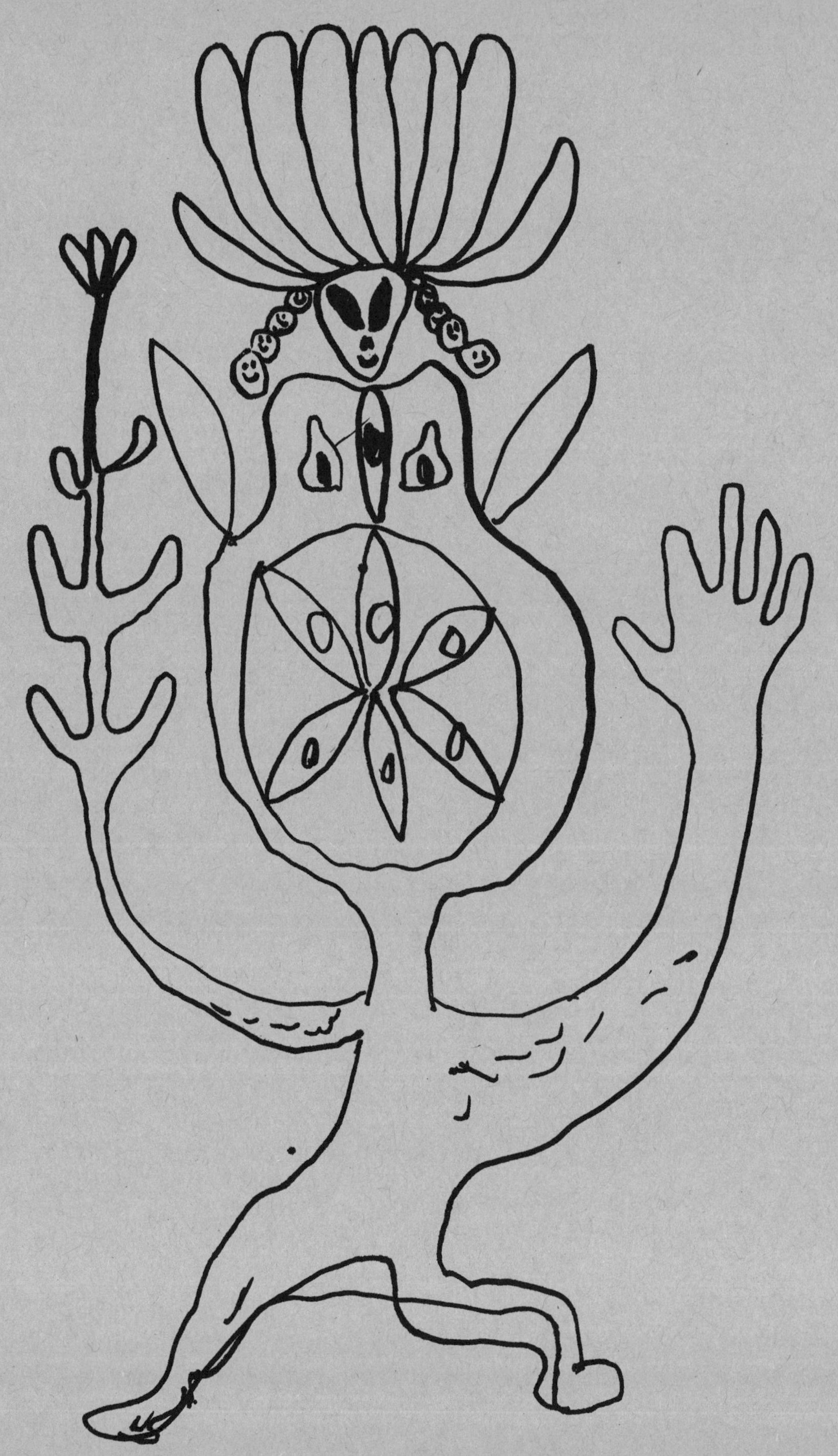

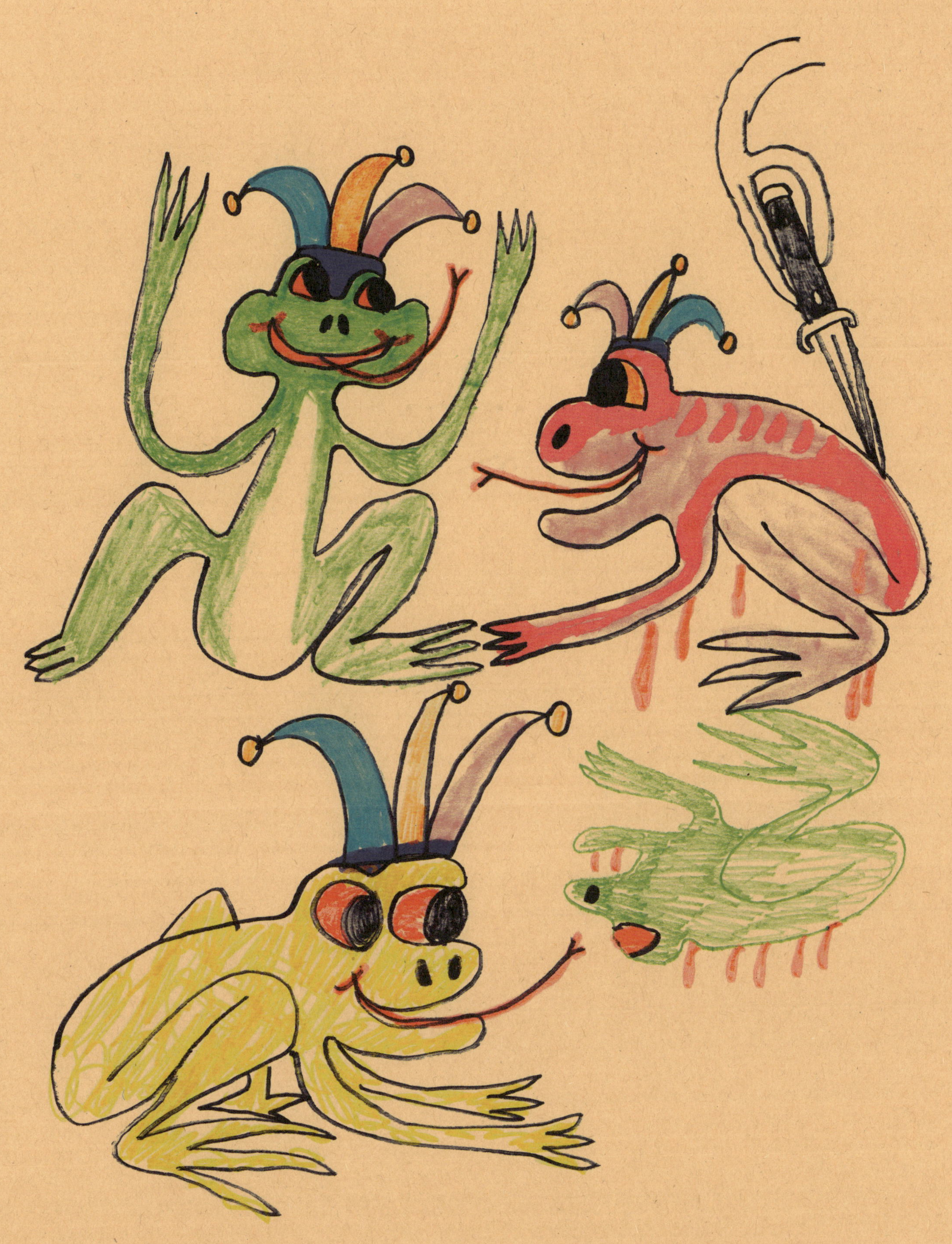

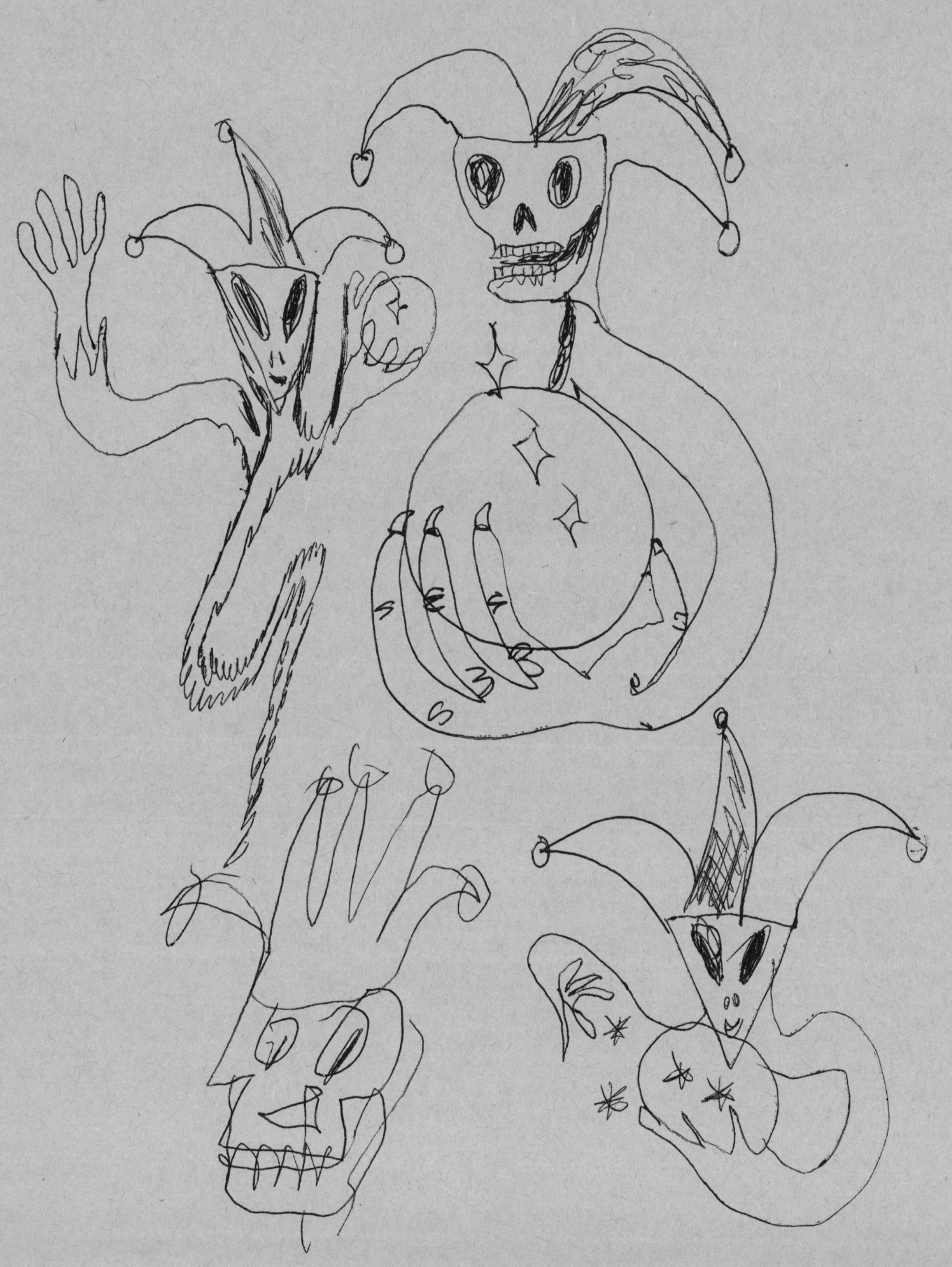

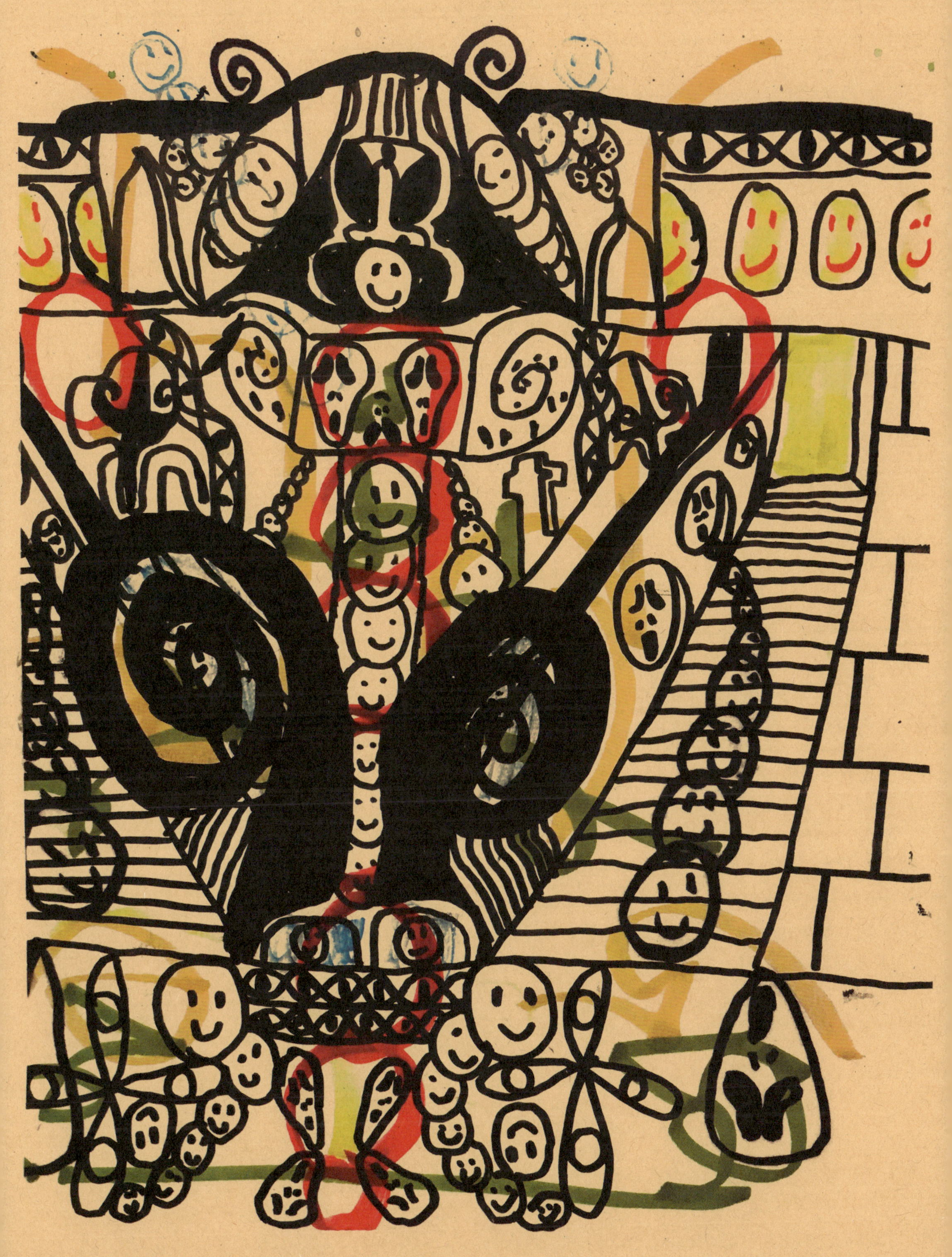

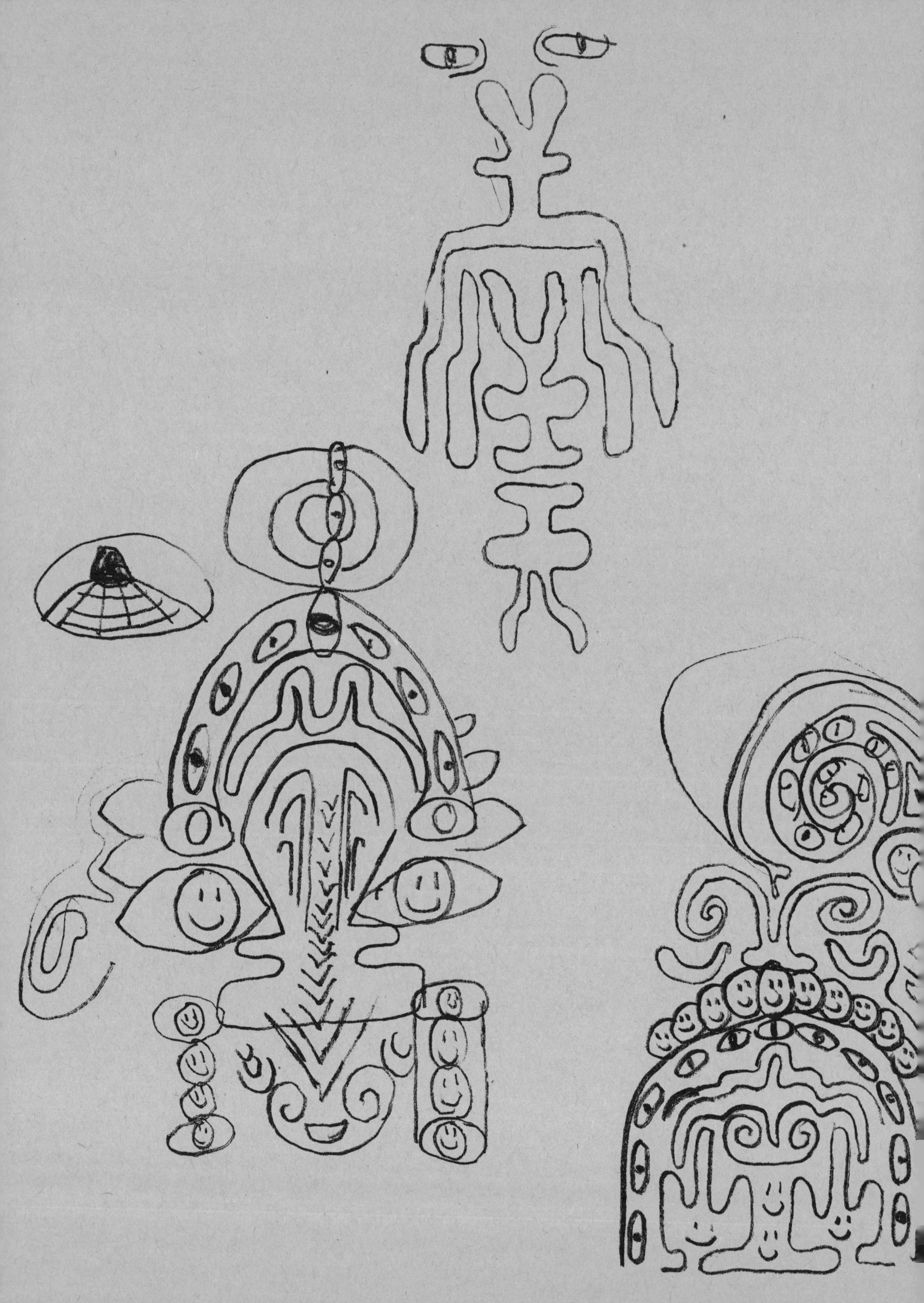

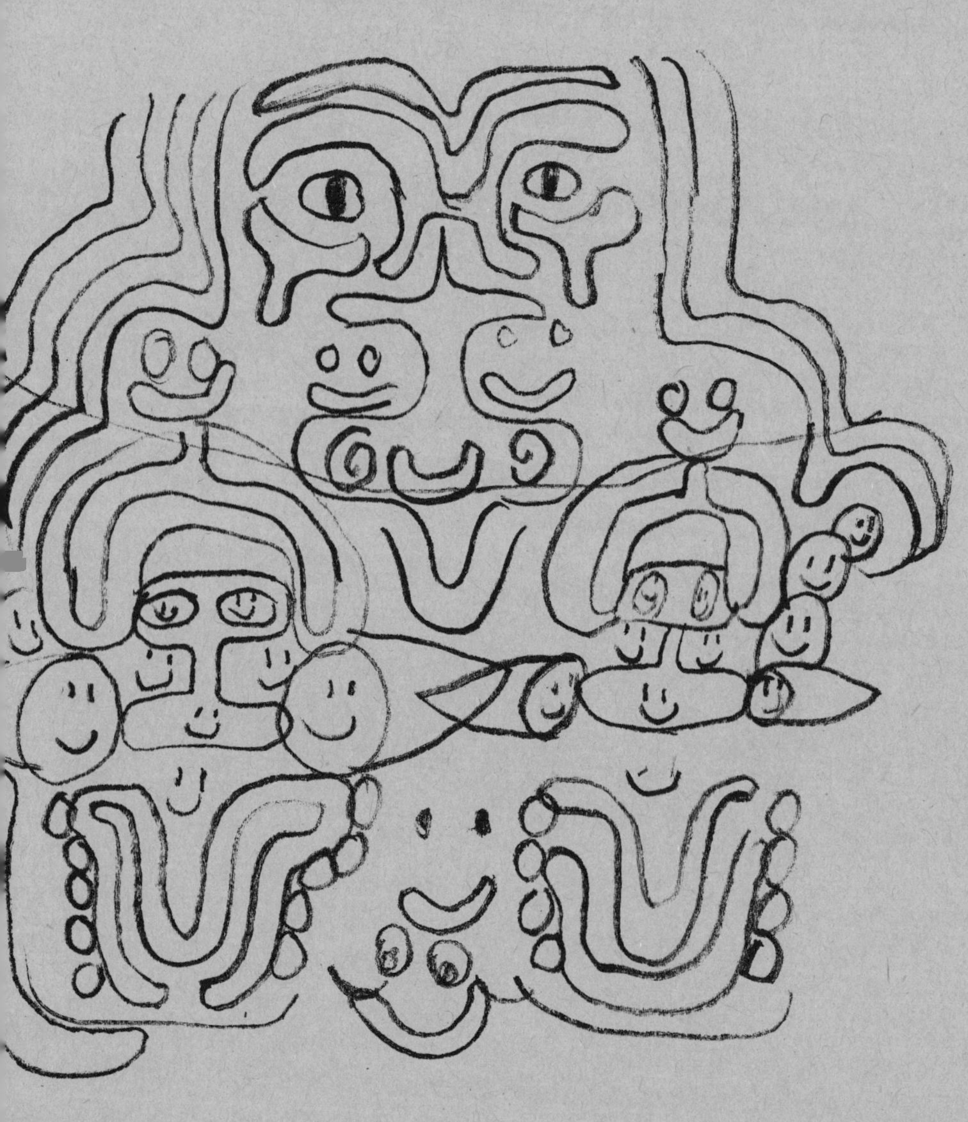

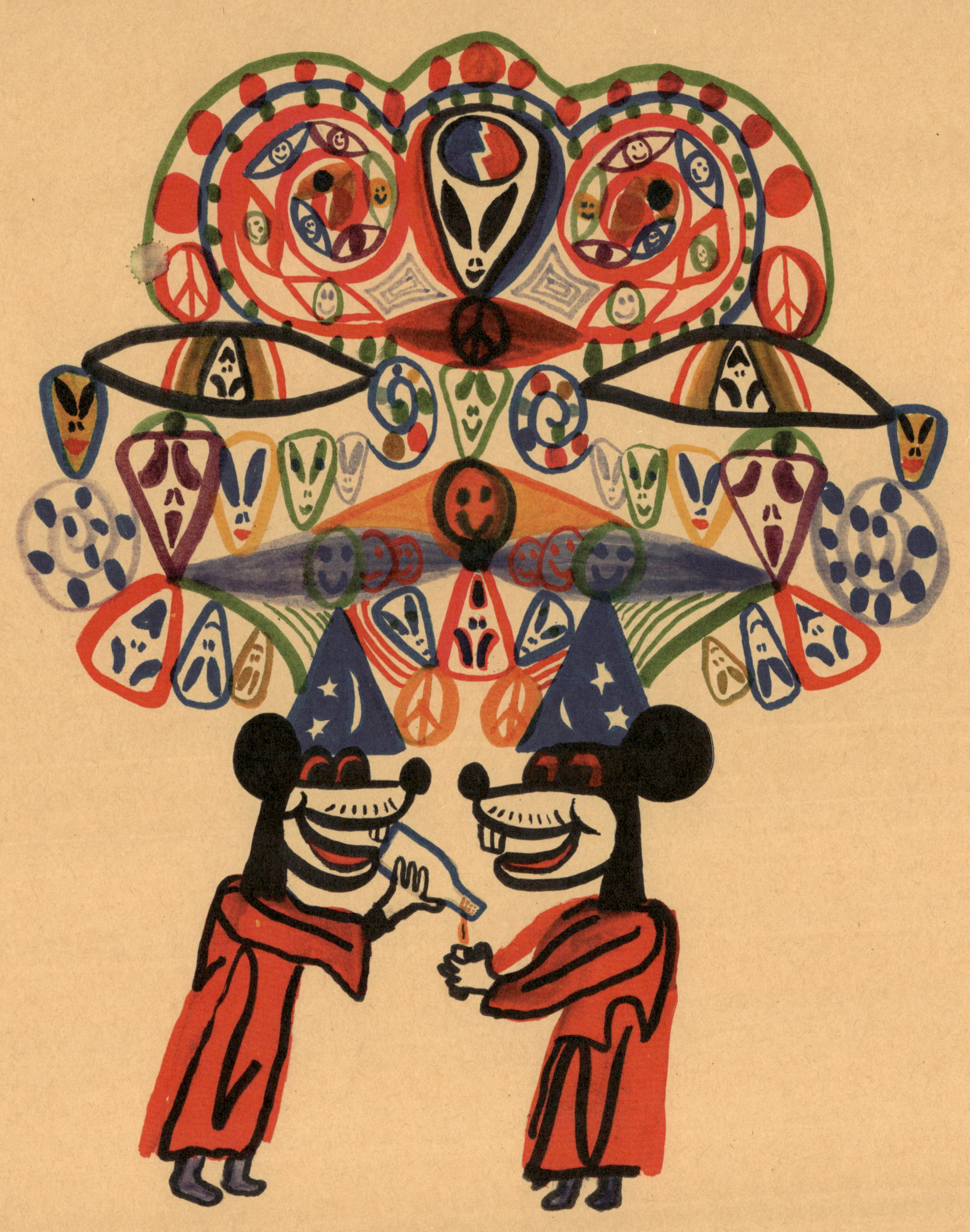

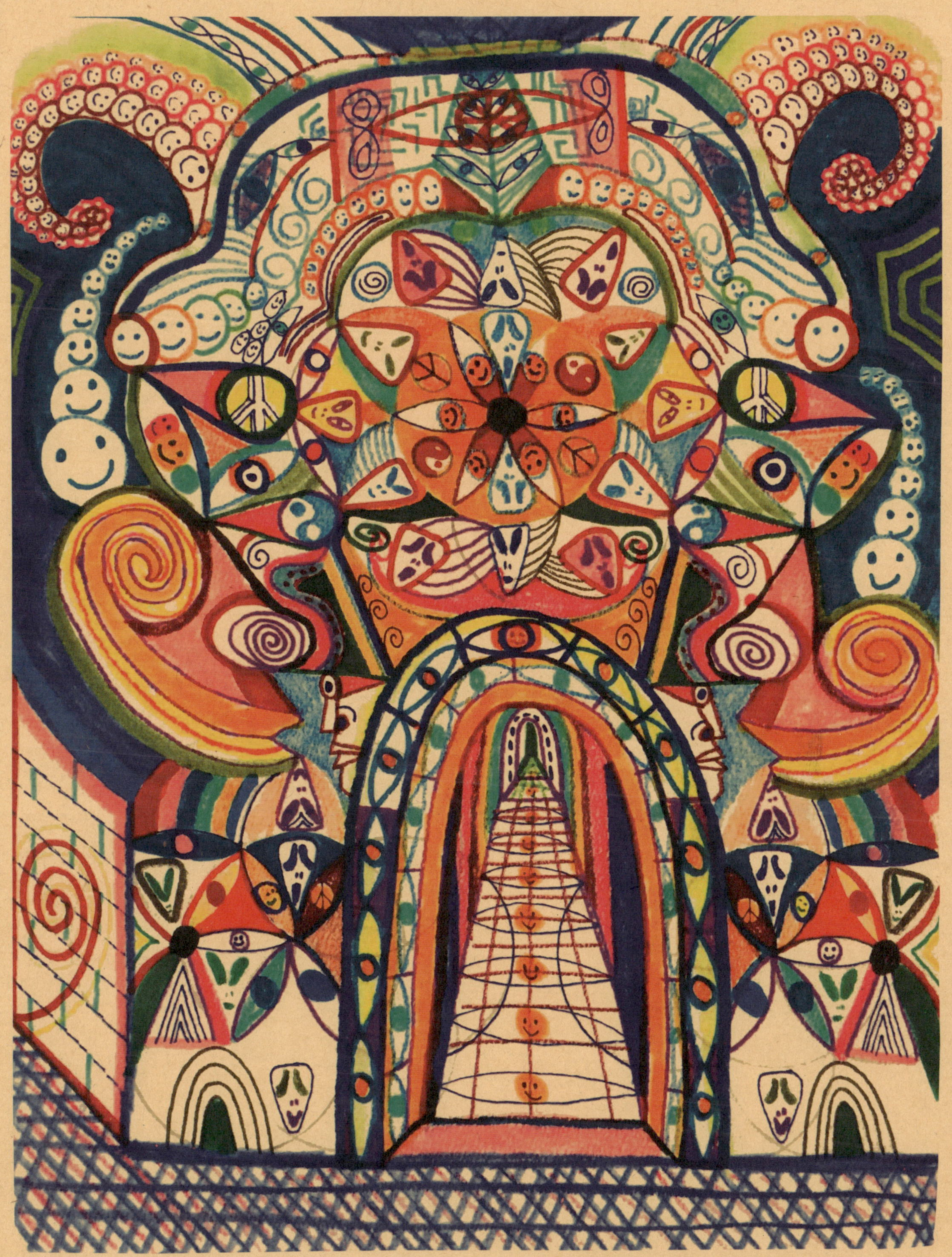

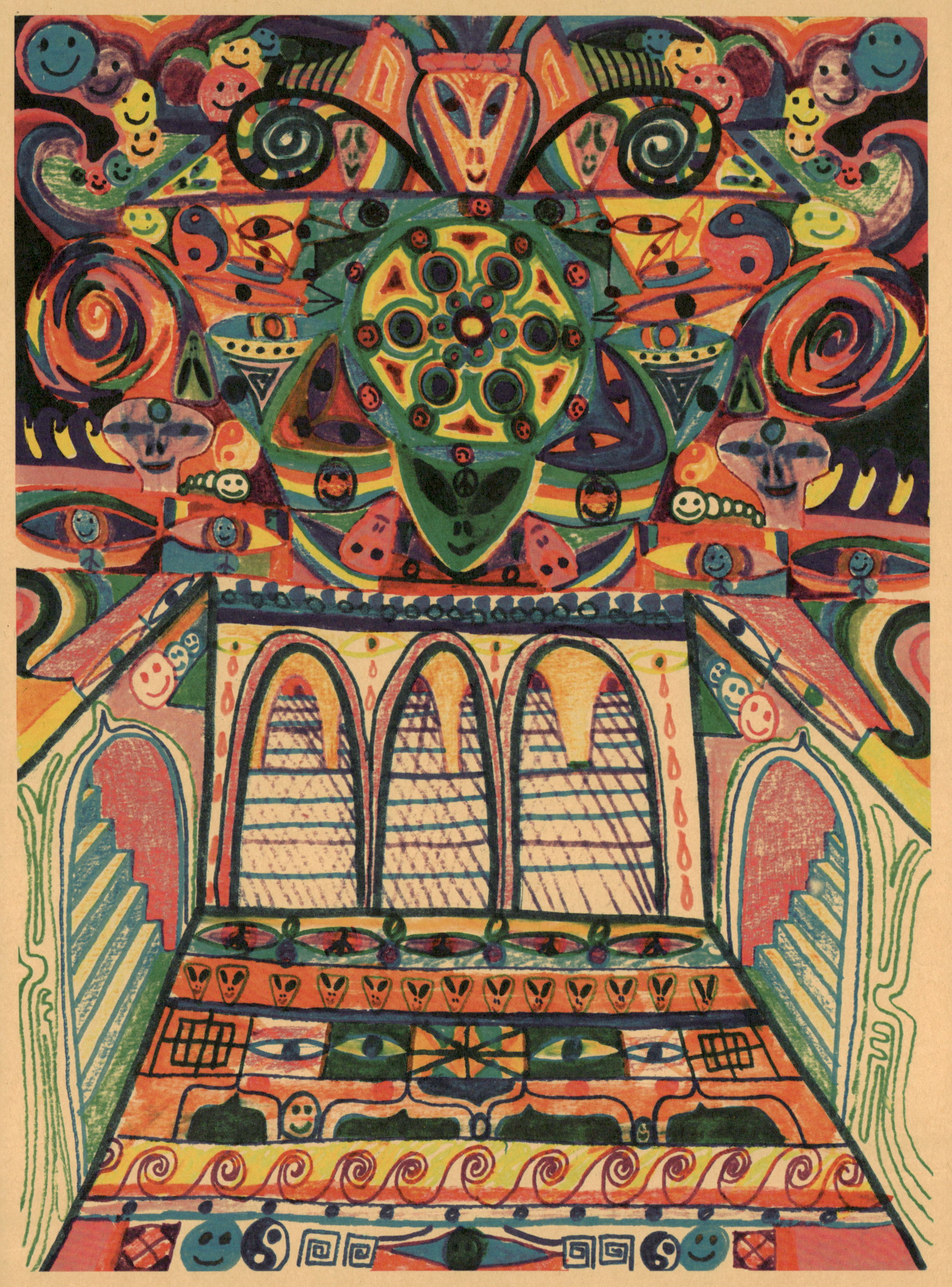

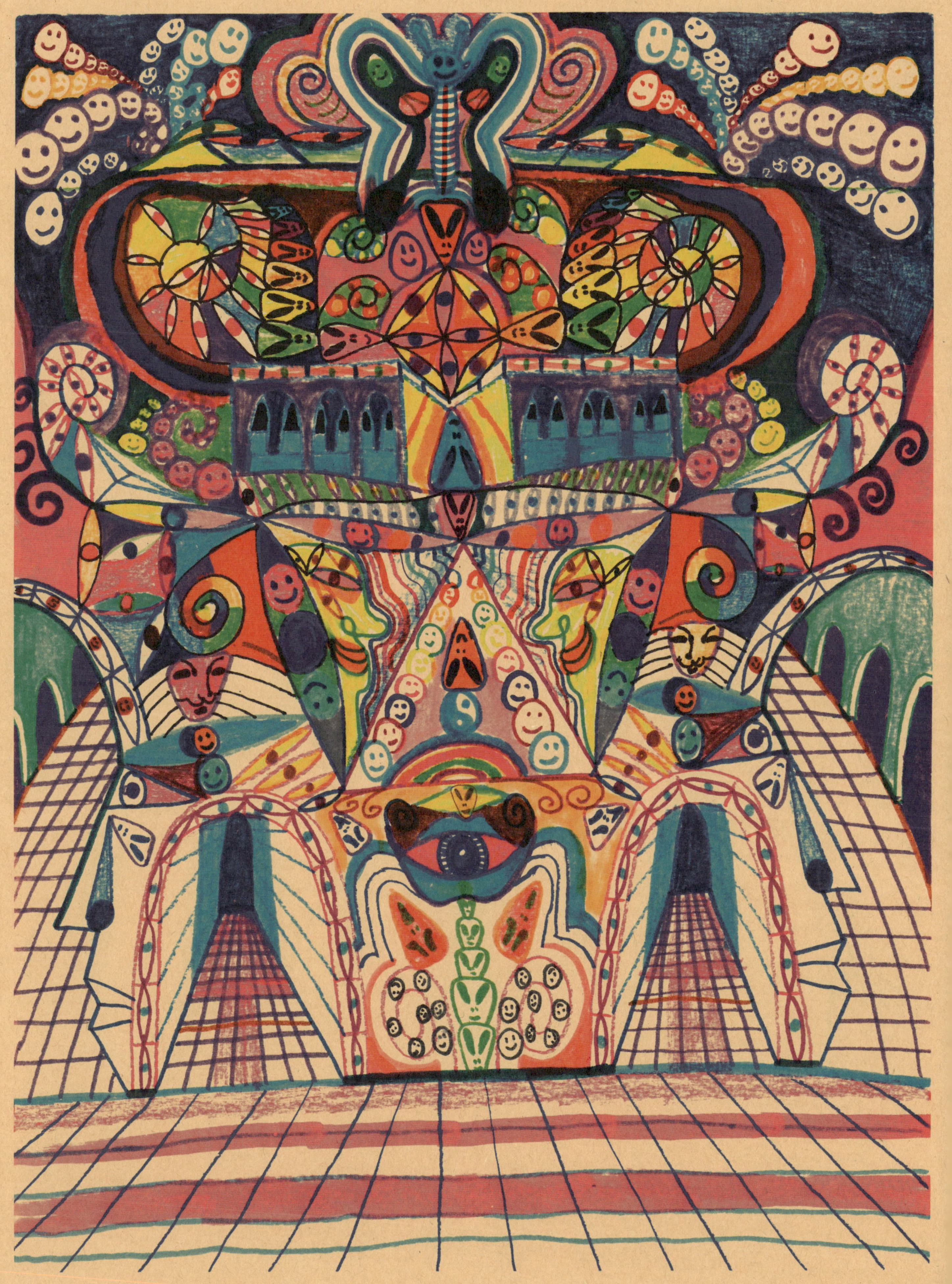

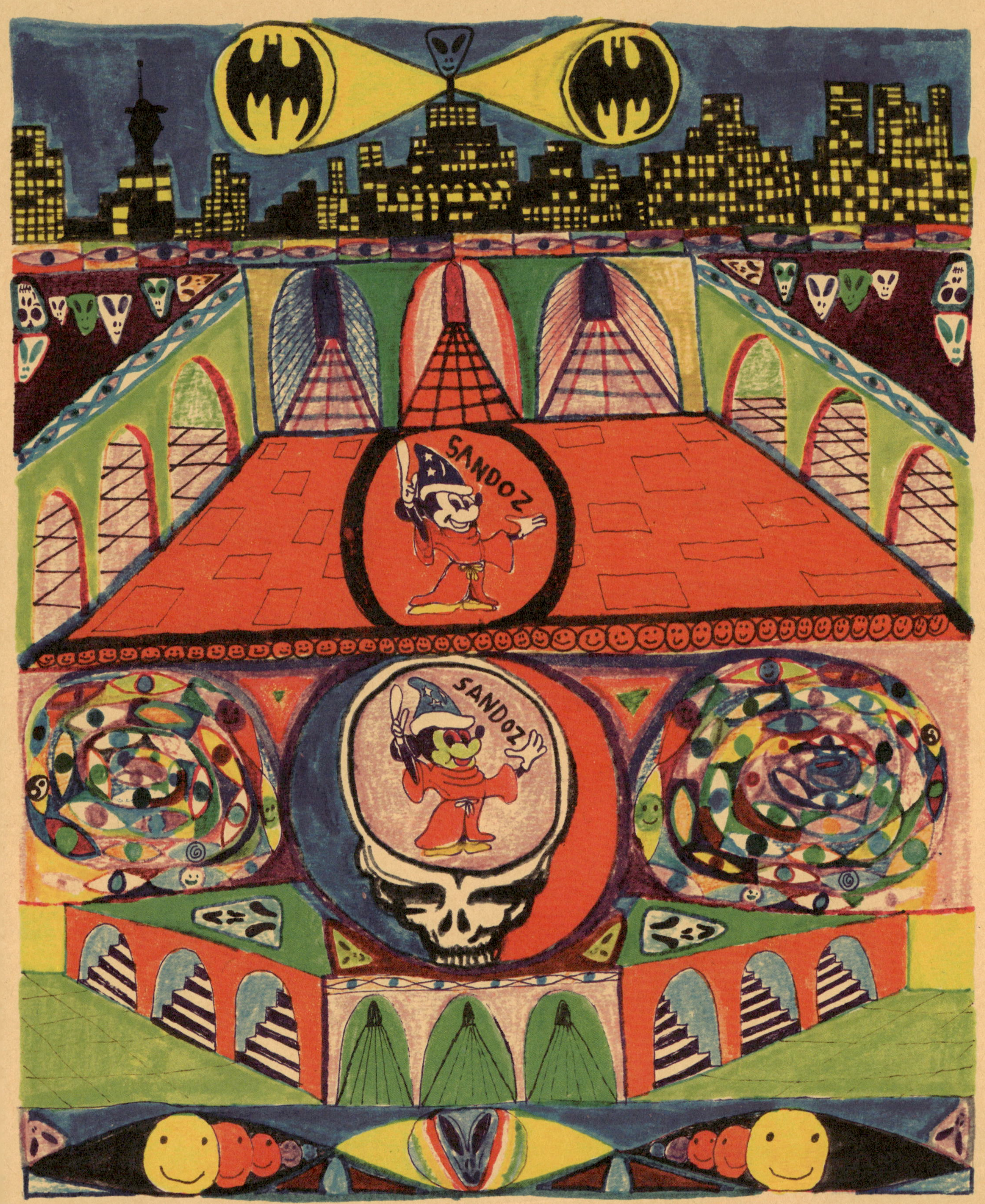
SANDOZ
SANDOZ

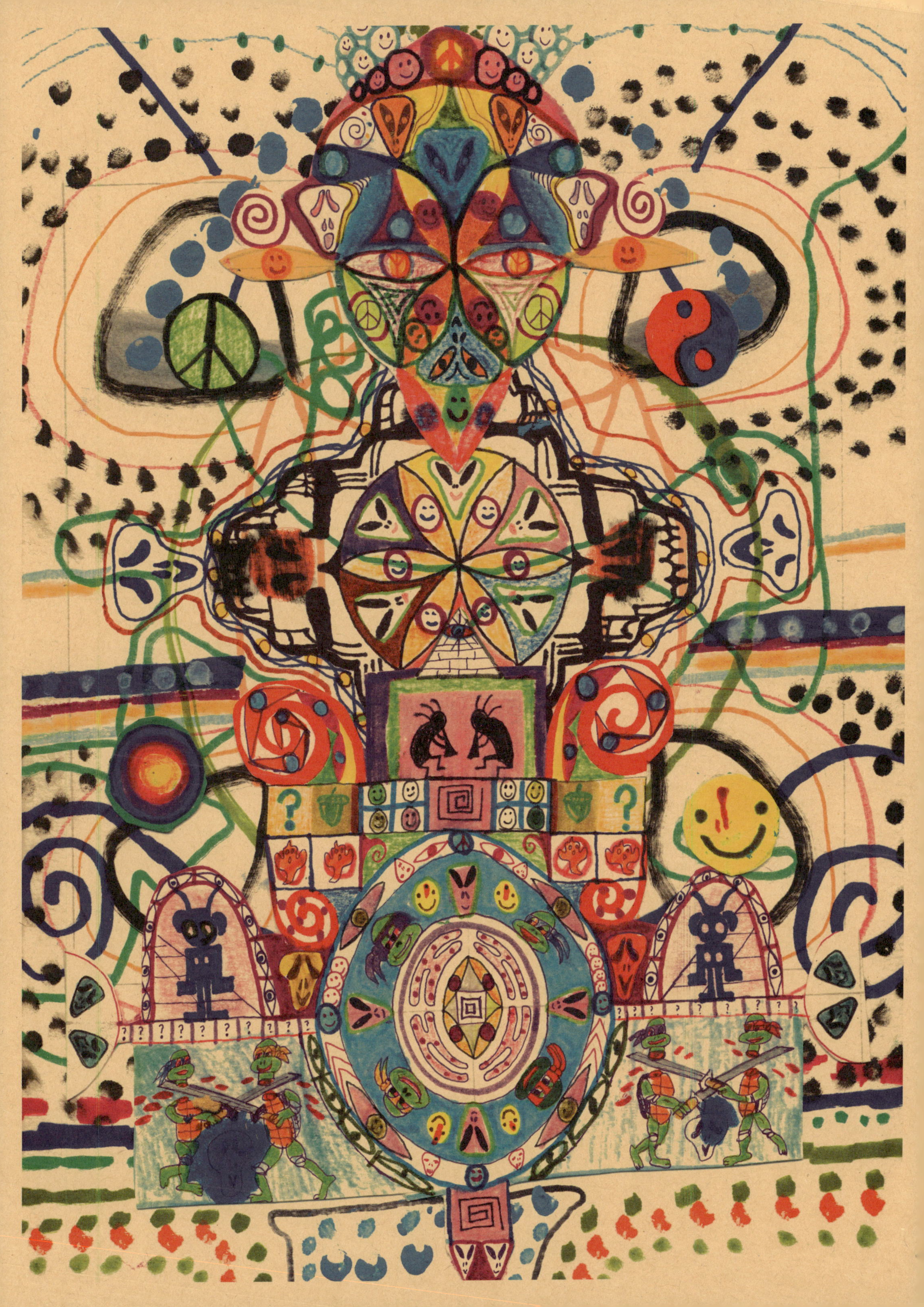

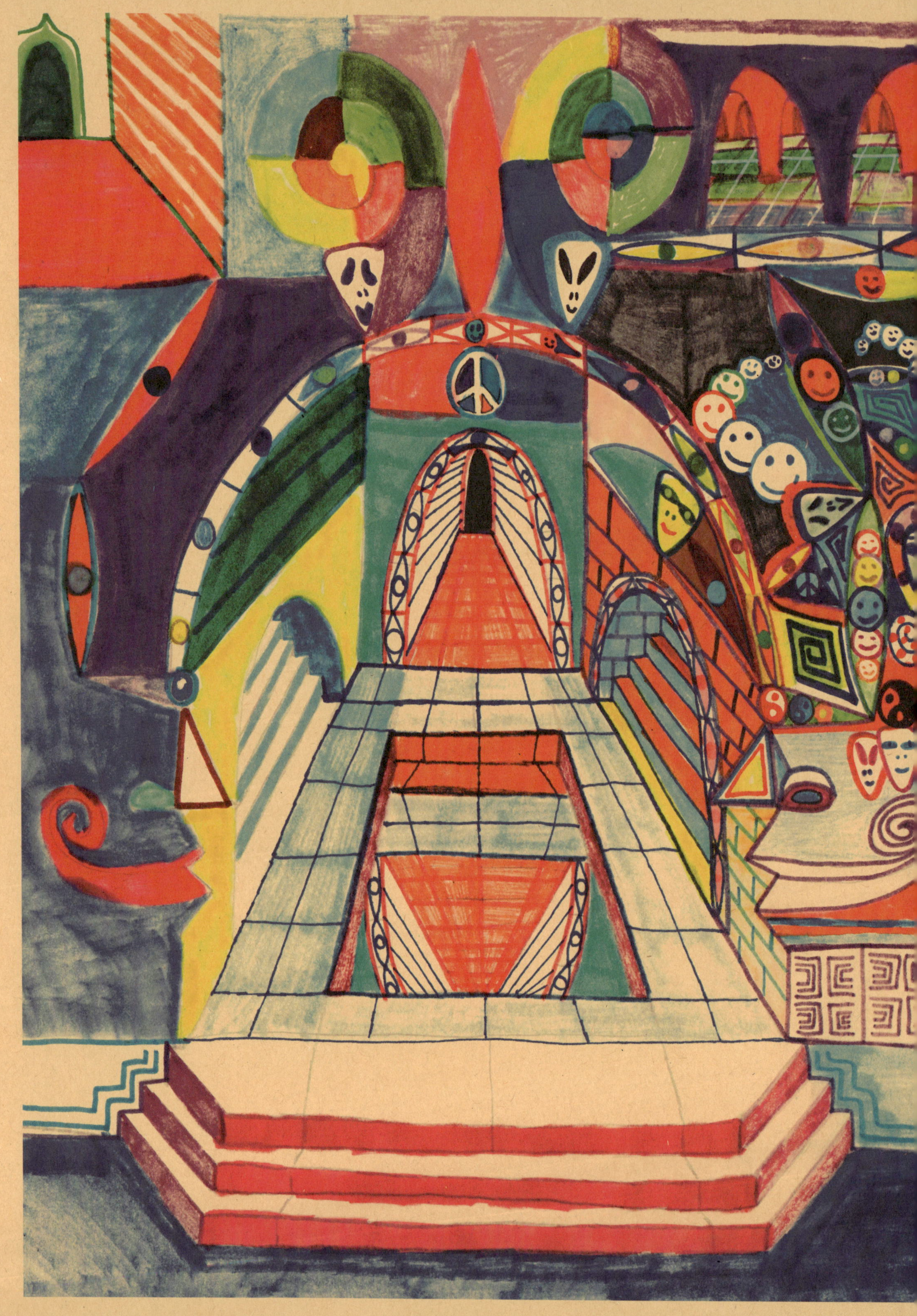

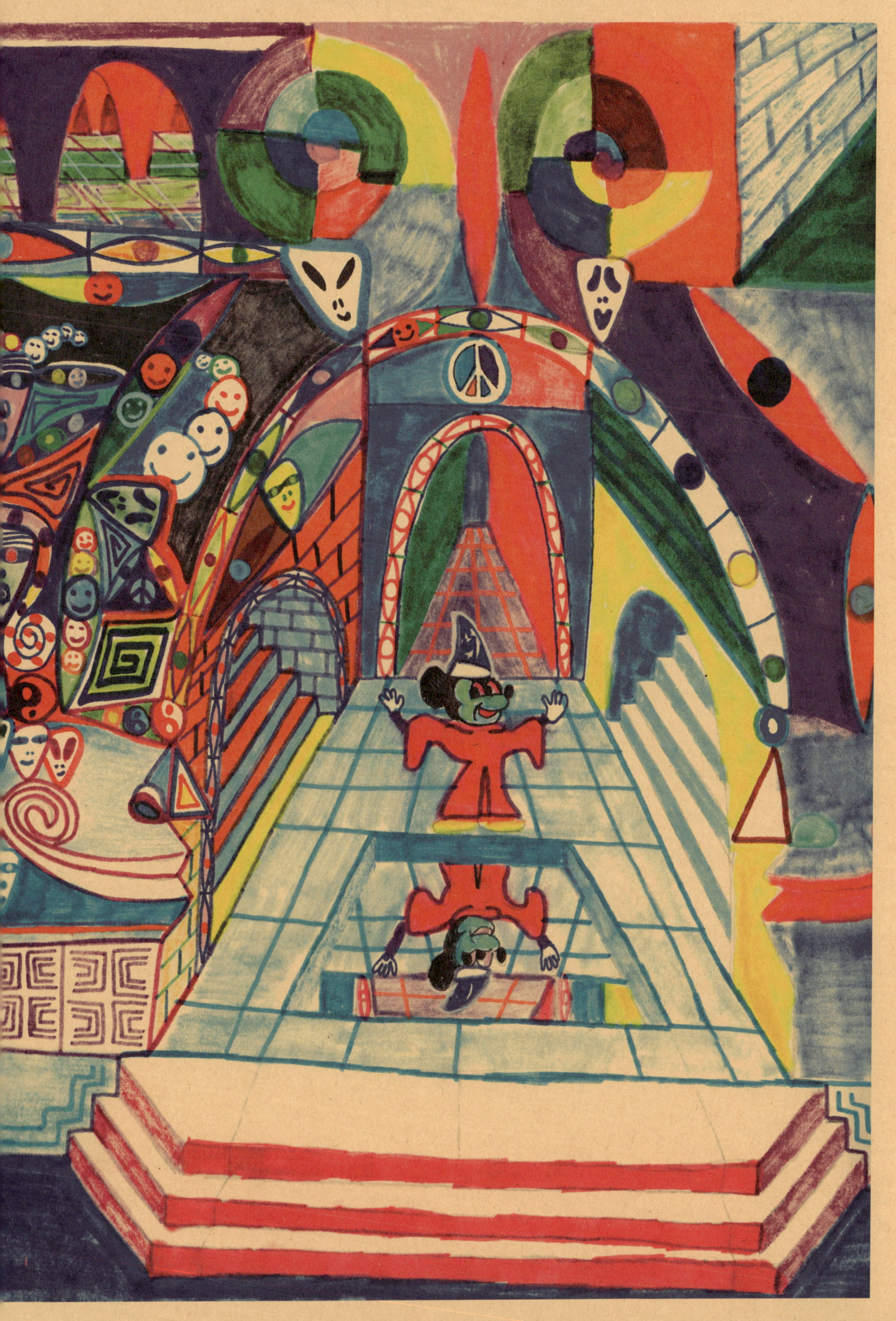

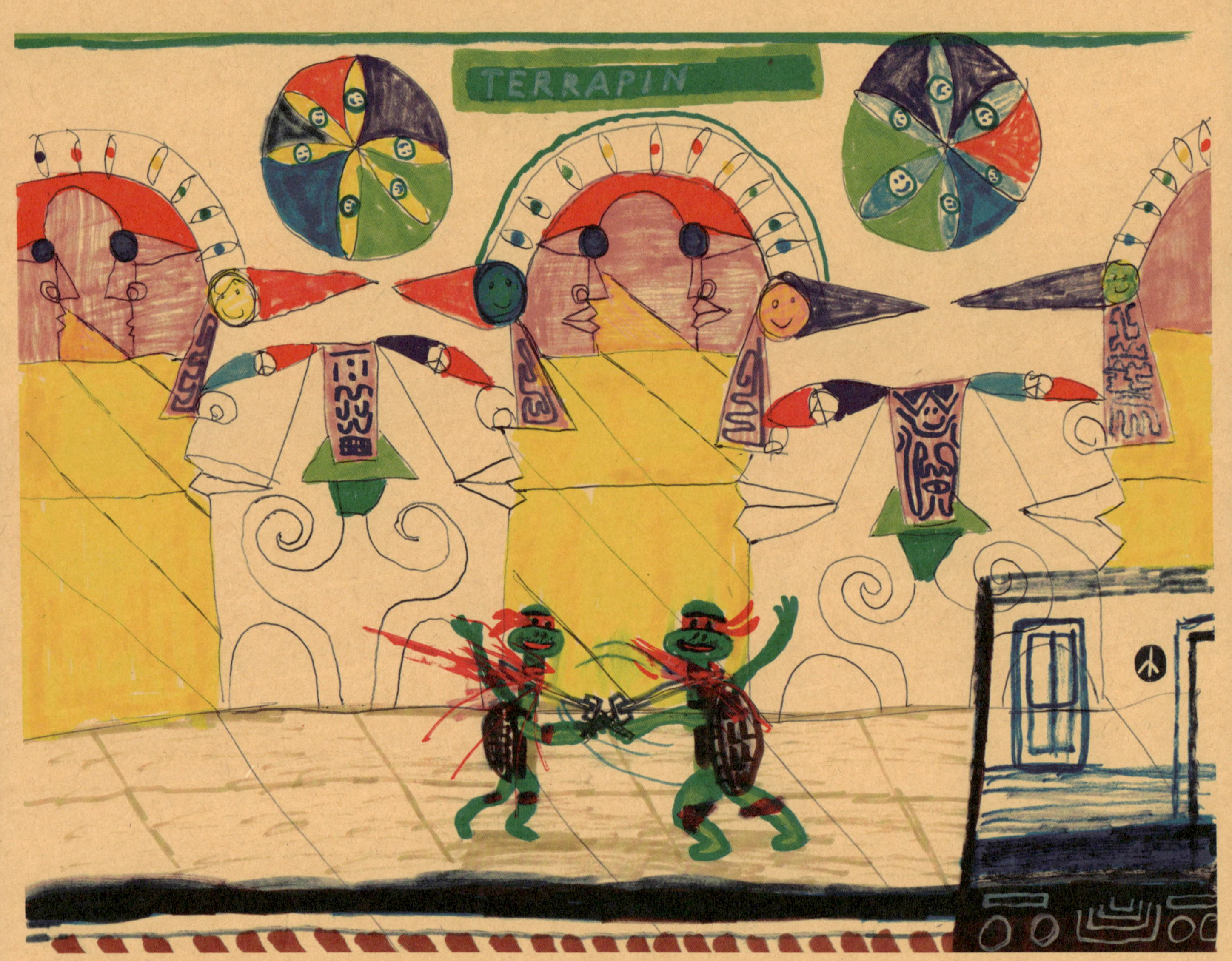

TERRAPIN

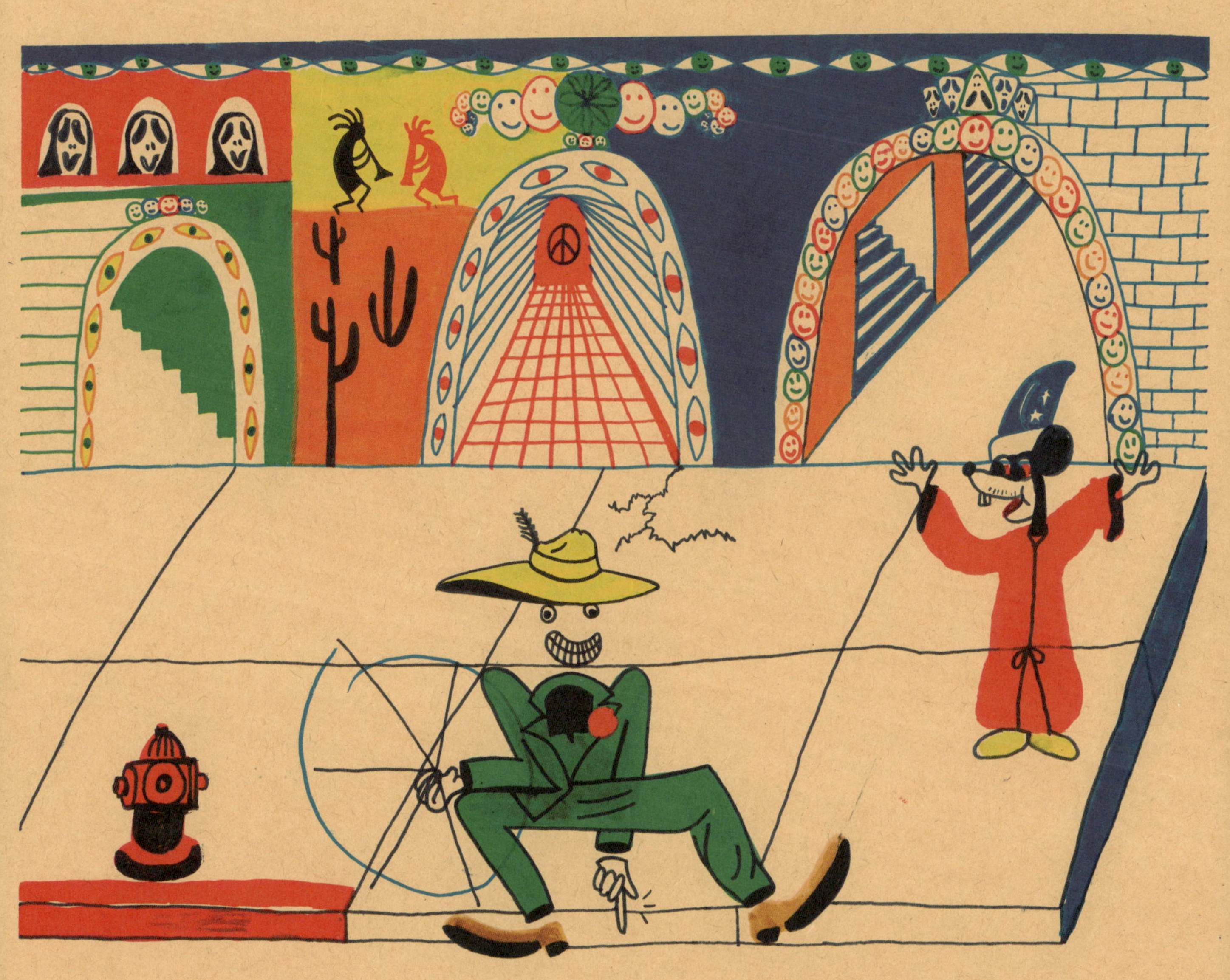

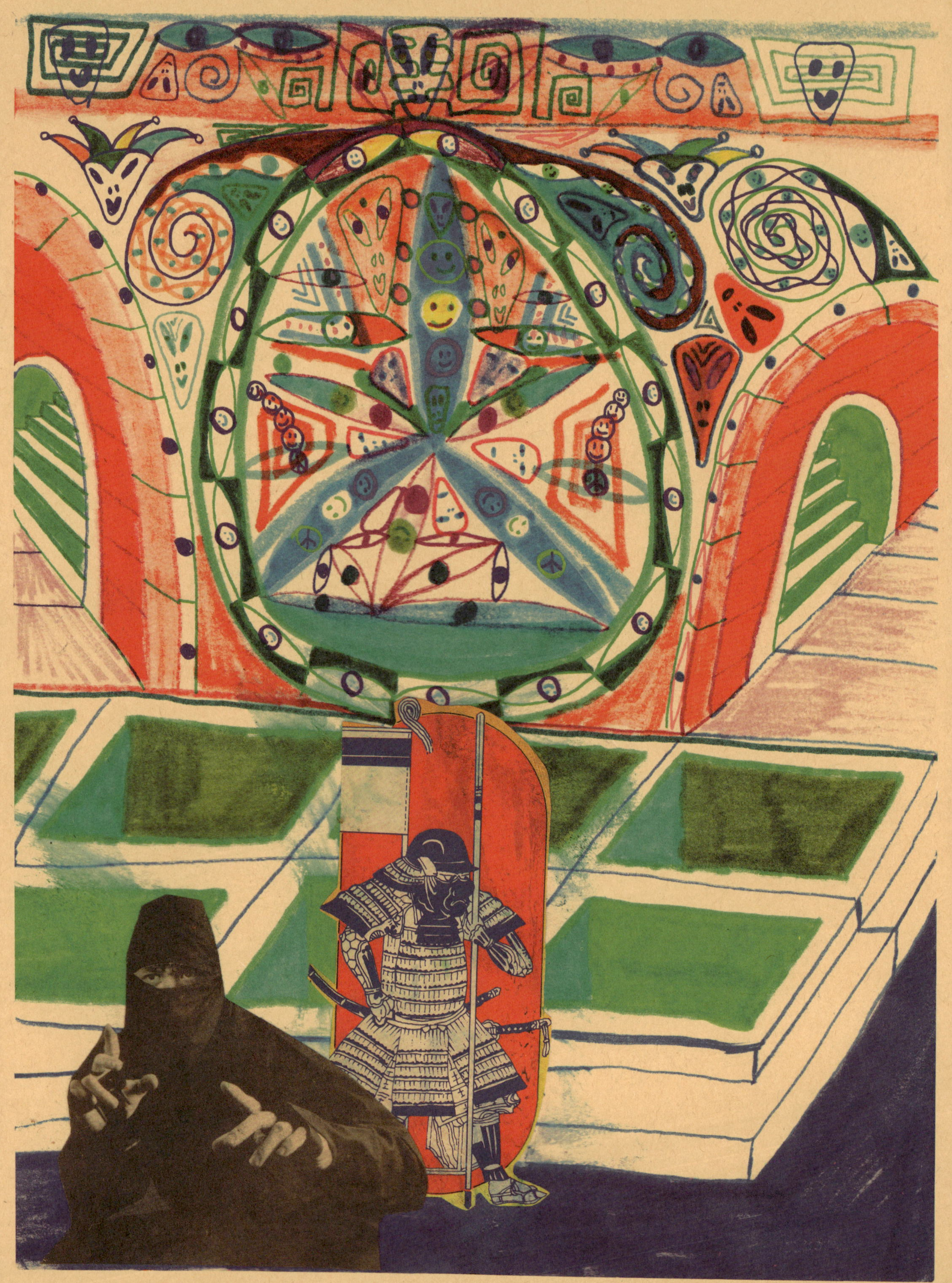

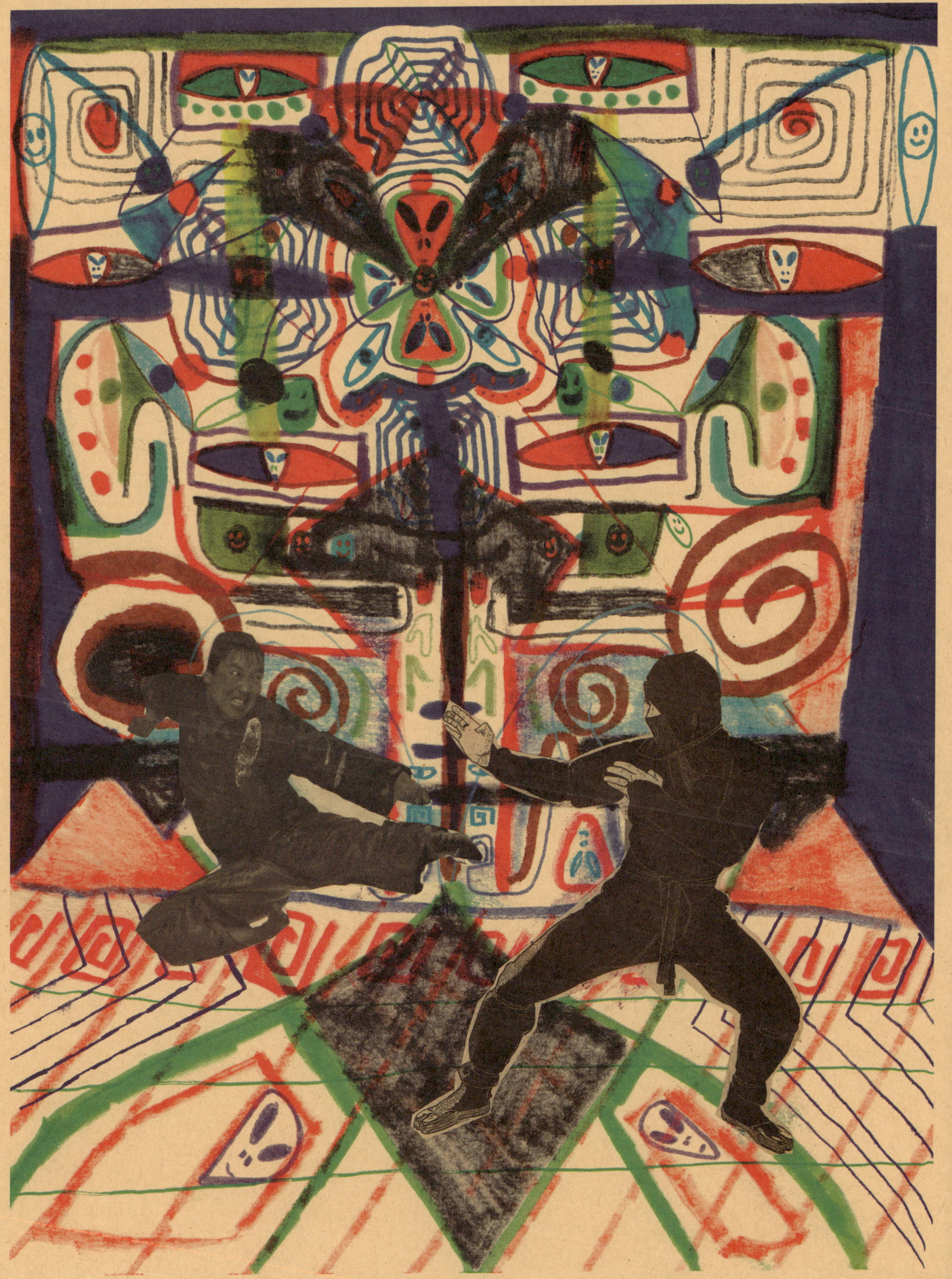

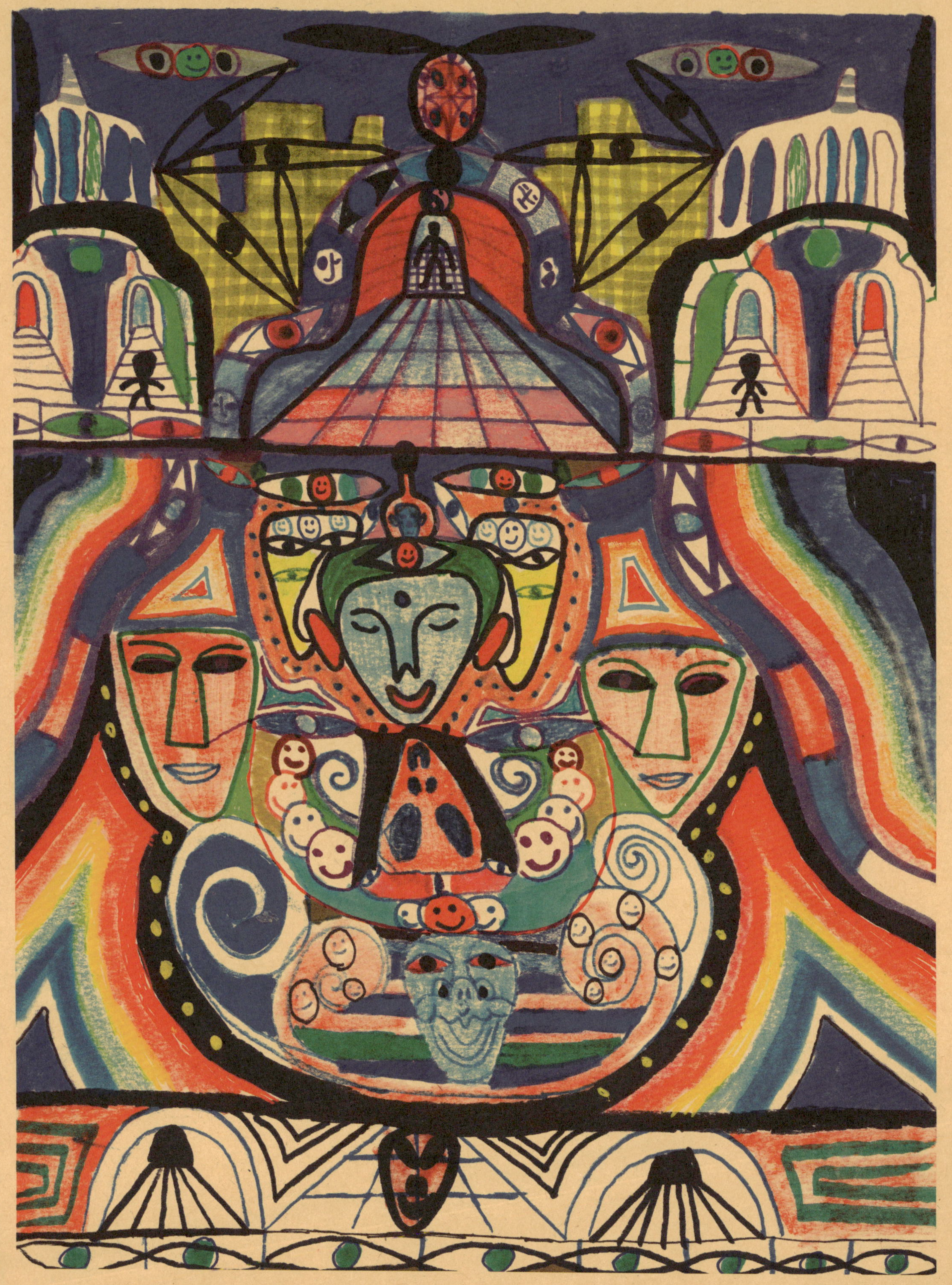

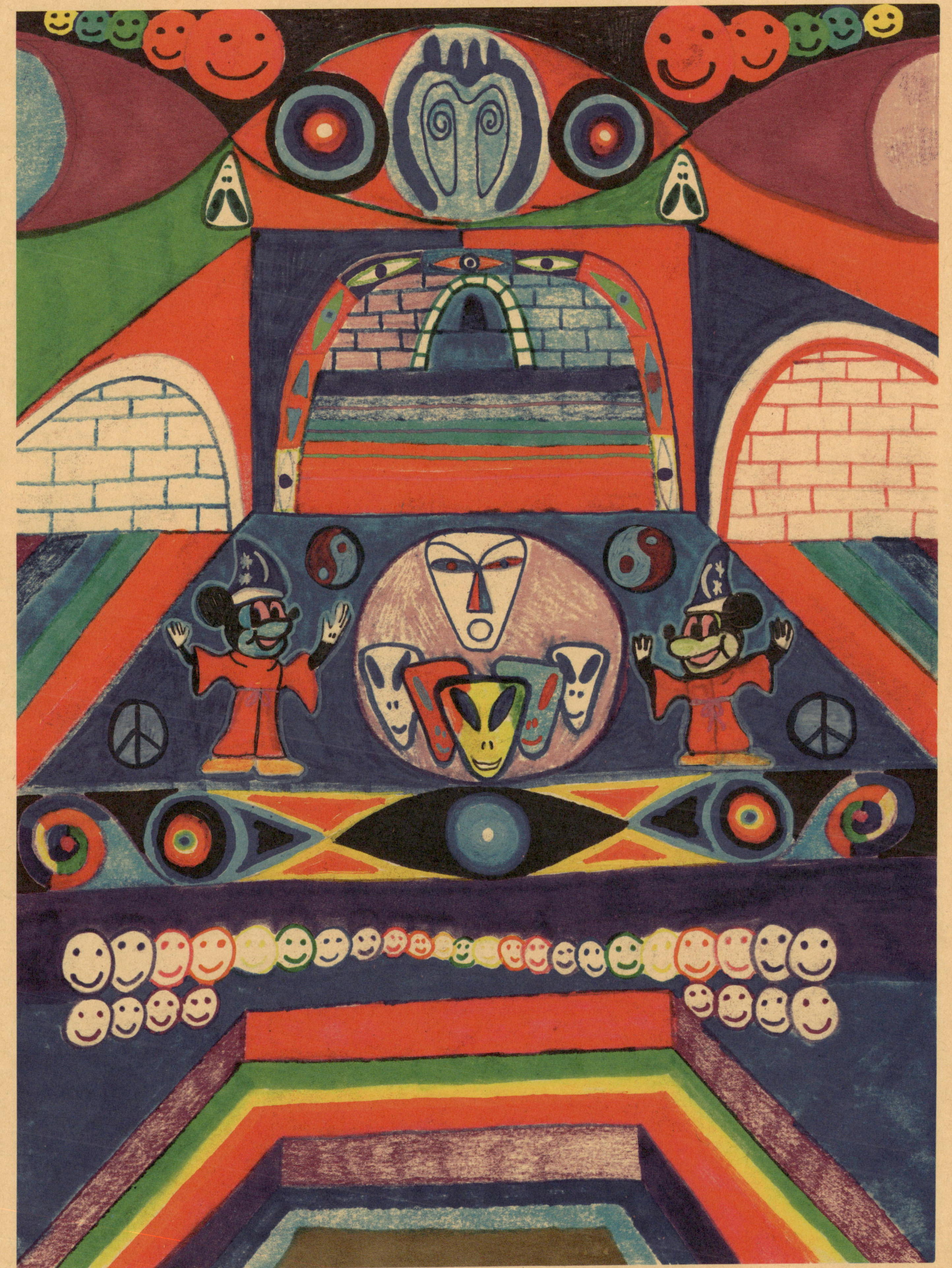

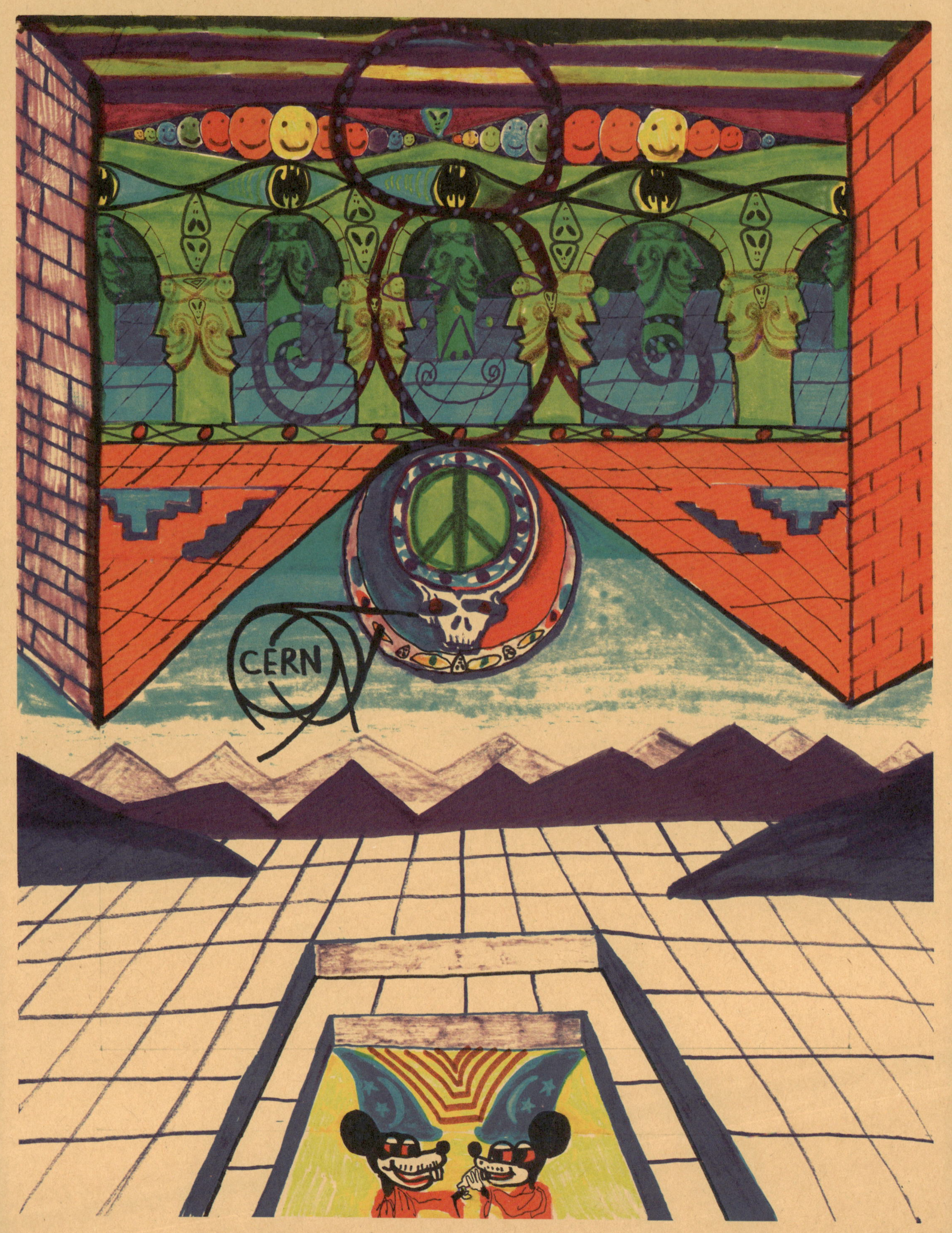

CERN

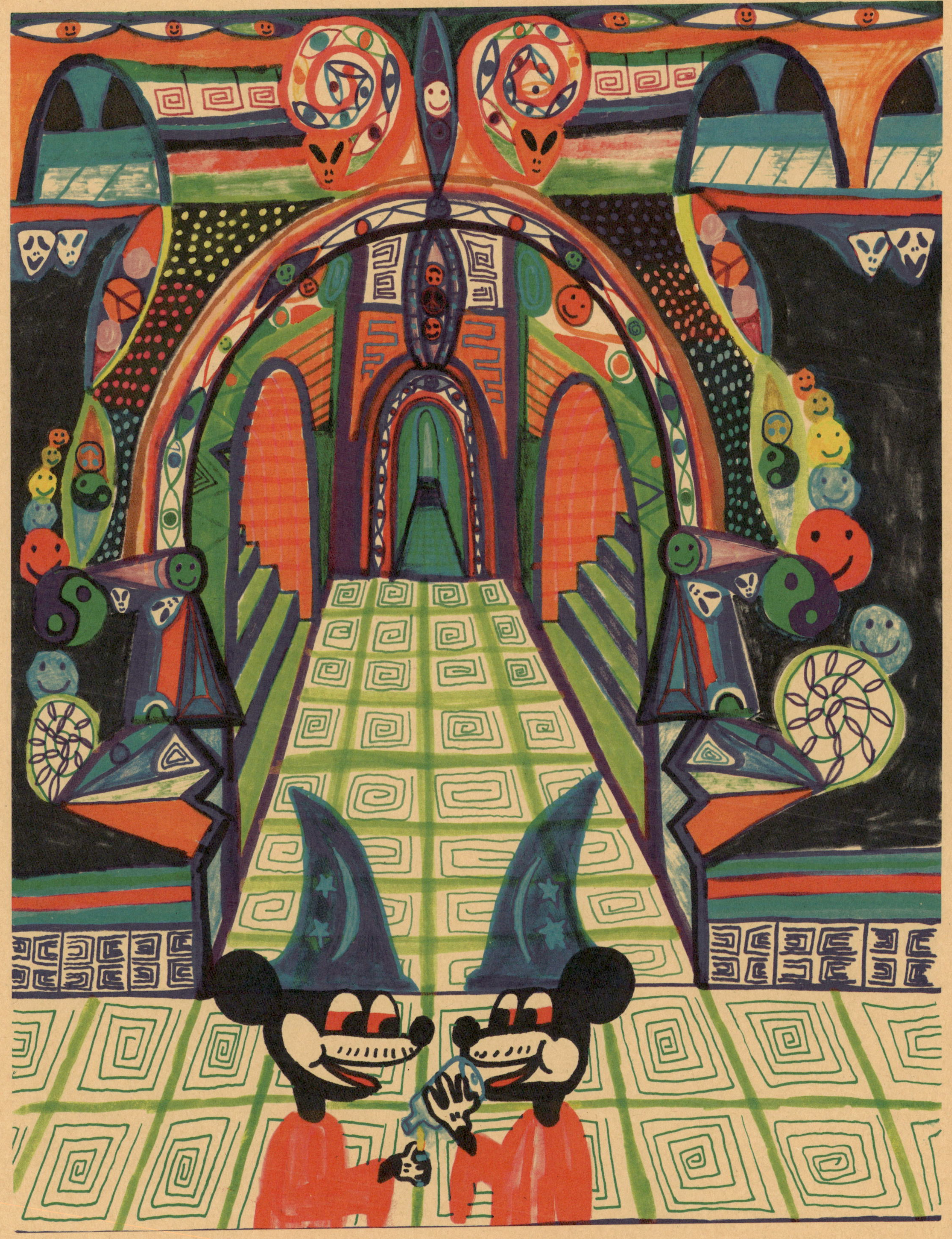

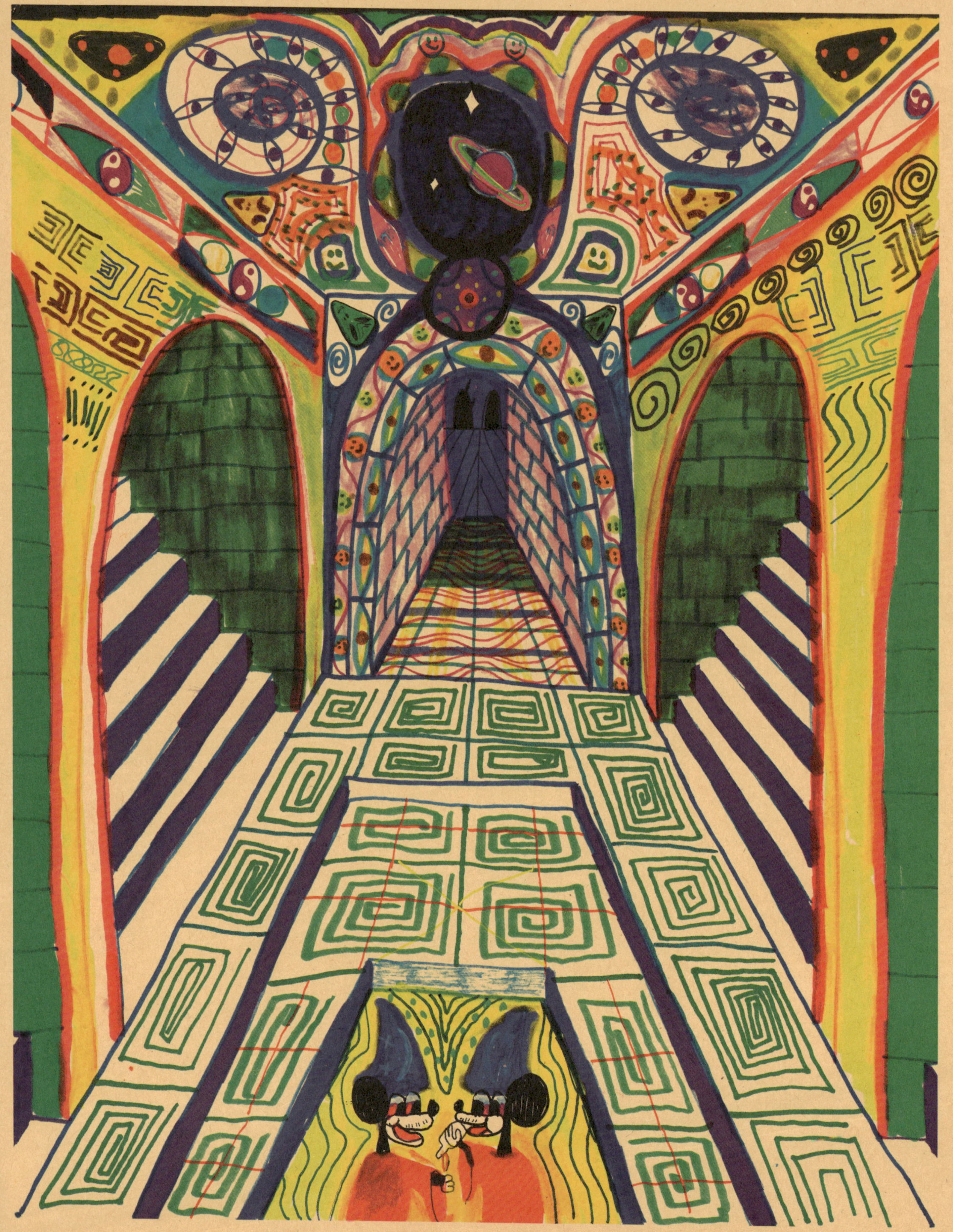

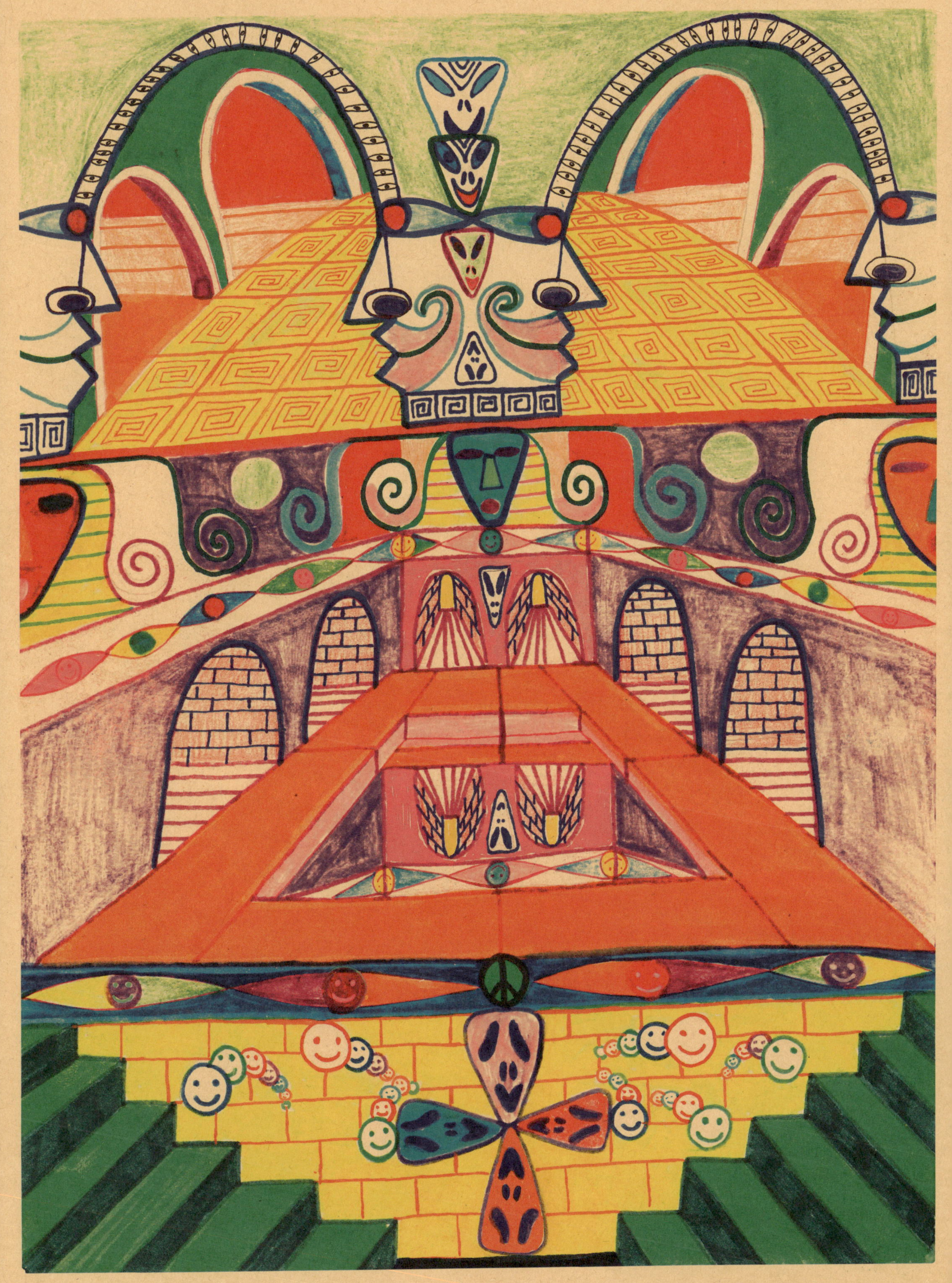

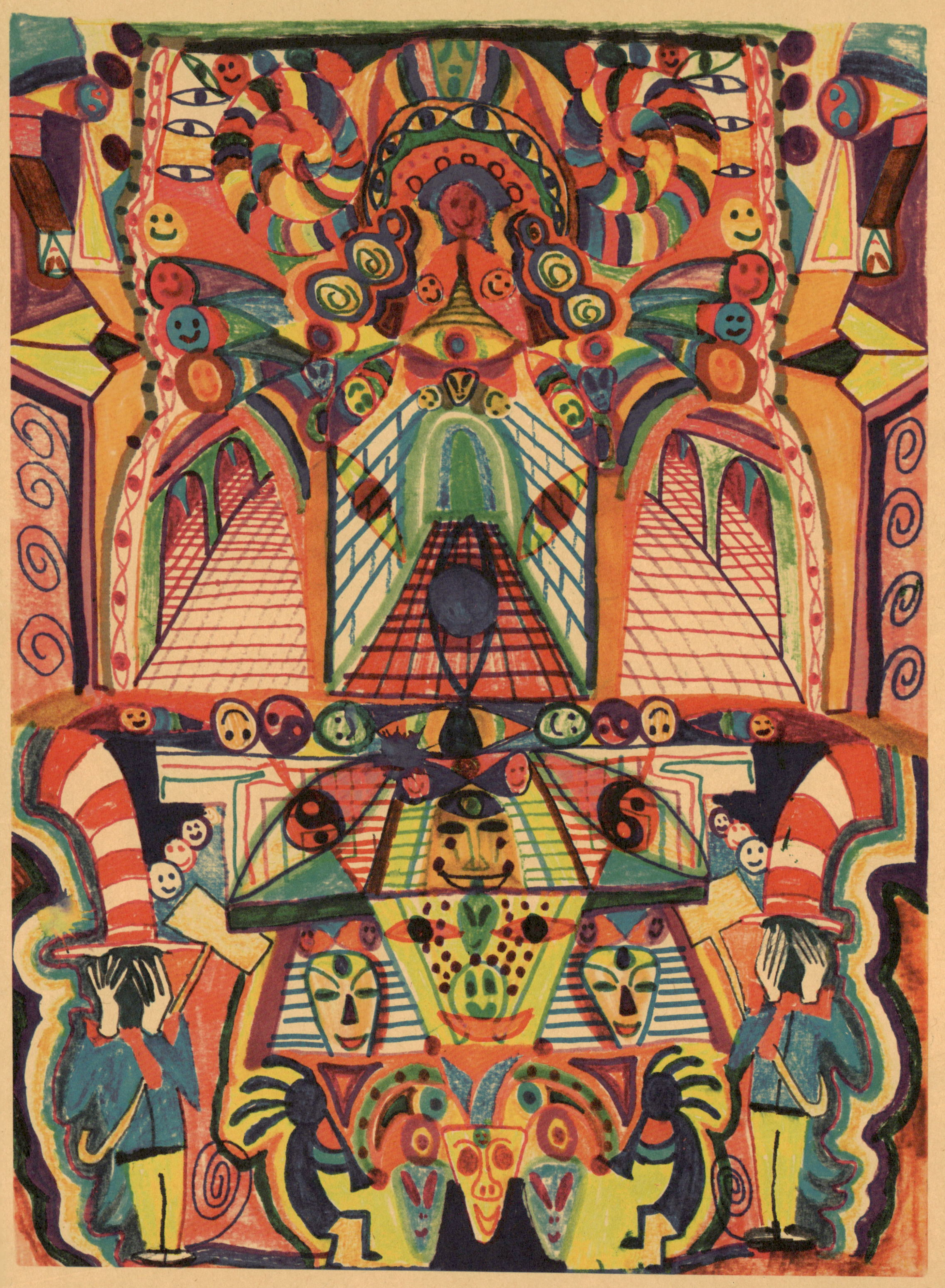

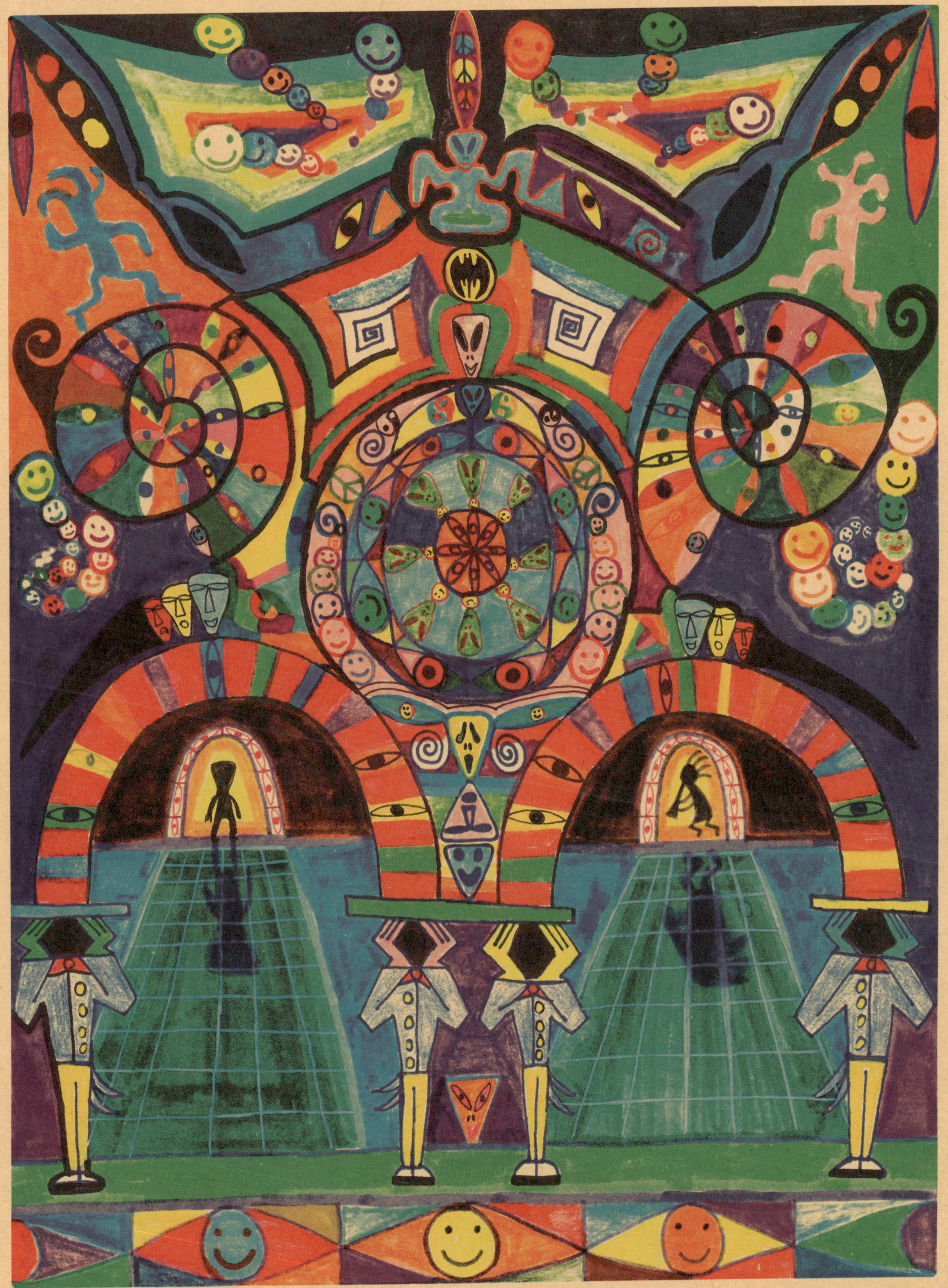

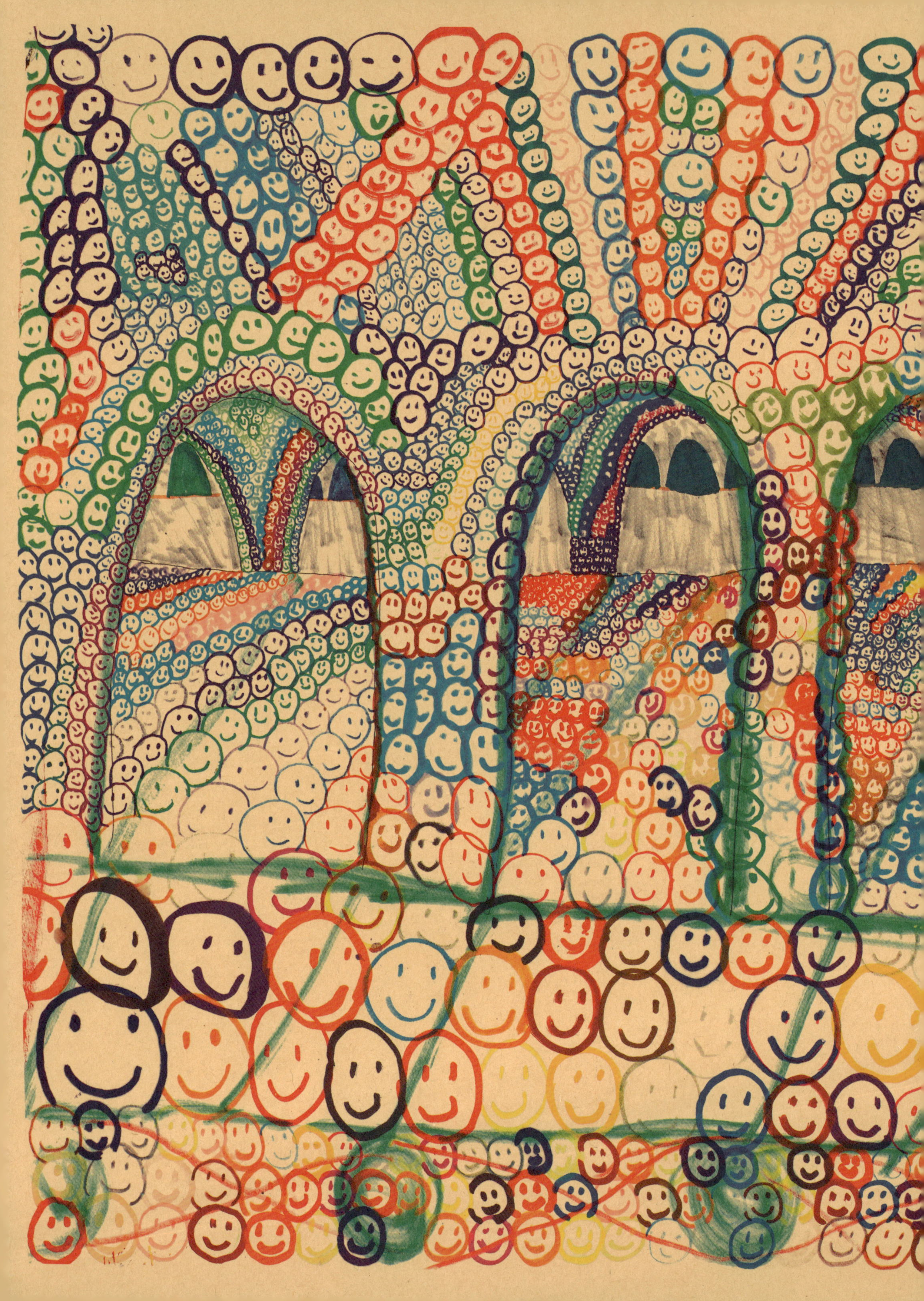

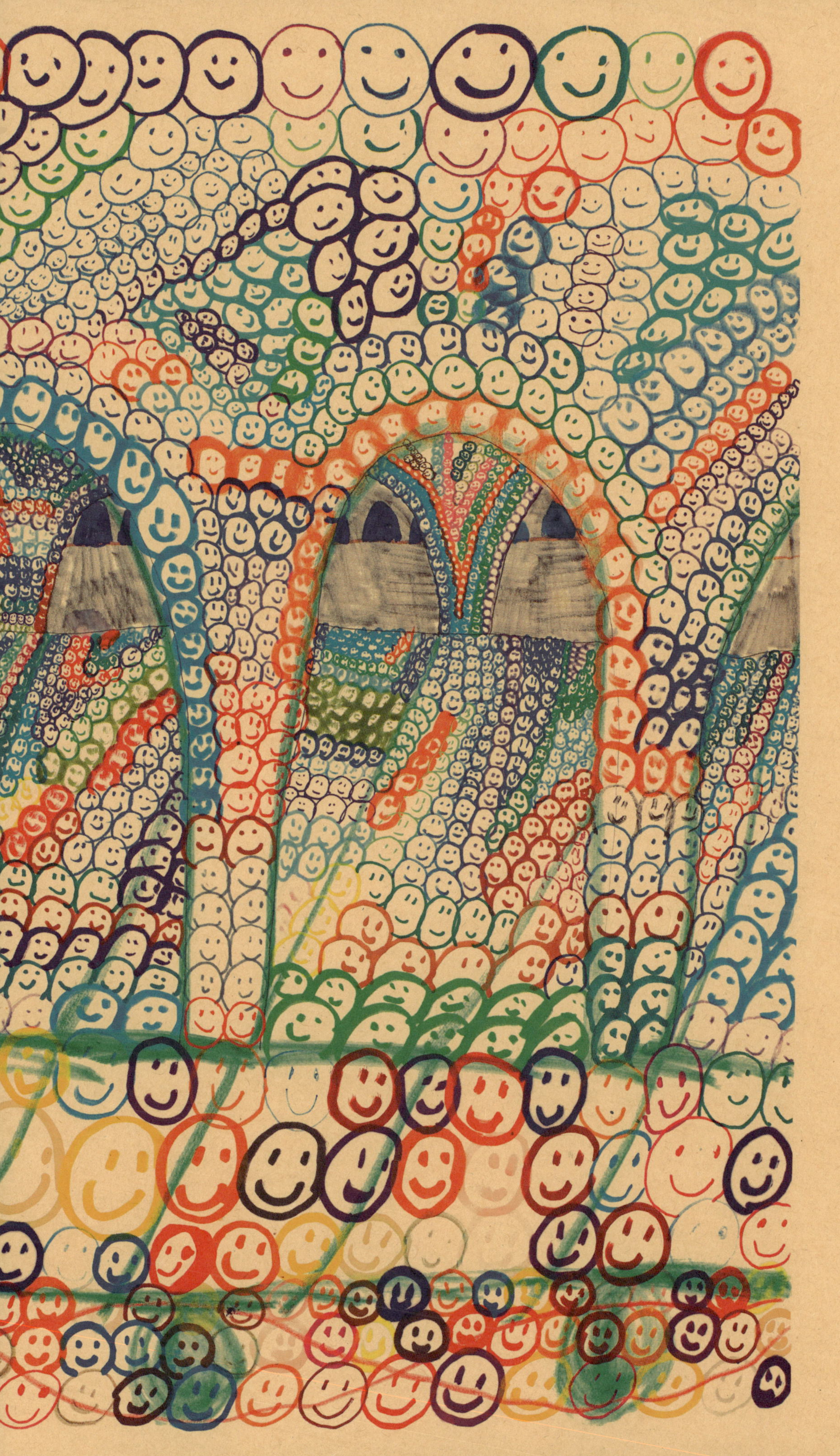

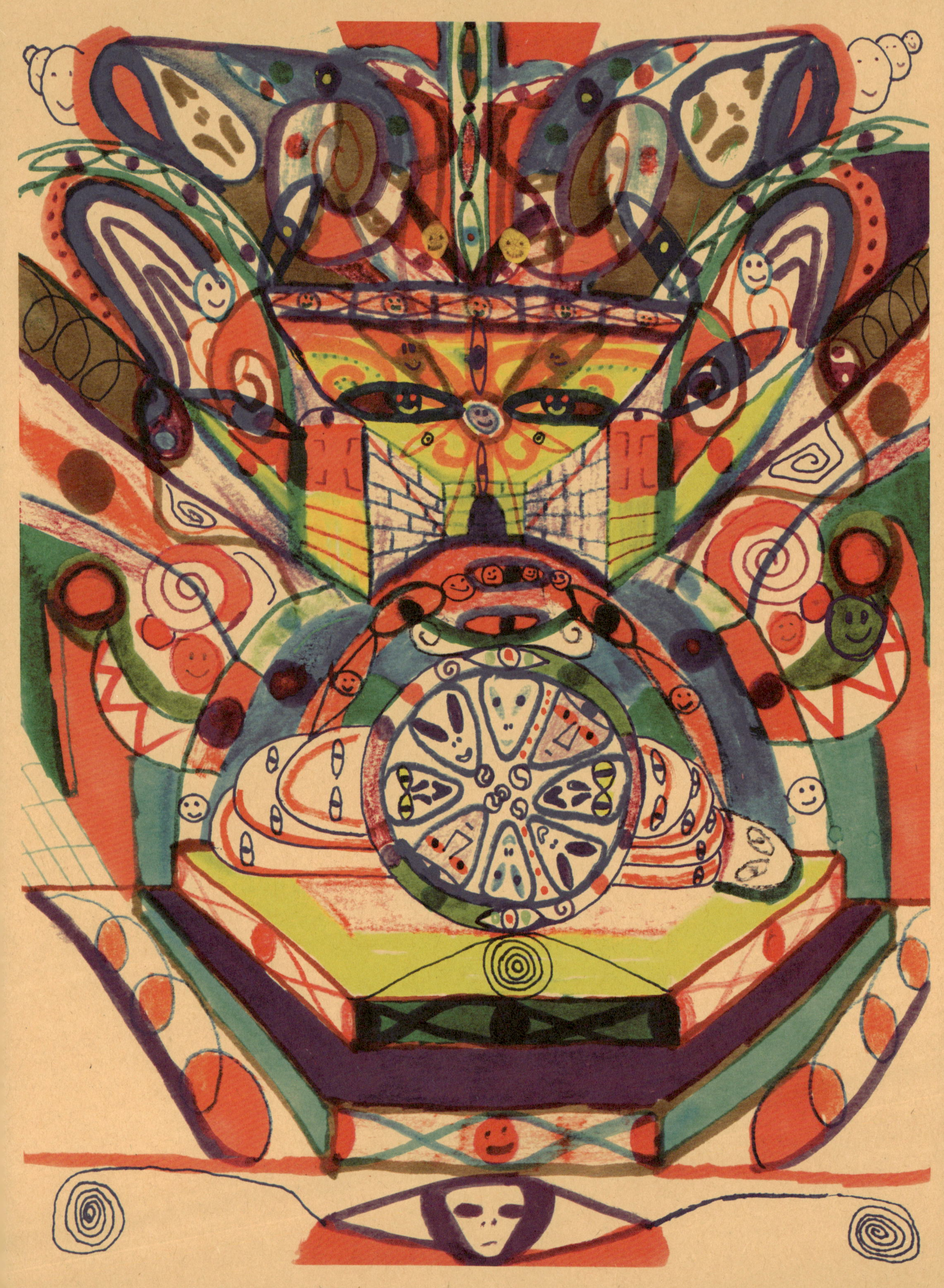

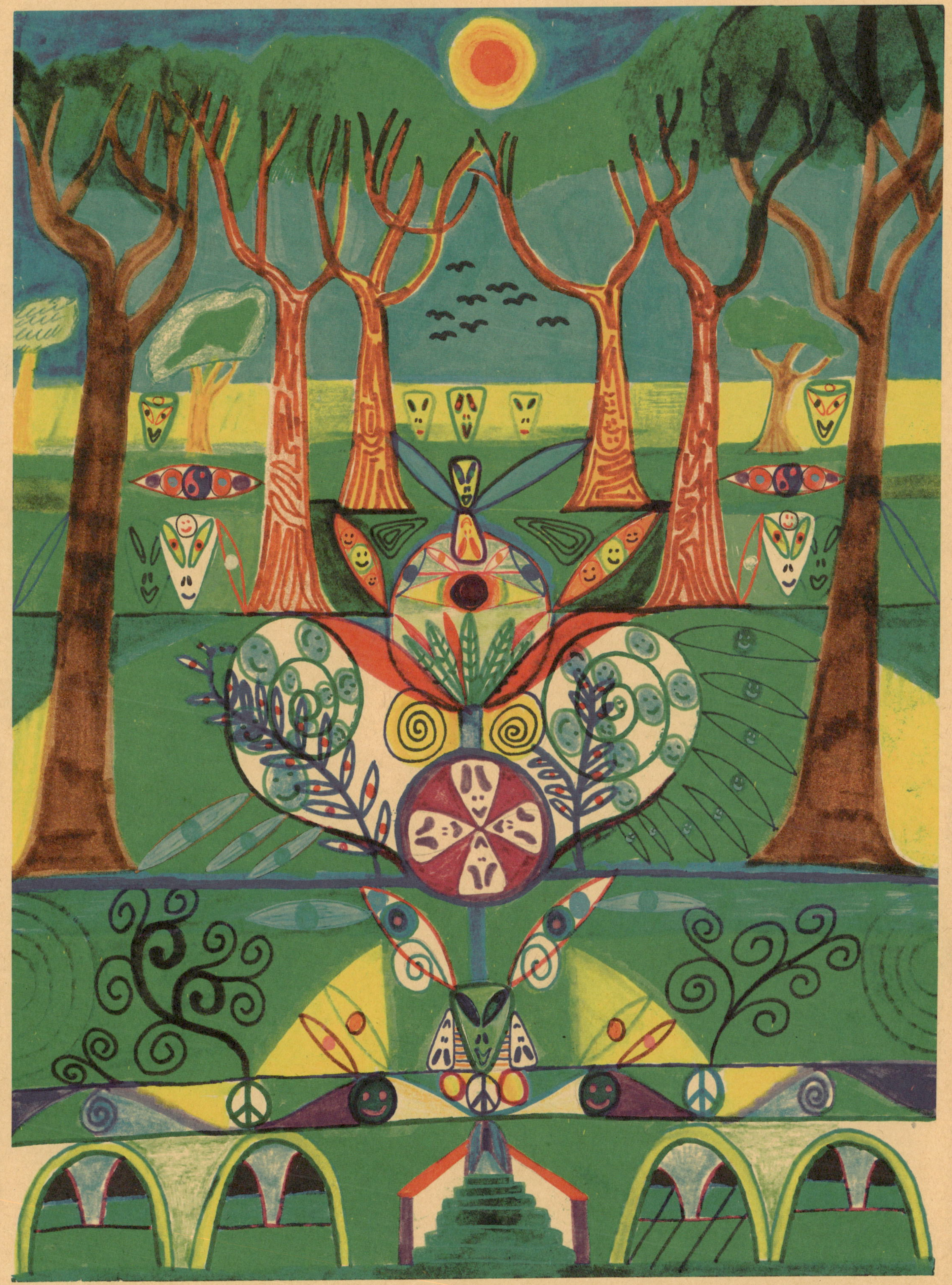

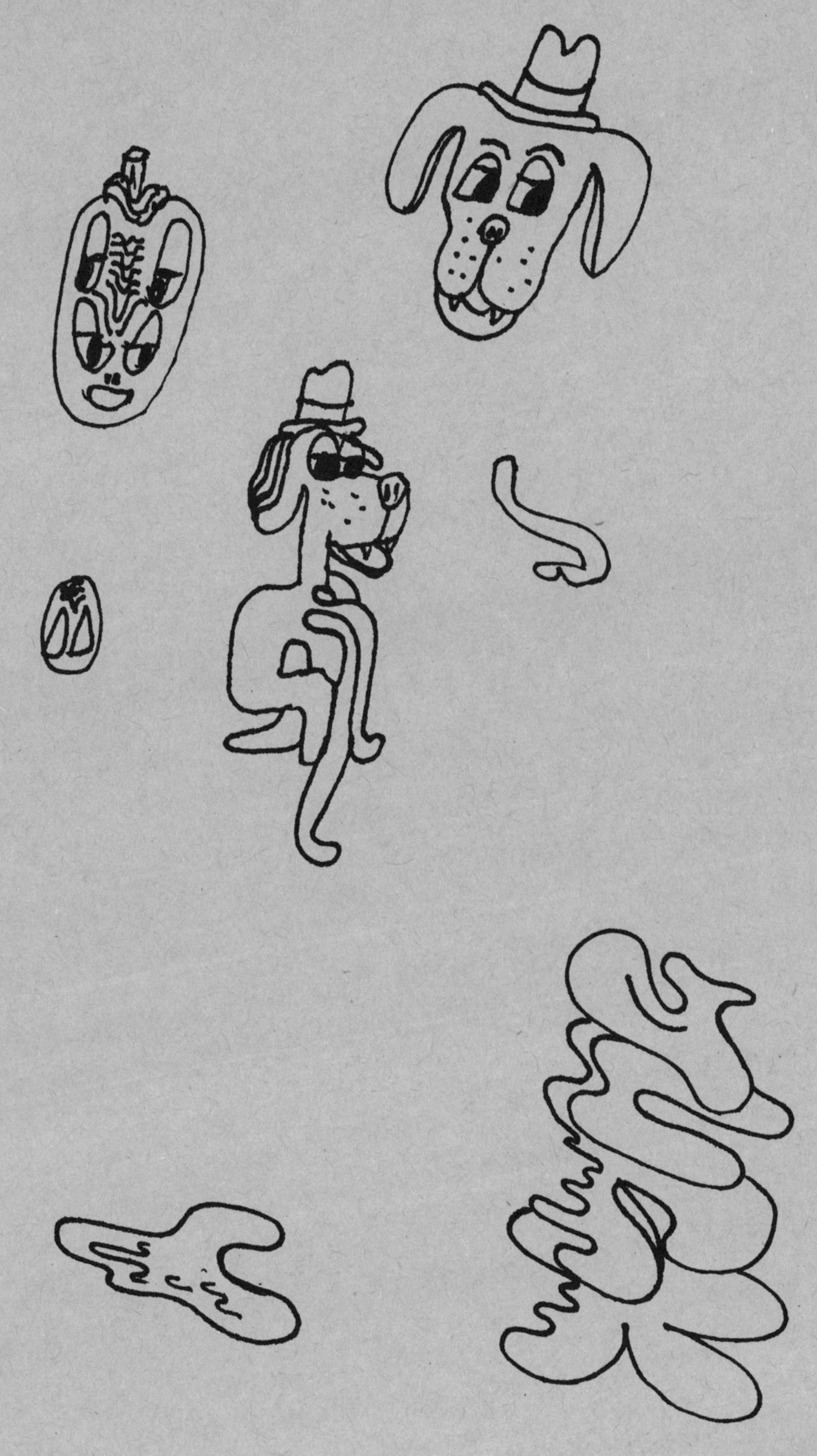

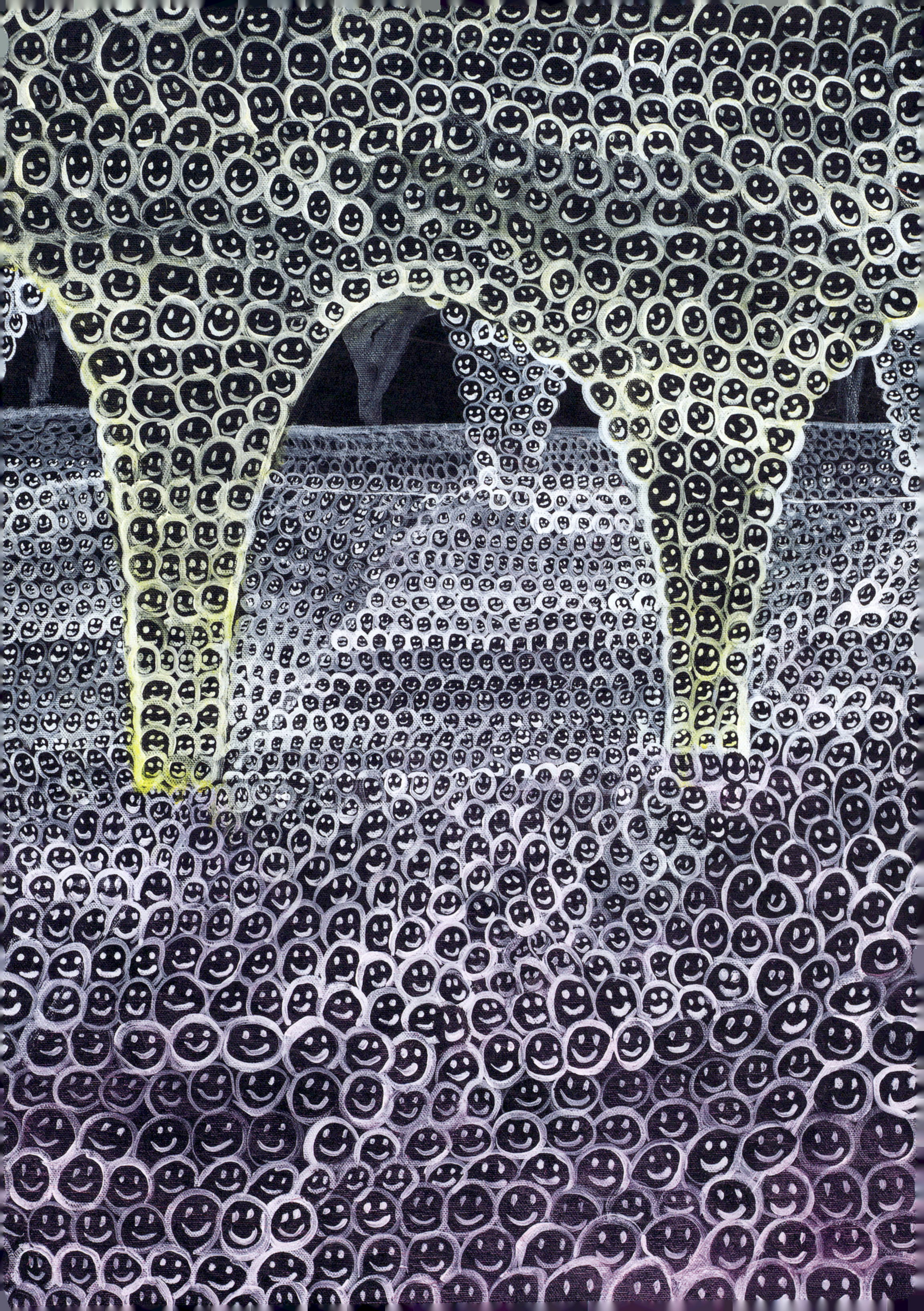

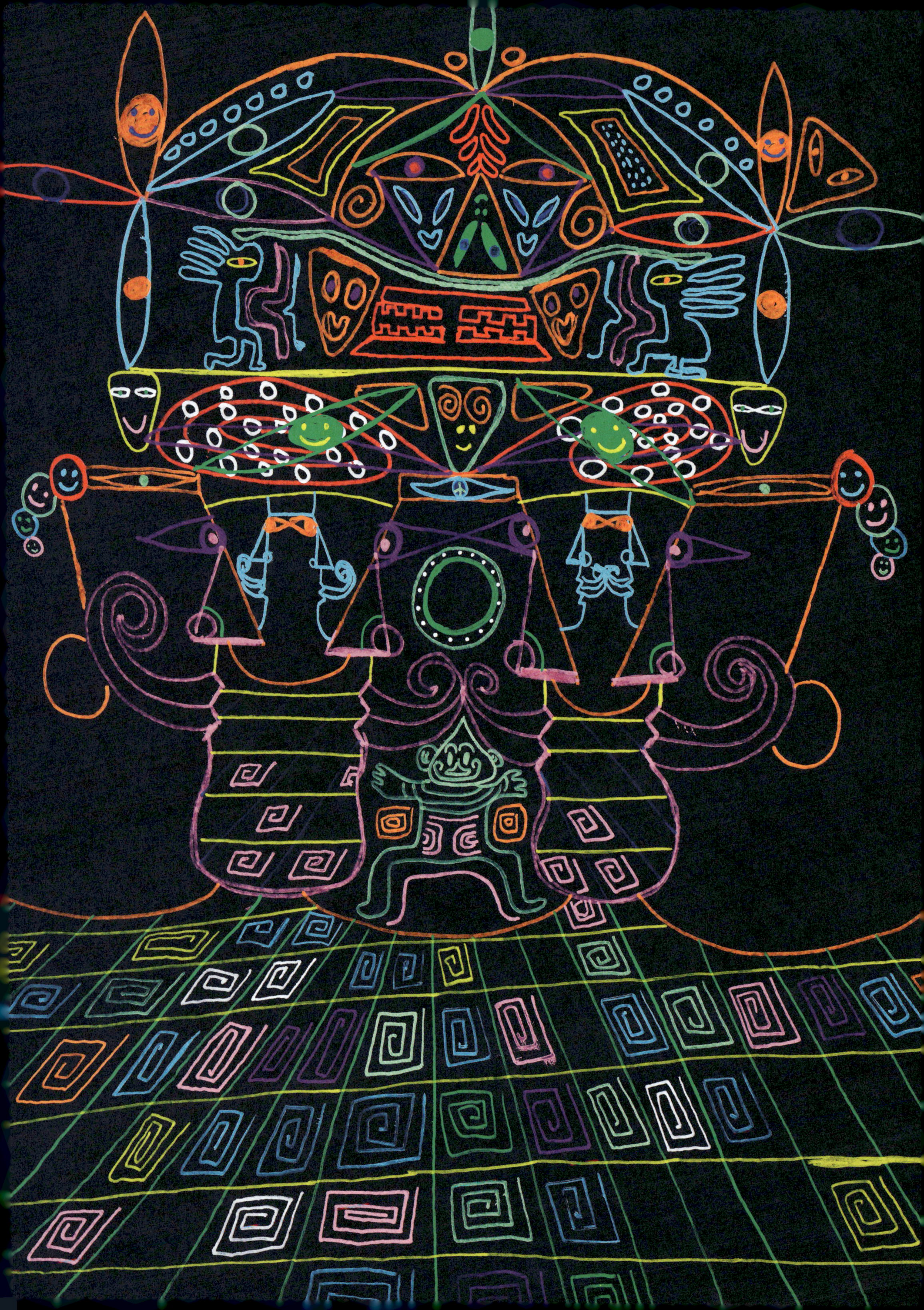

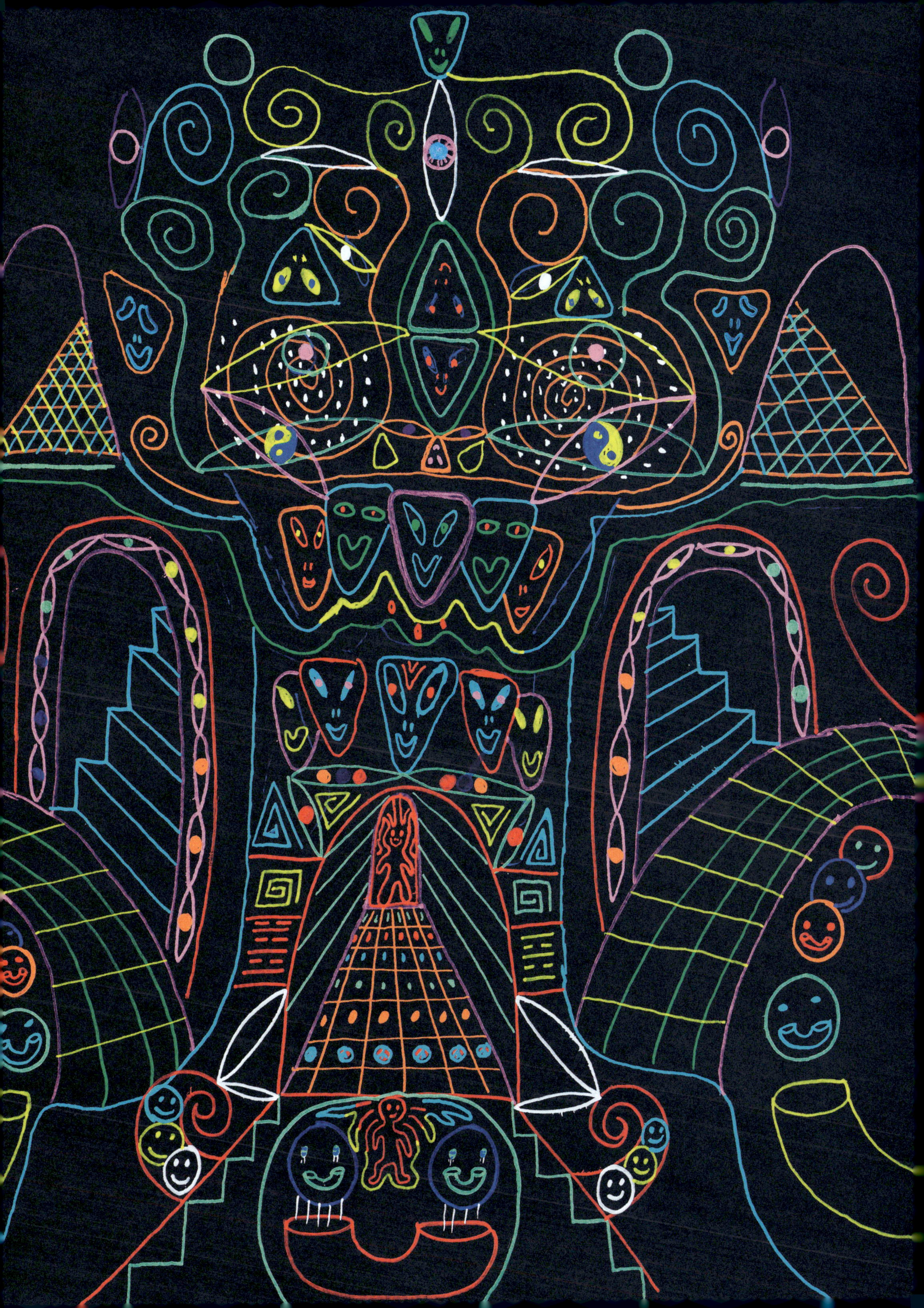

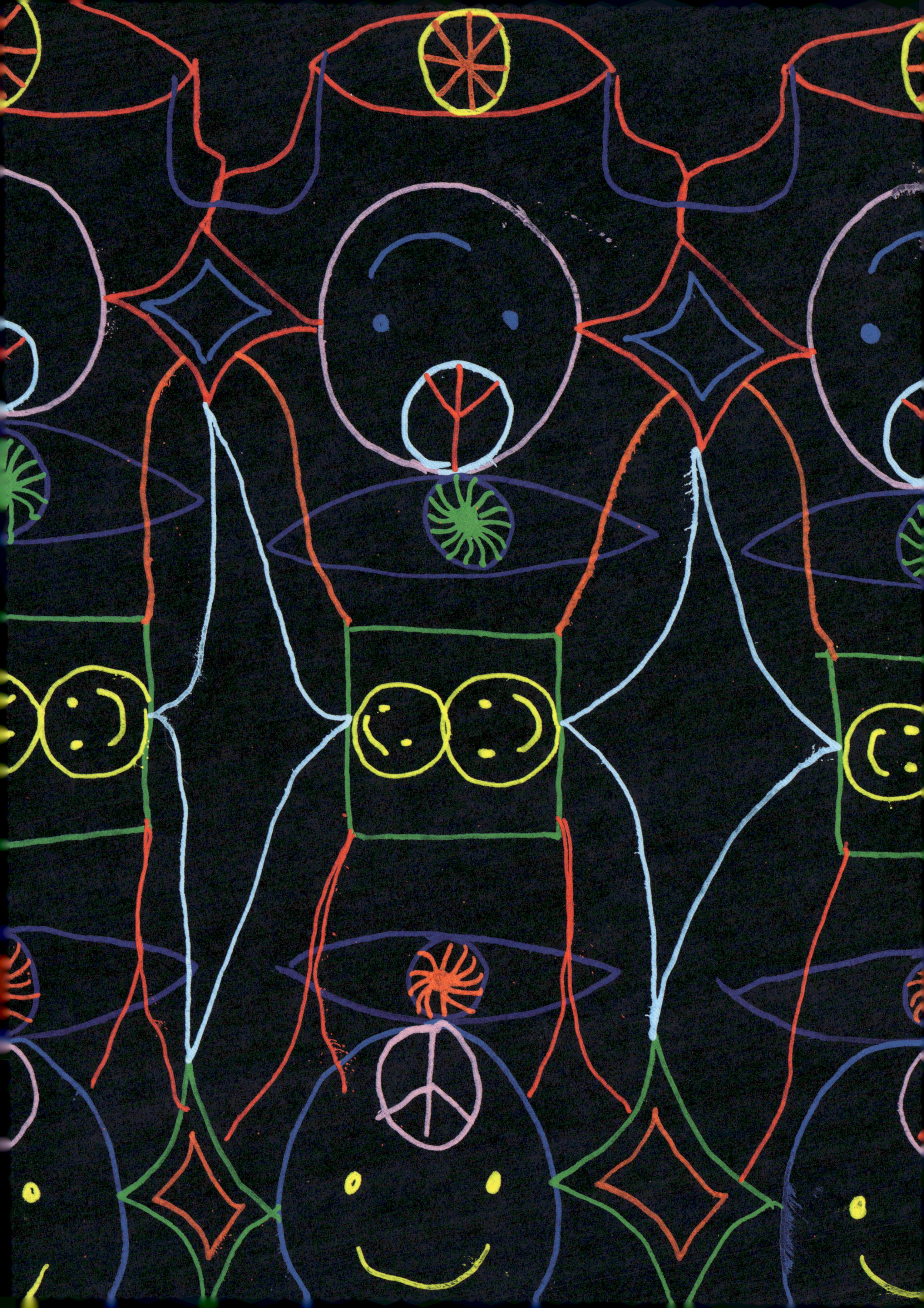

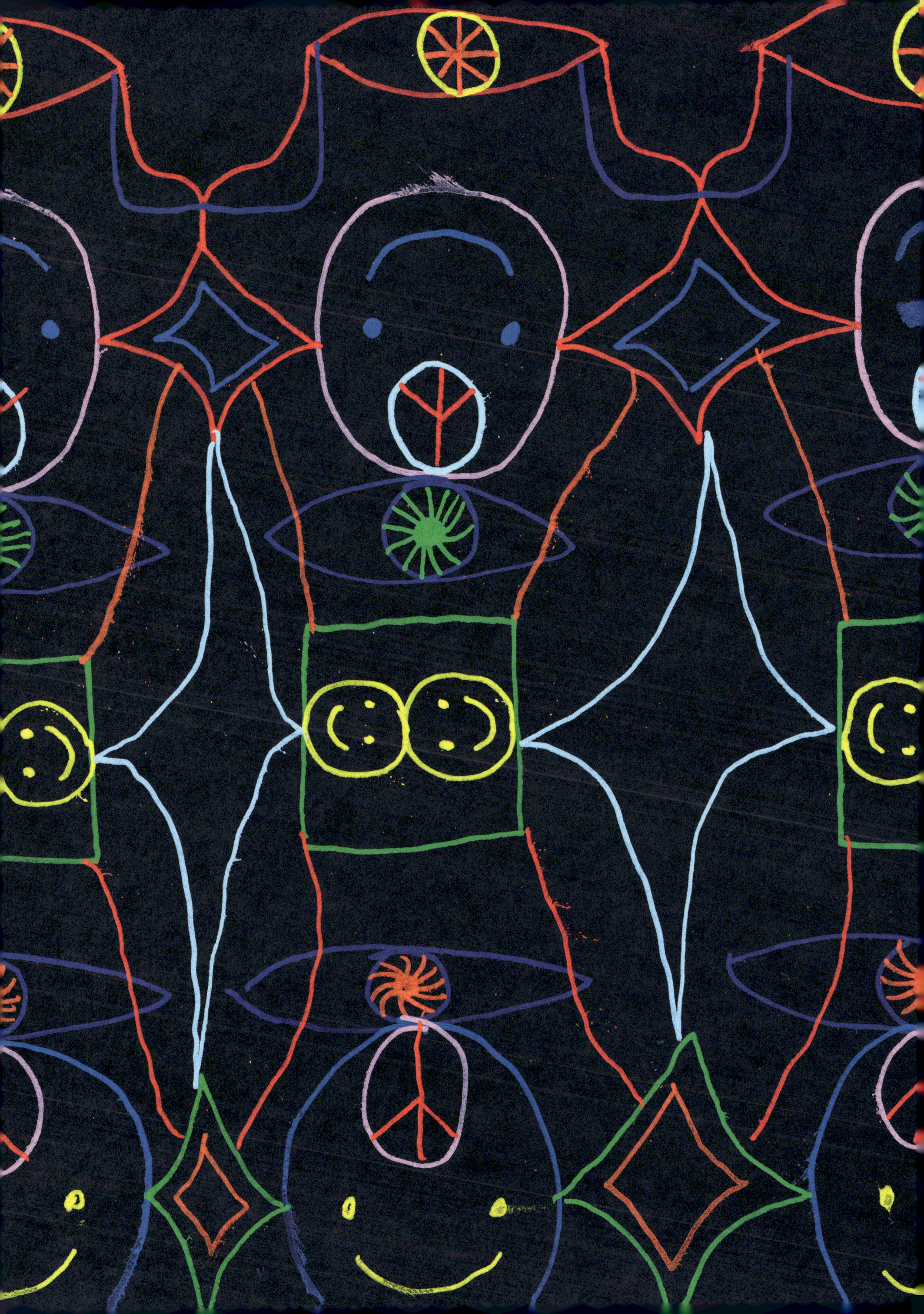

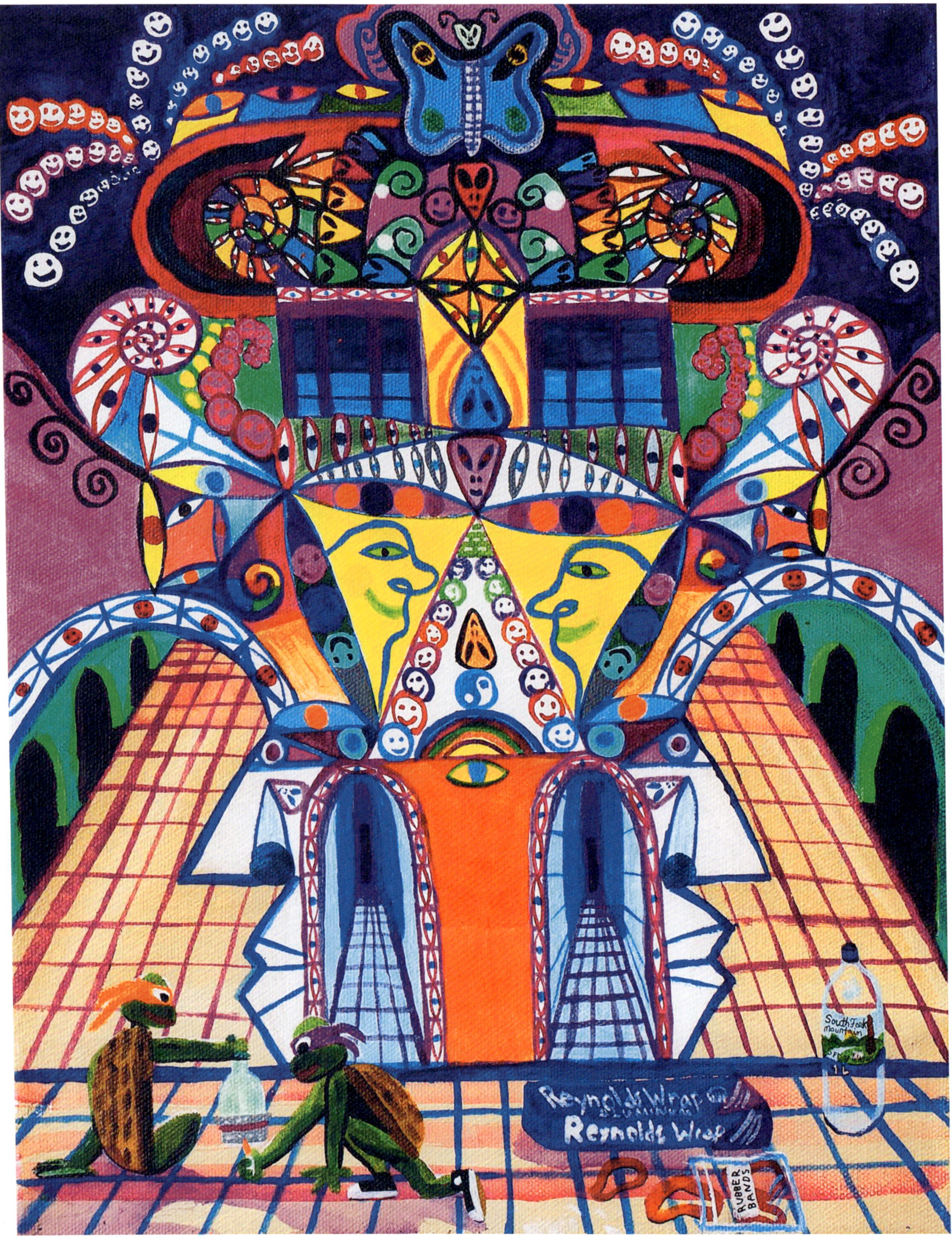

Reynolds Wrap
Reynolds Wrap
South Fork Mountain
SPRING
1 L
RUBBER BANDS

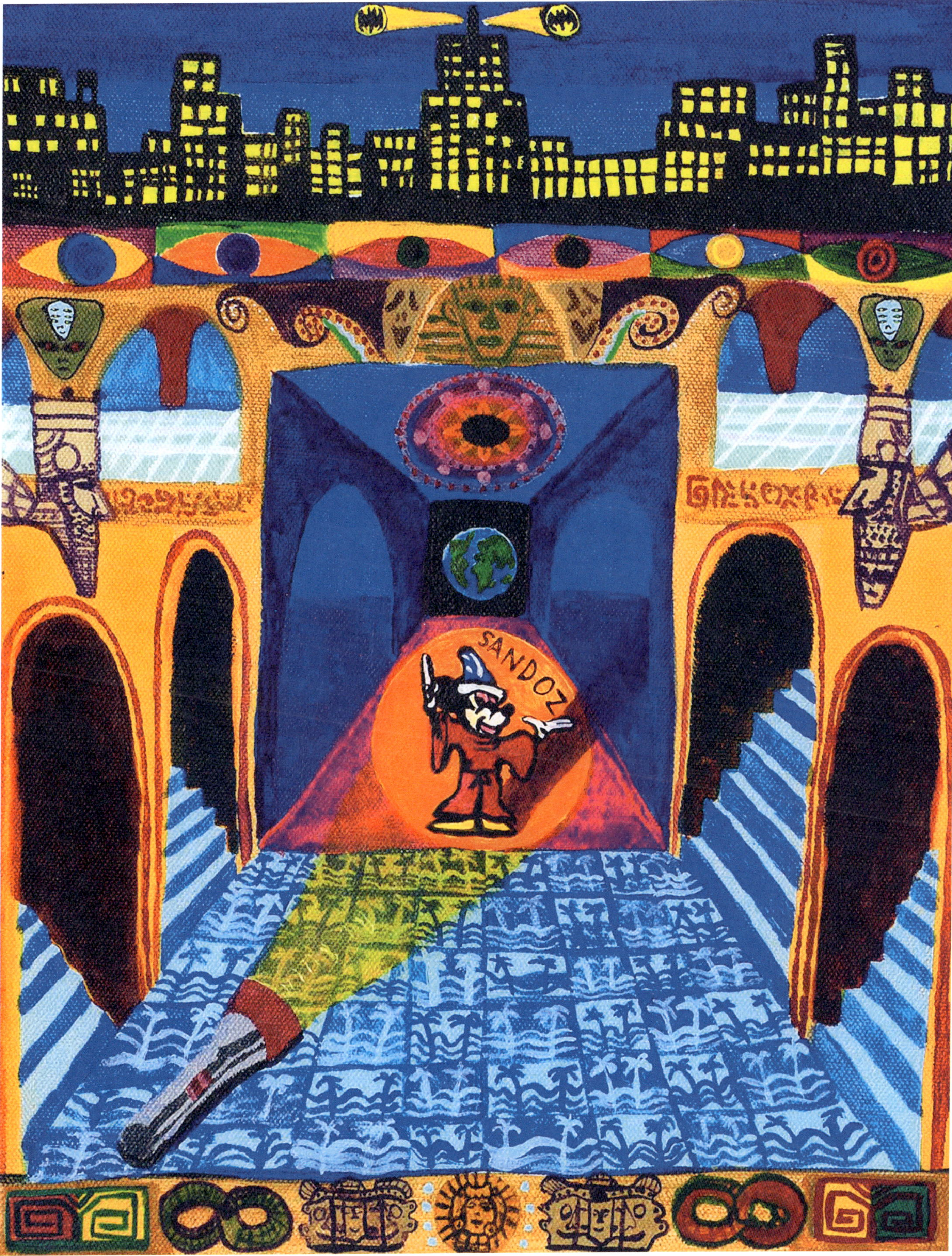

SANDOZ

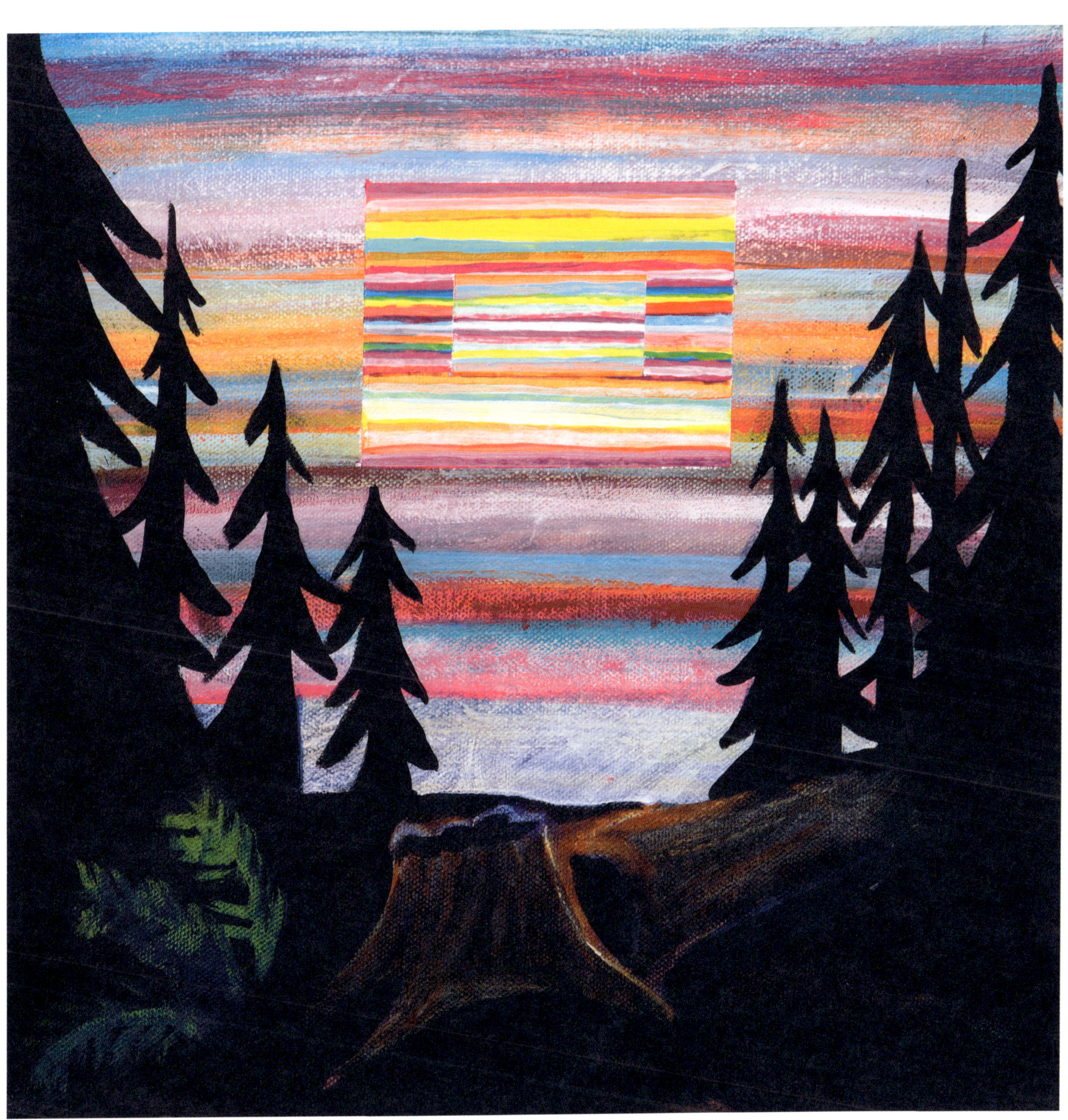

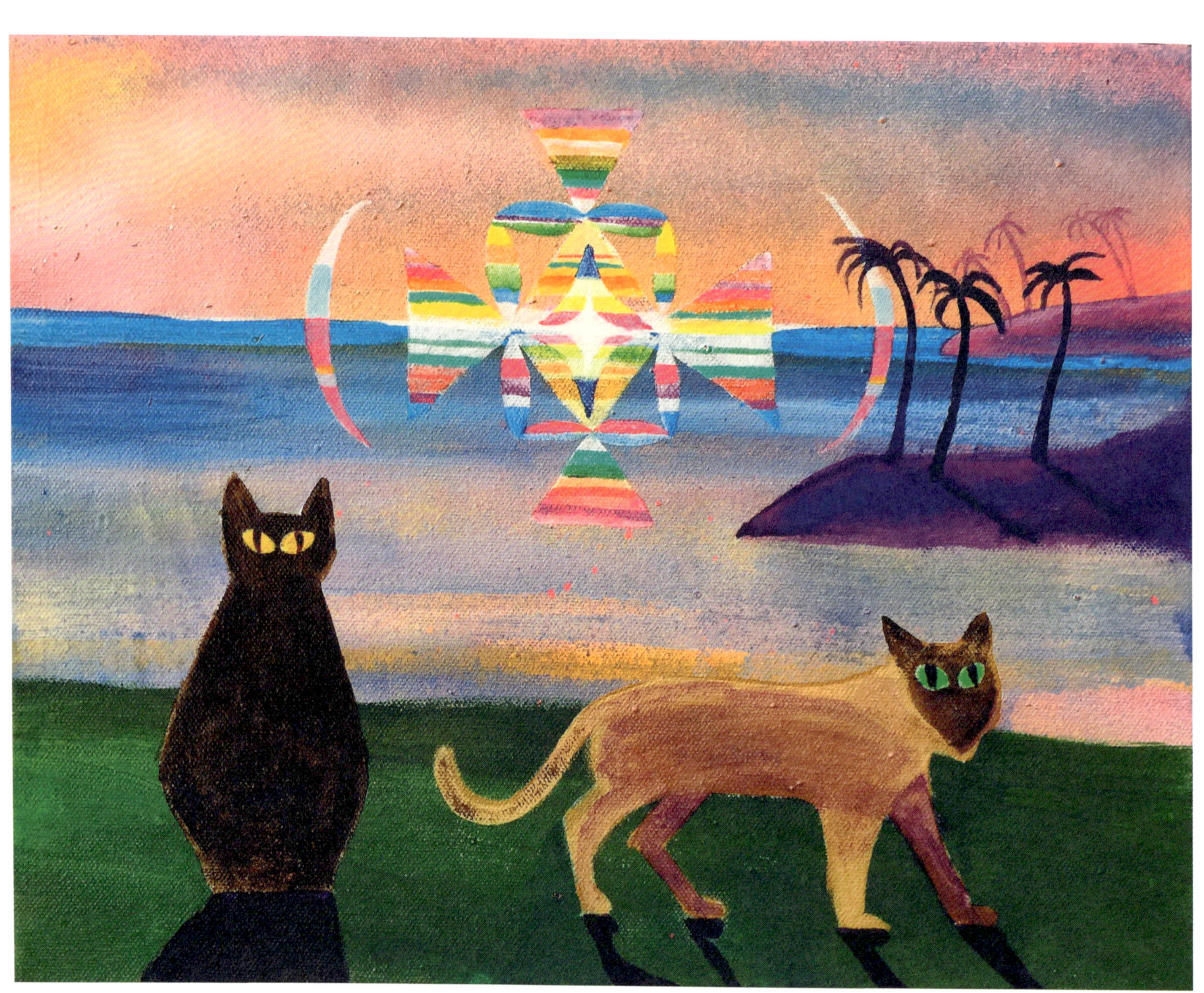

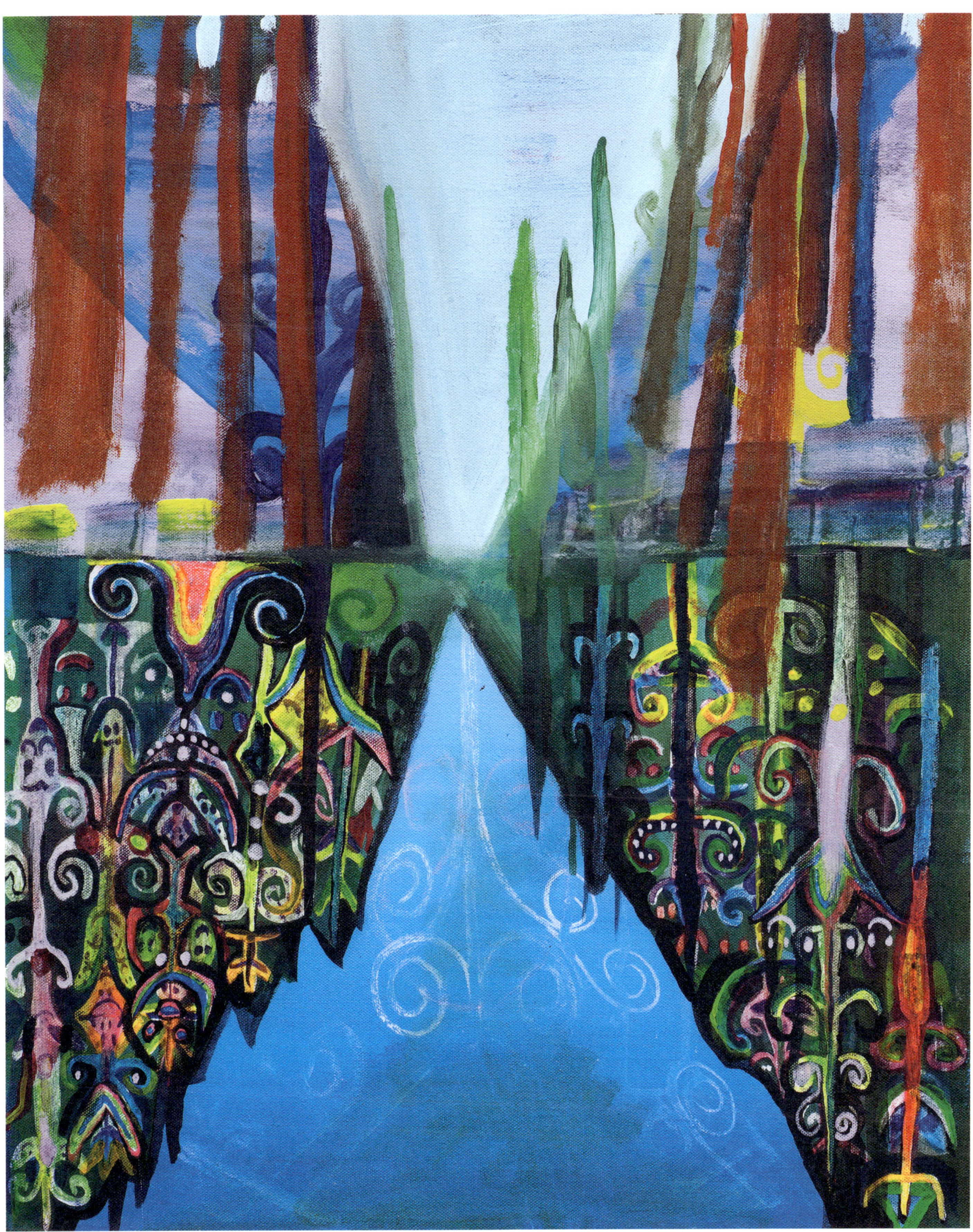

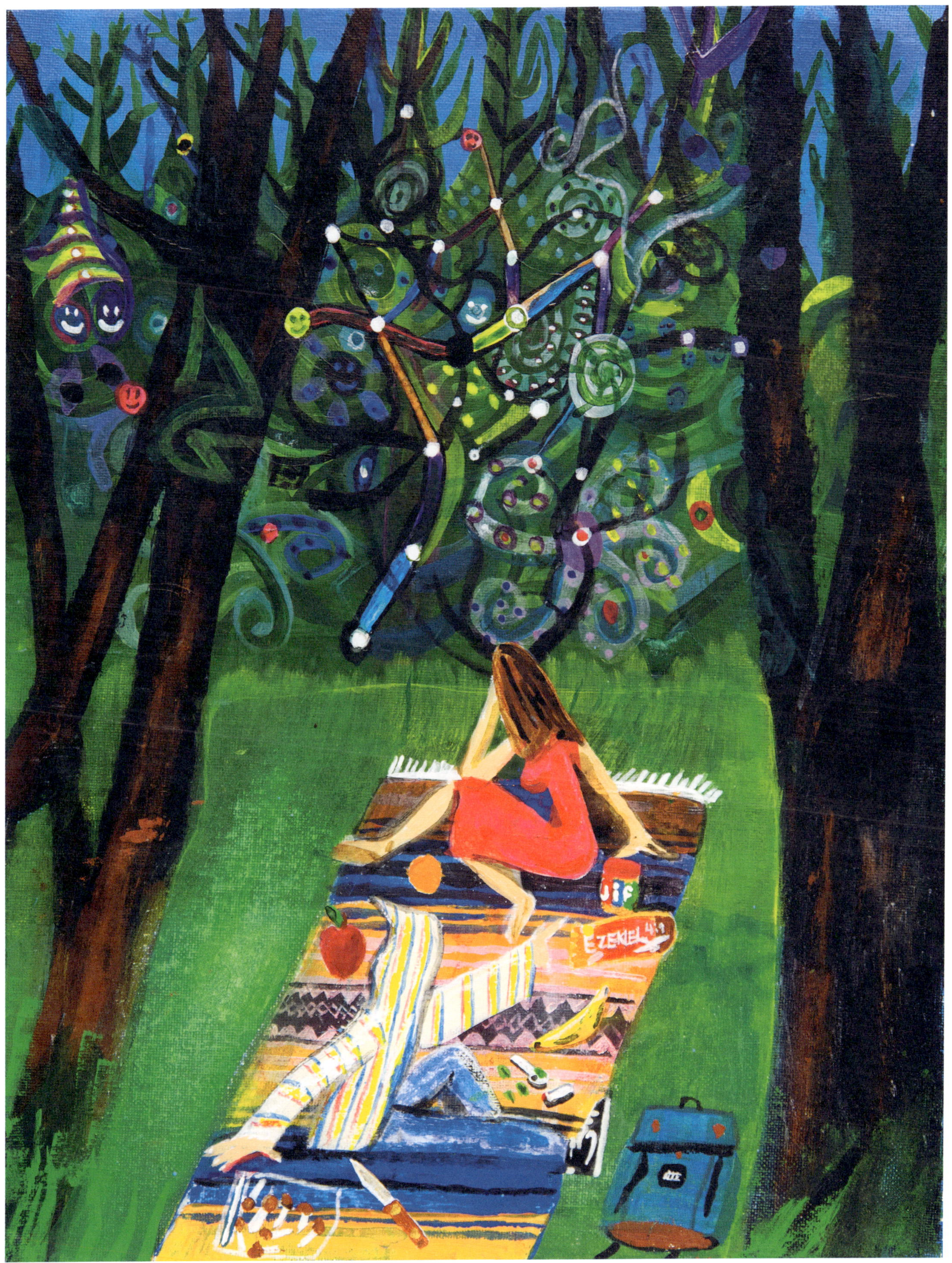
JIF
EZEKIEL 4:9
LIFE

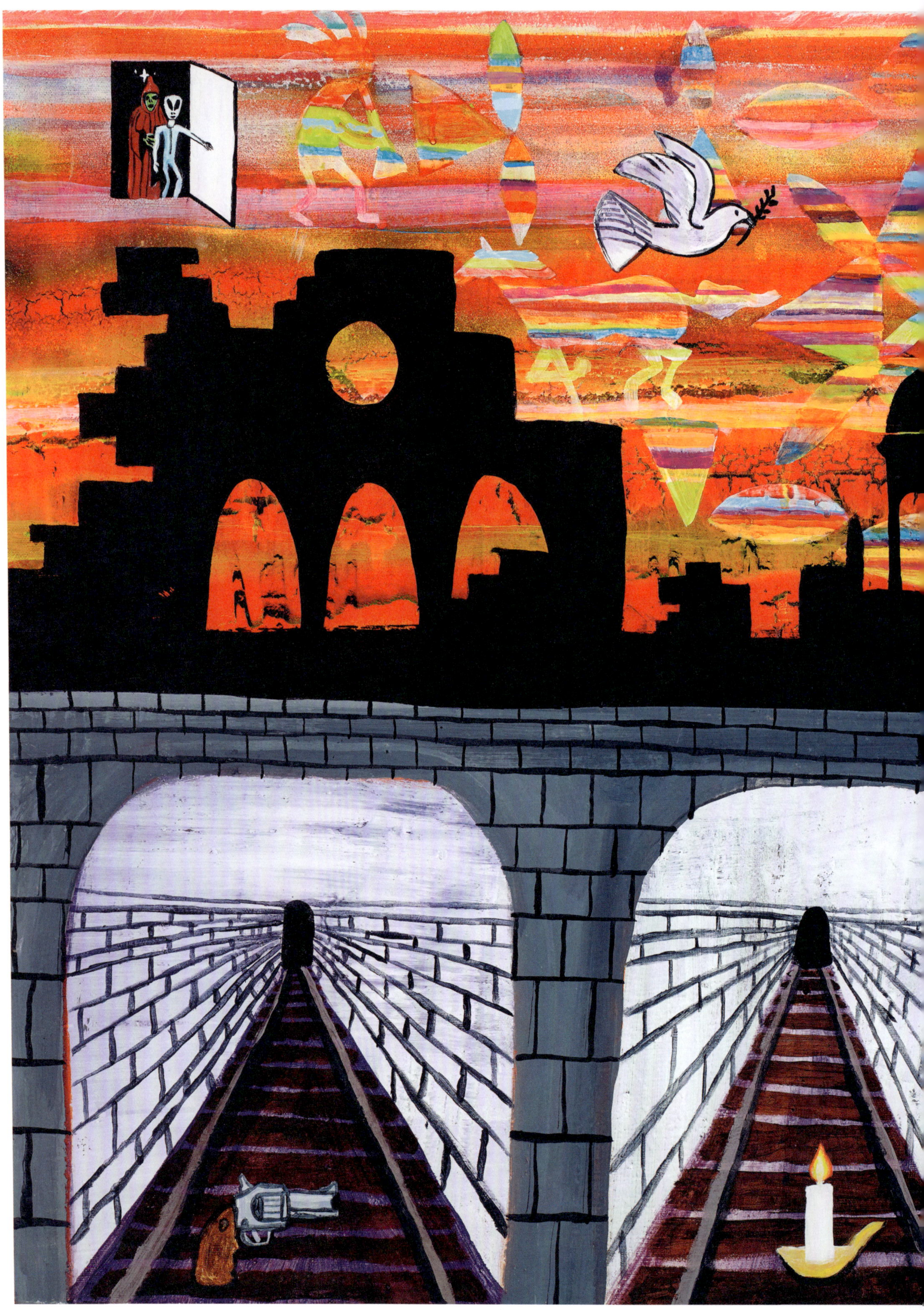

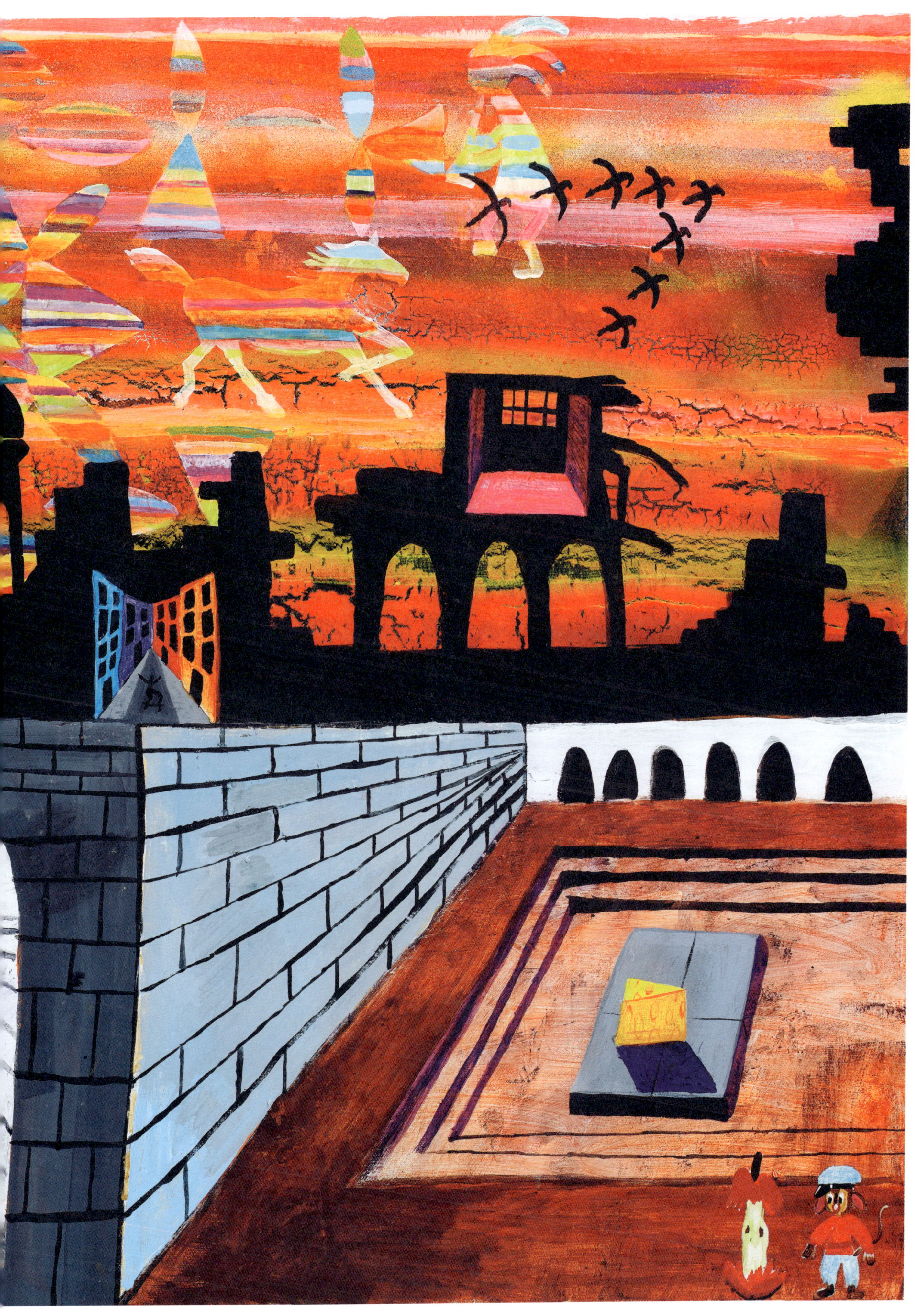

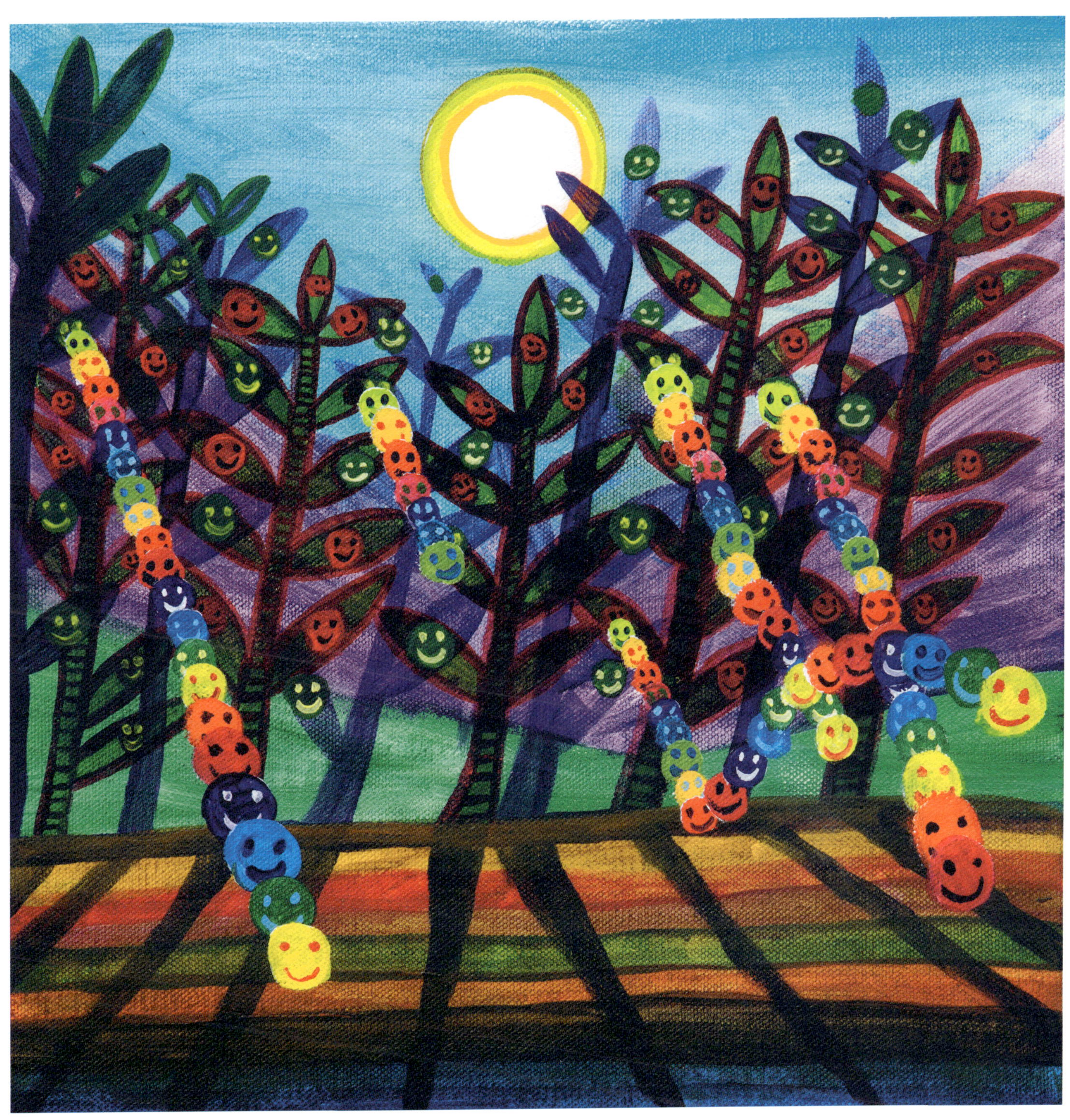

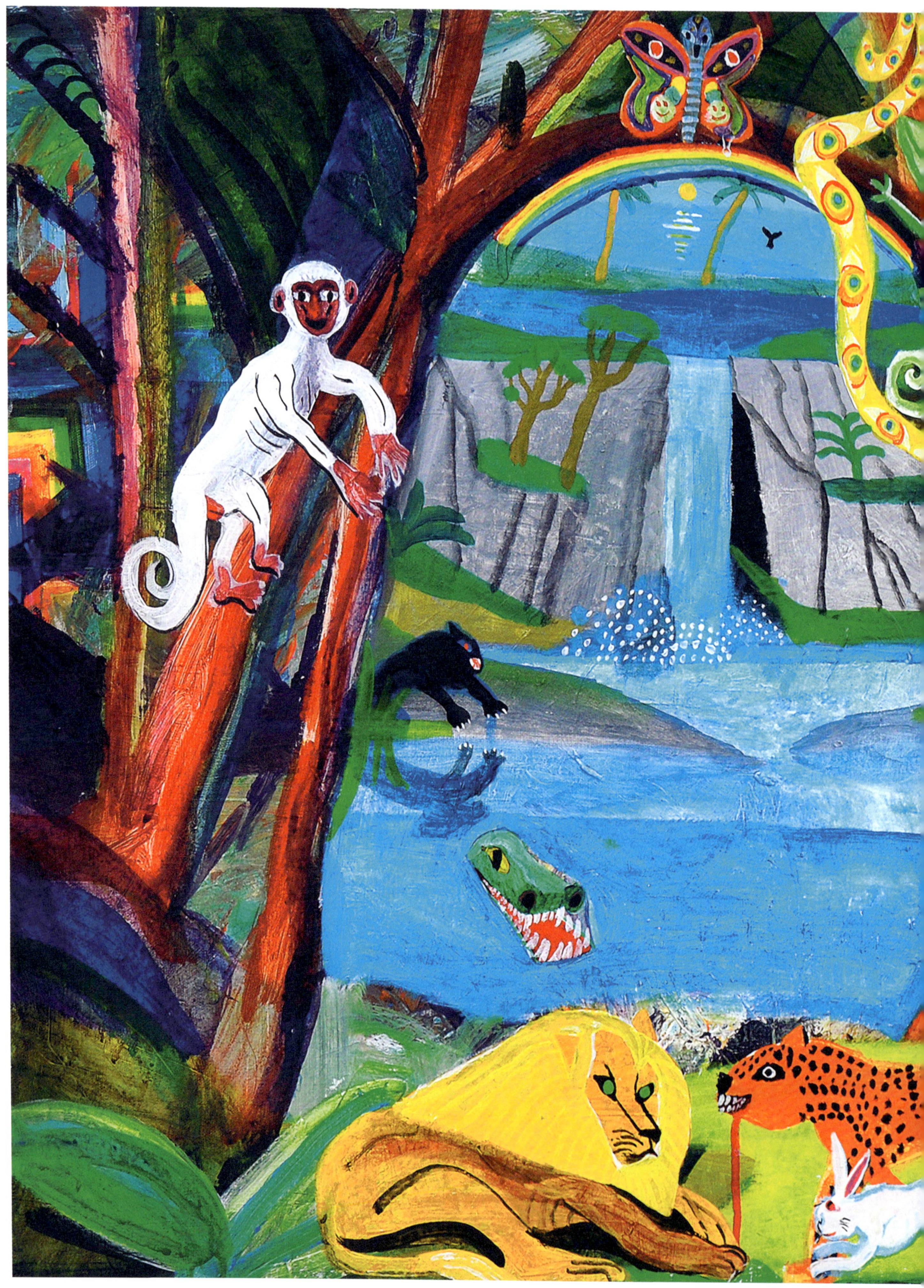

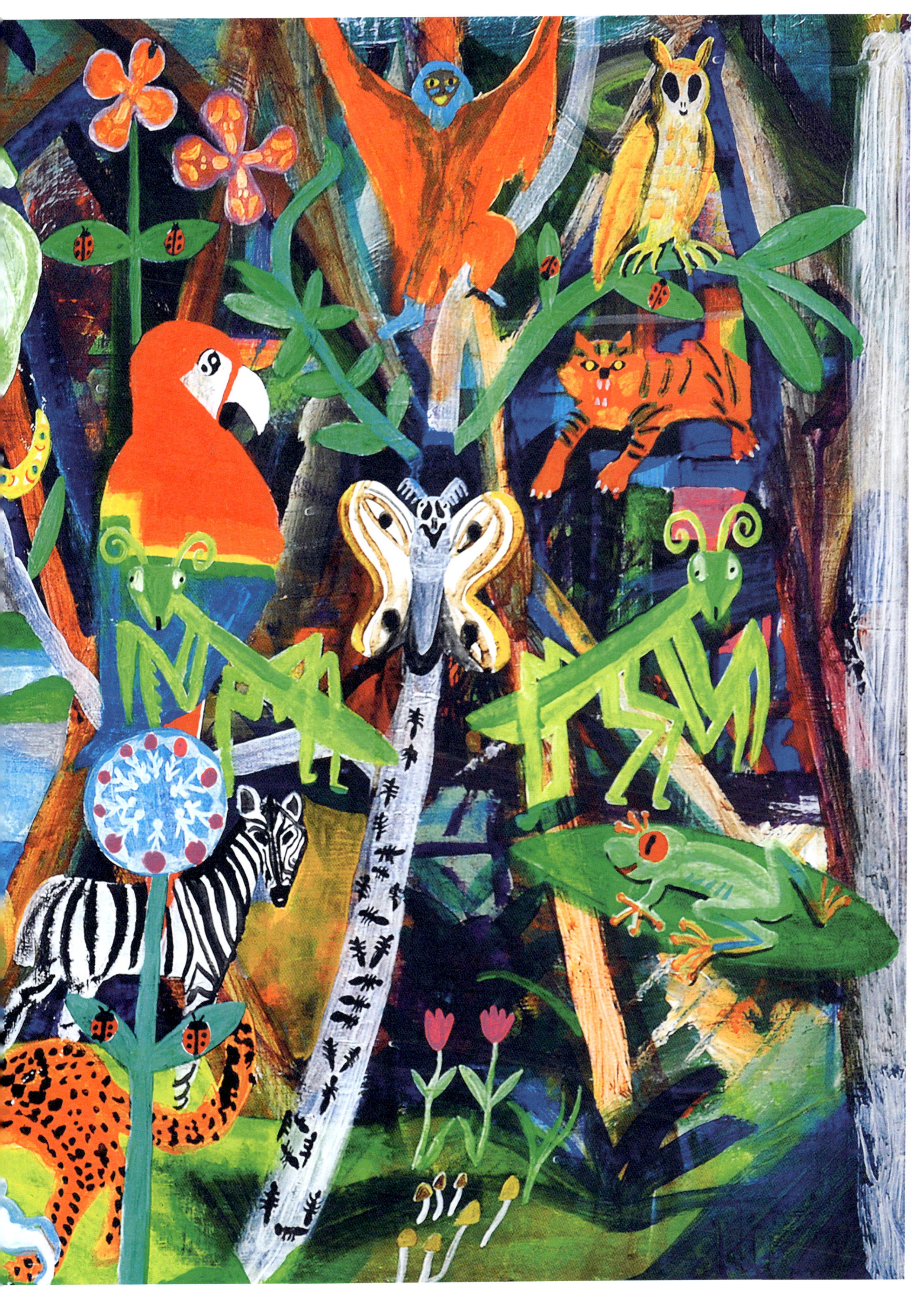

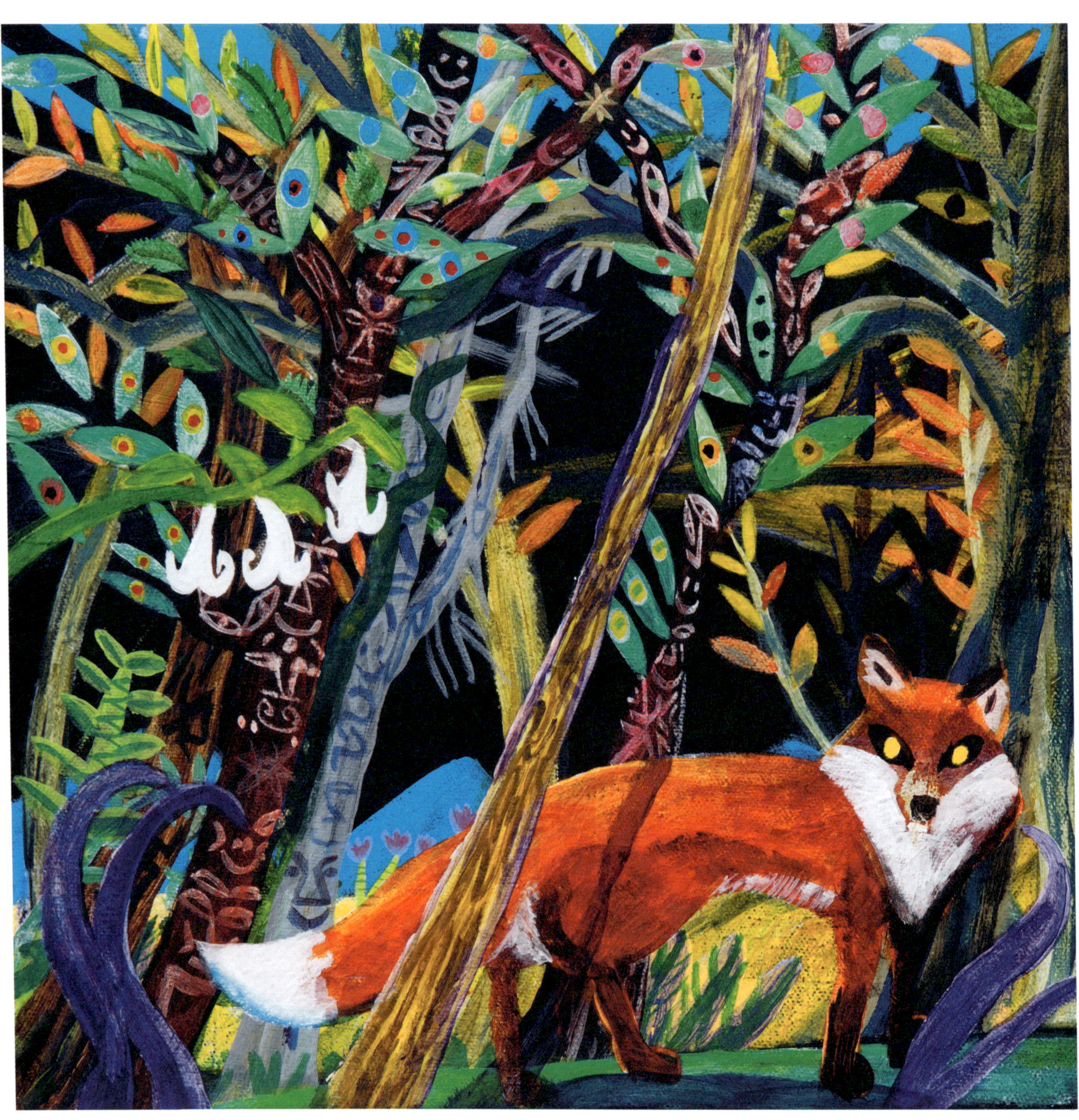

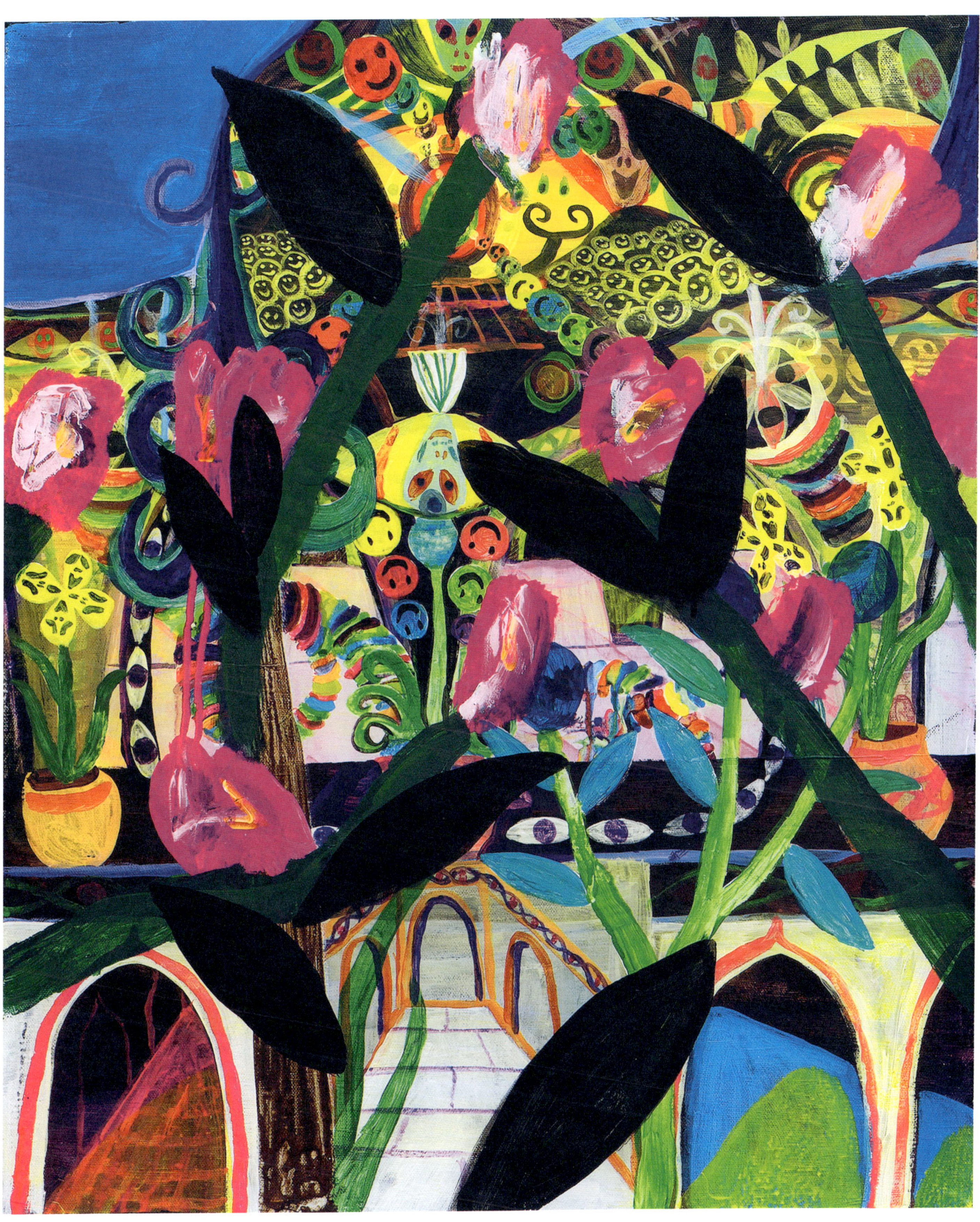

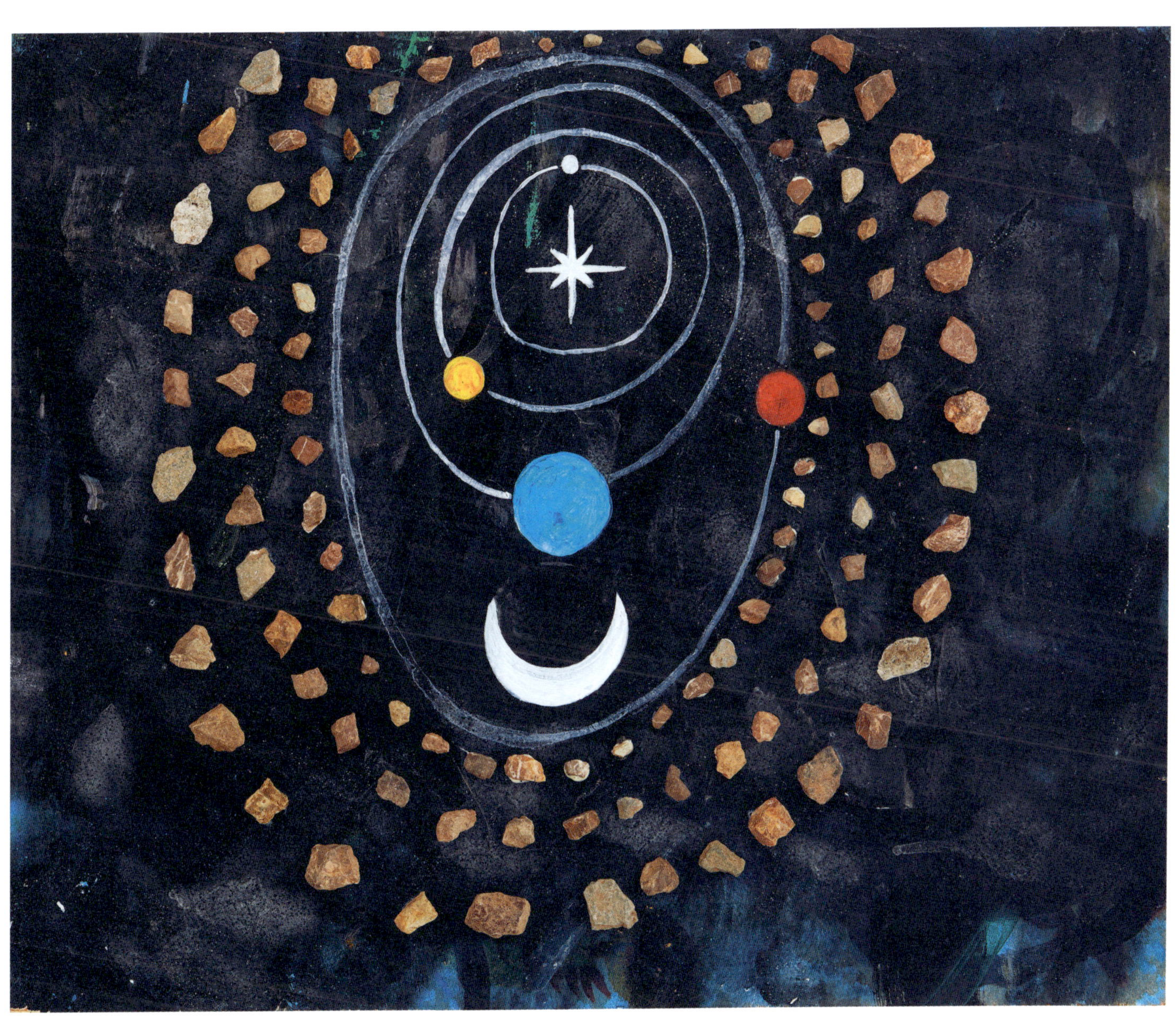

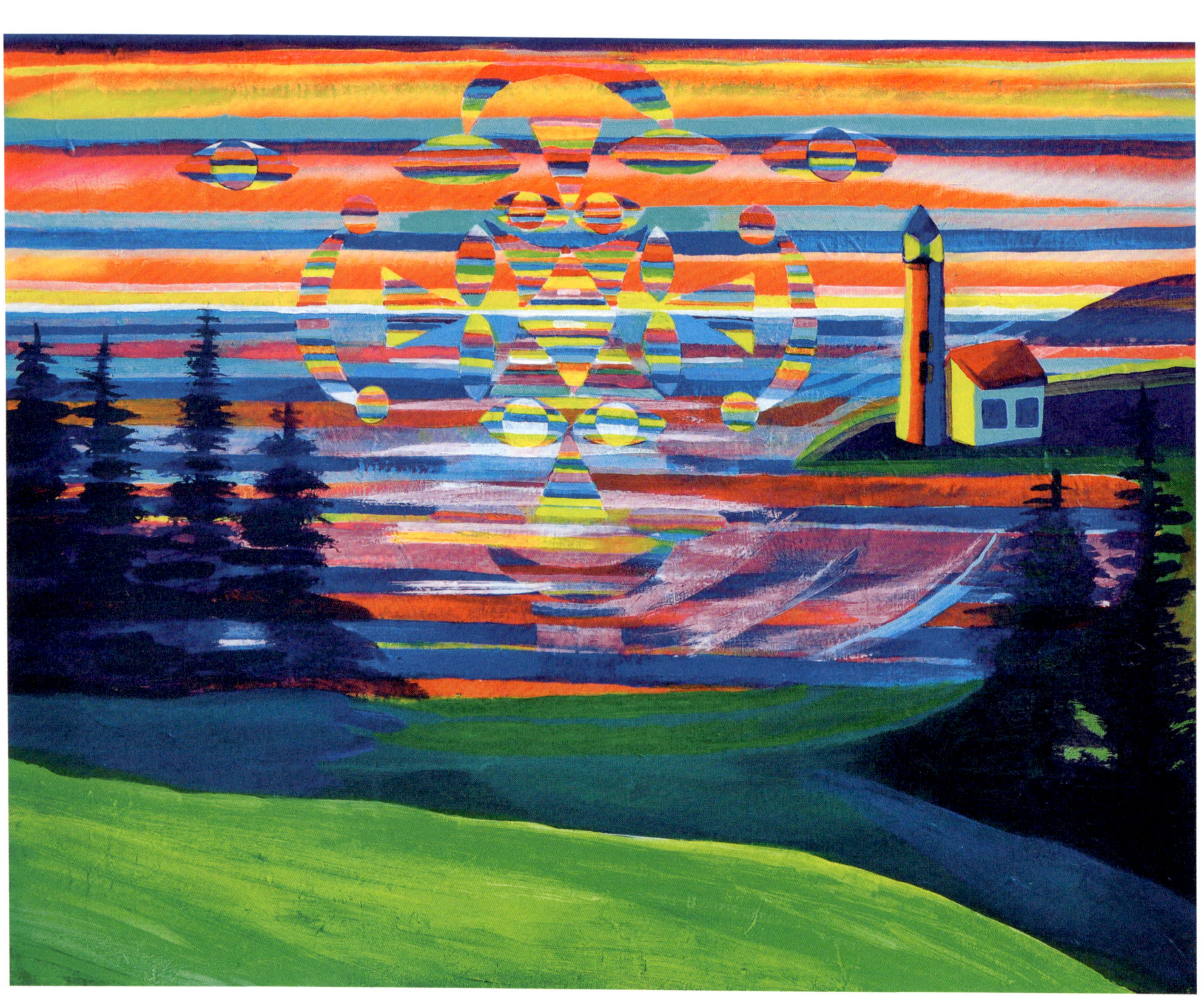

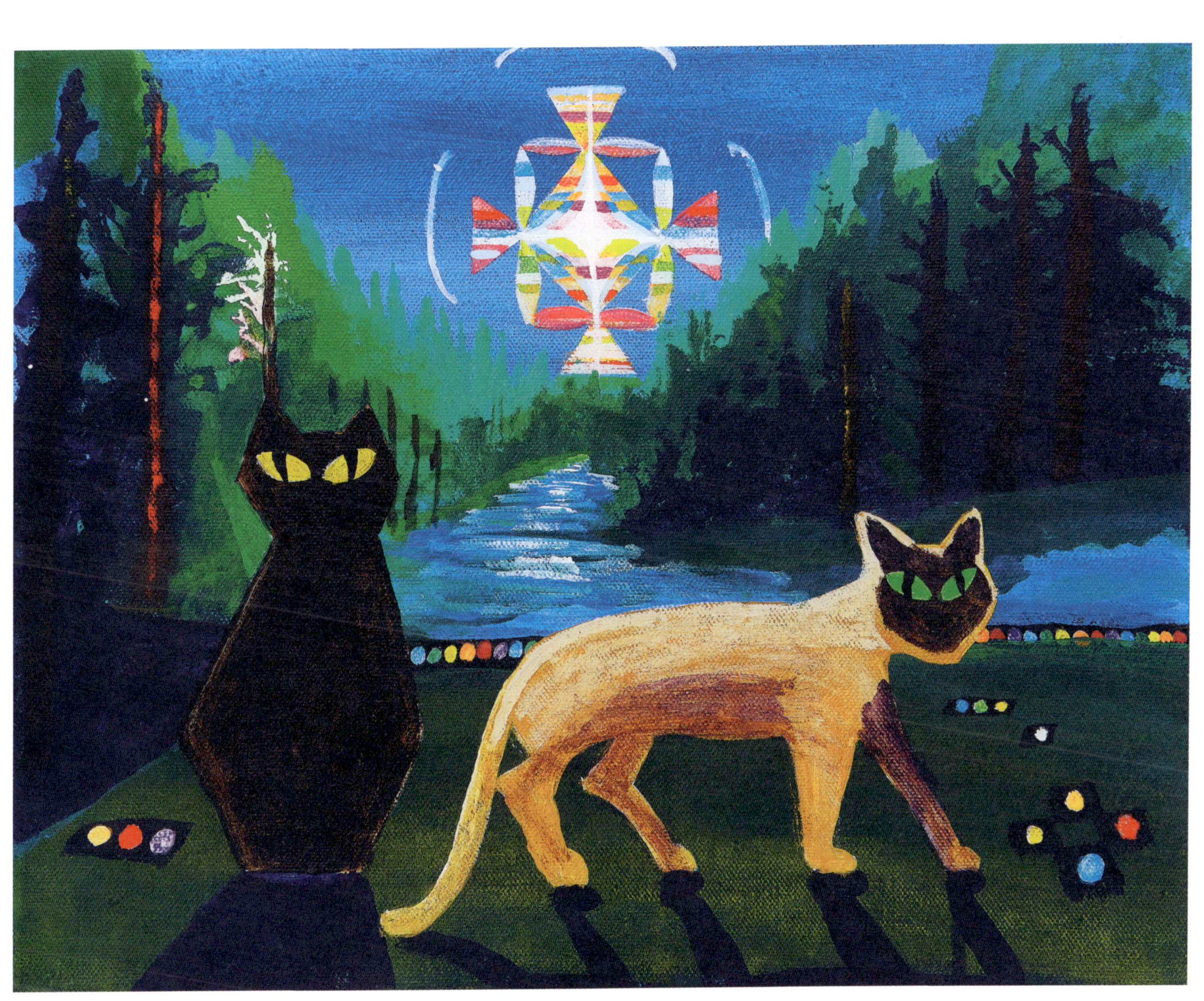

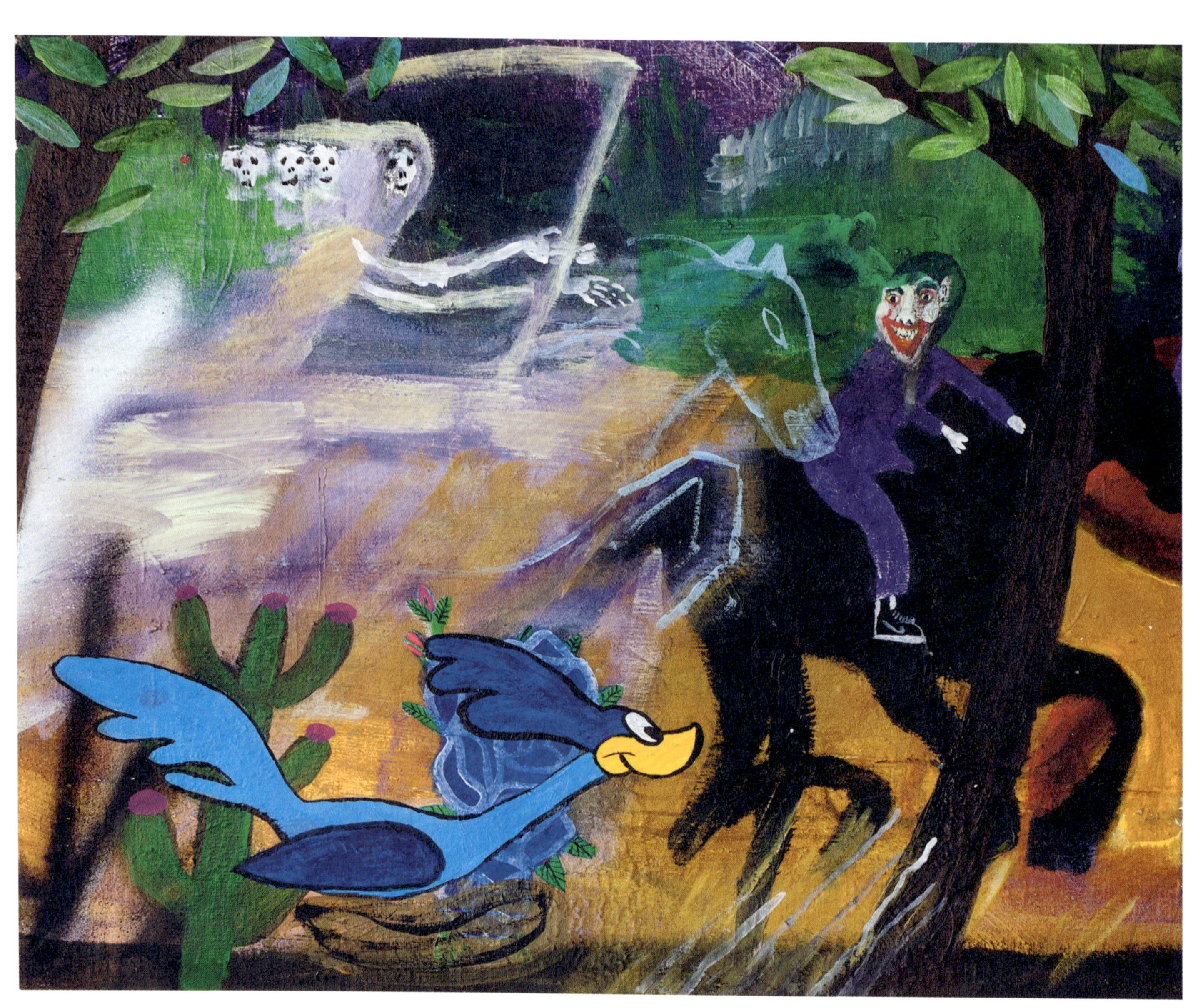

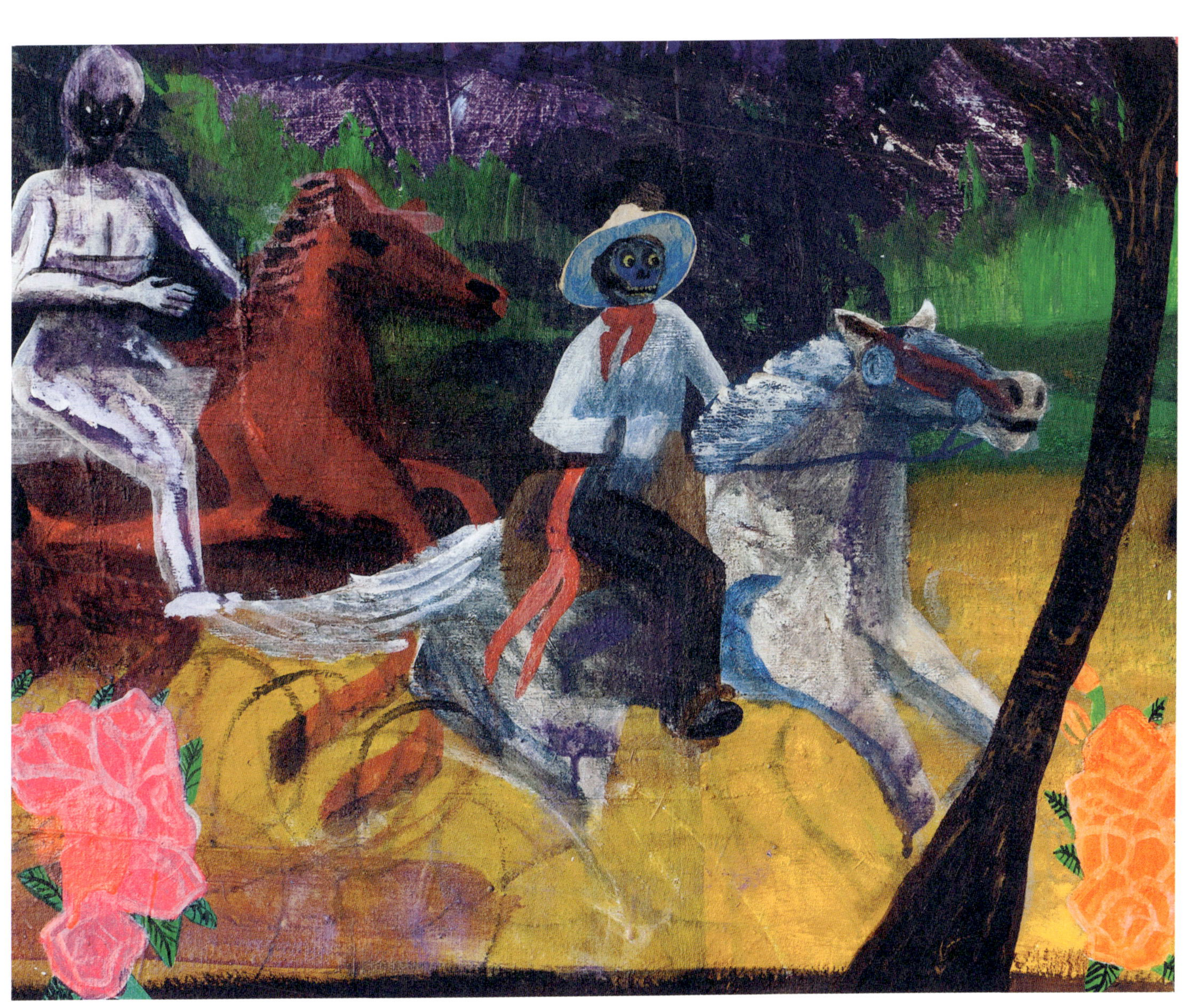

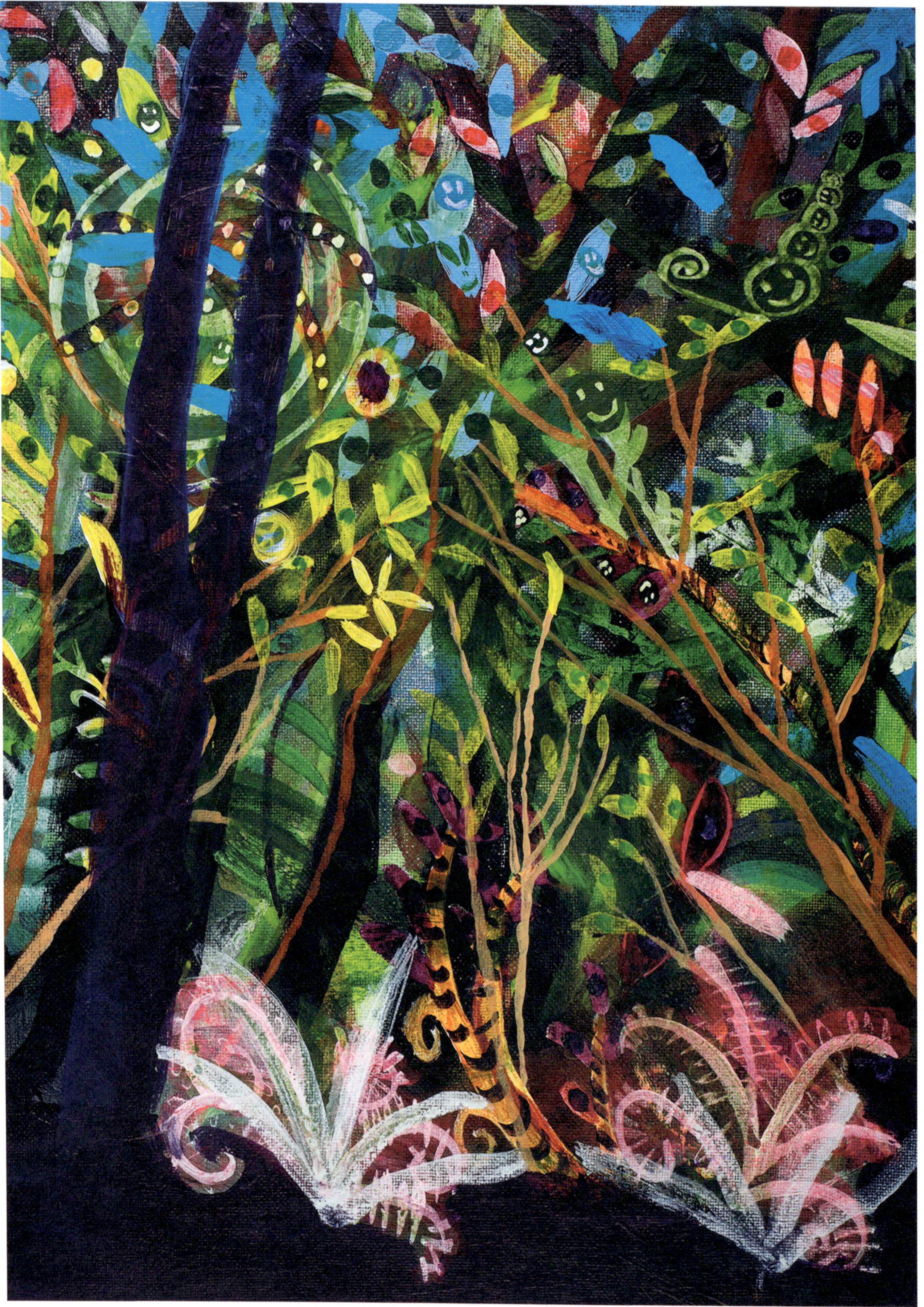

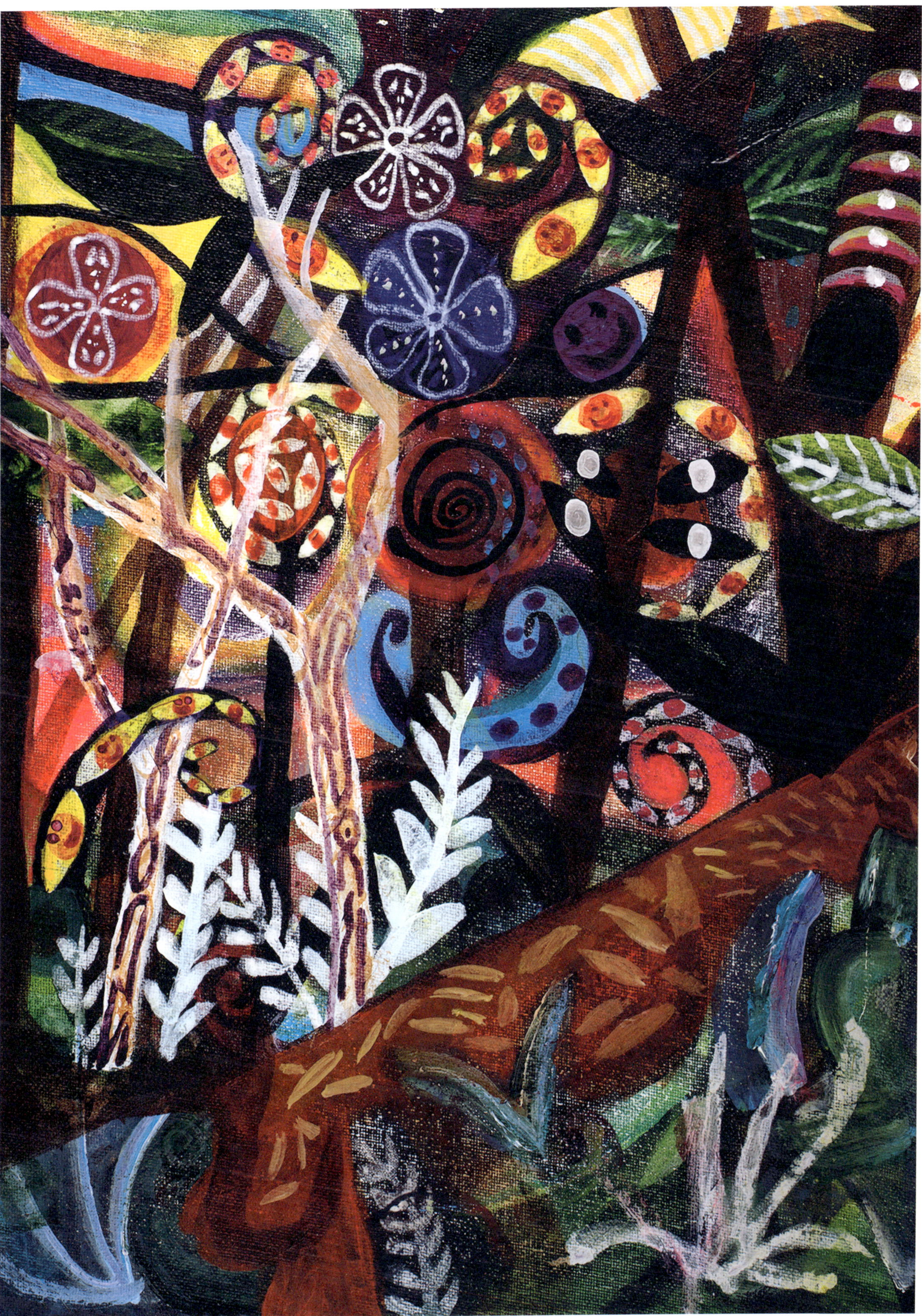

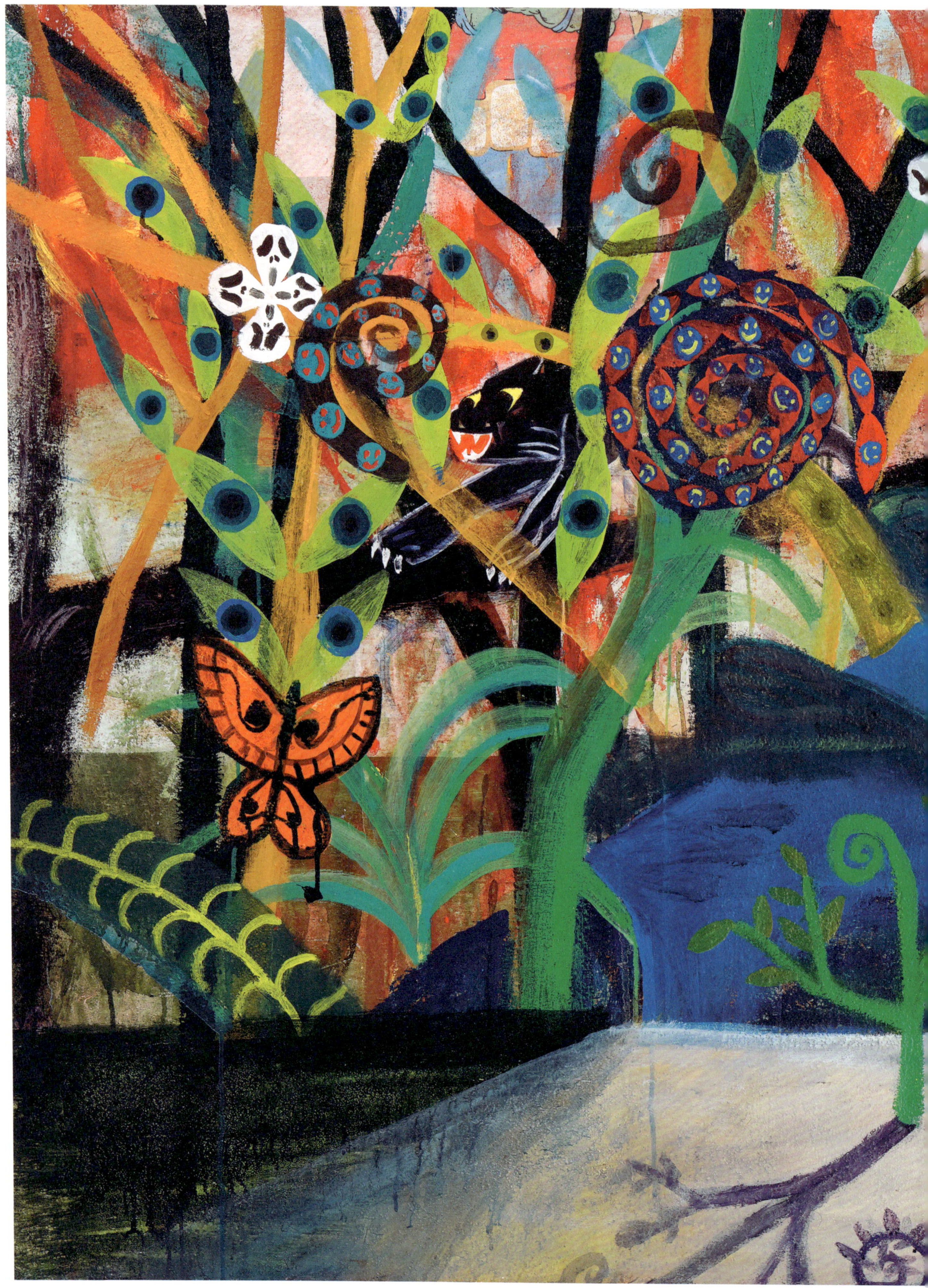

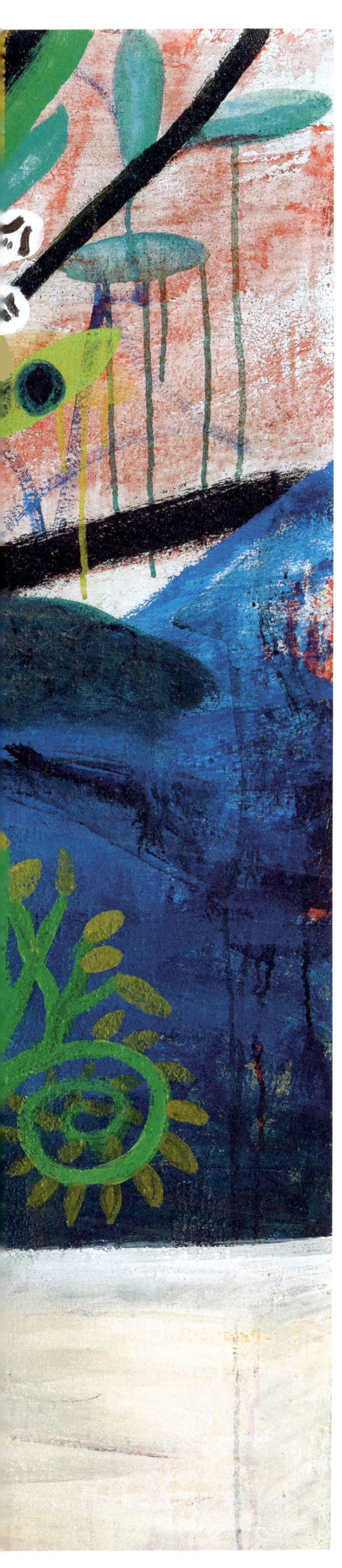

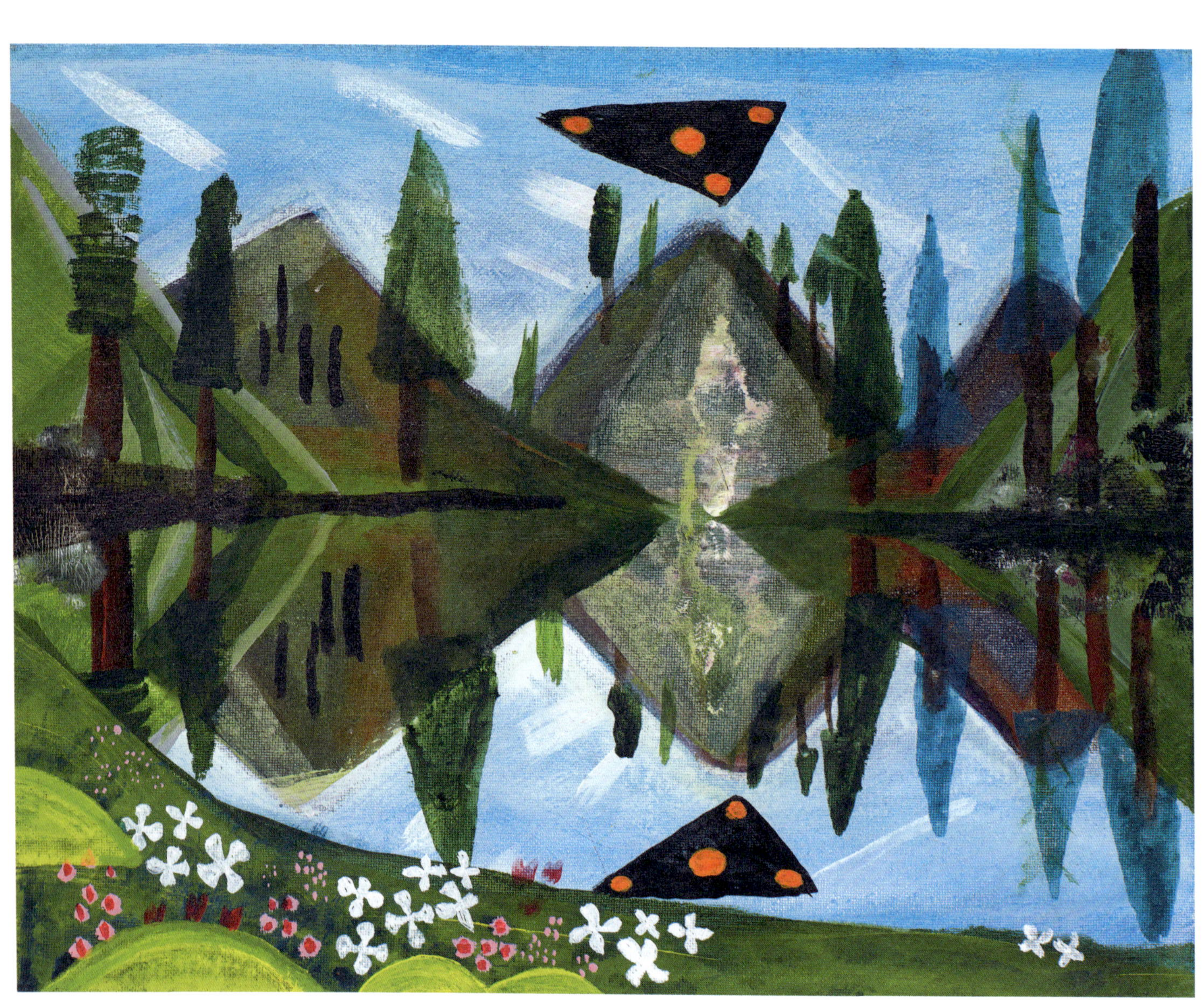

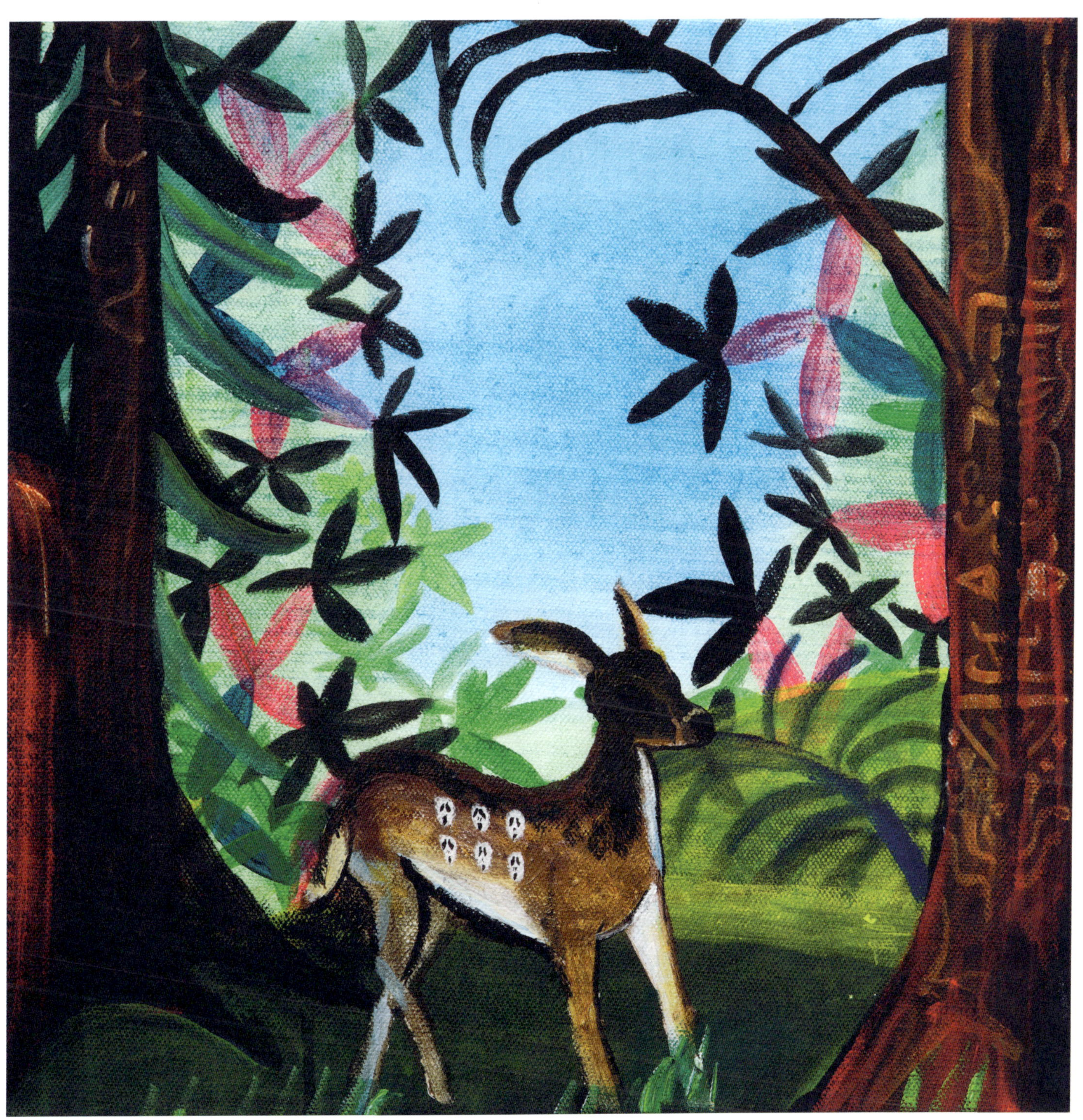

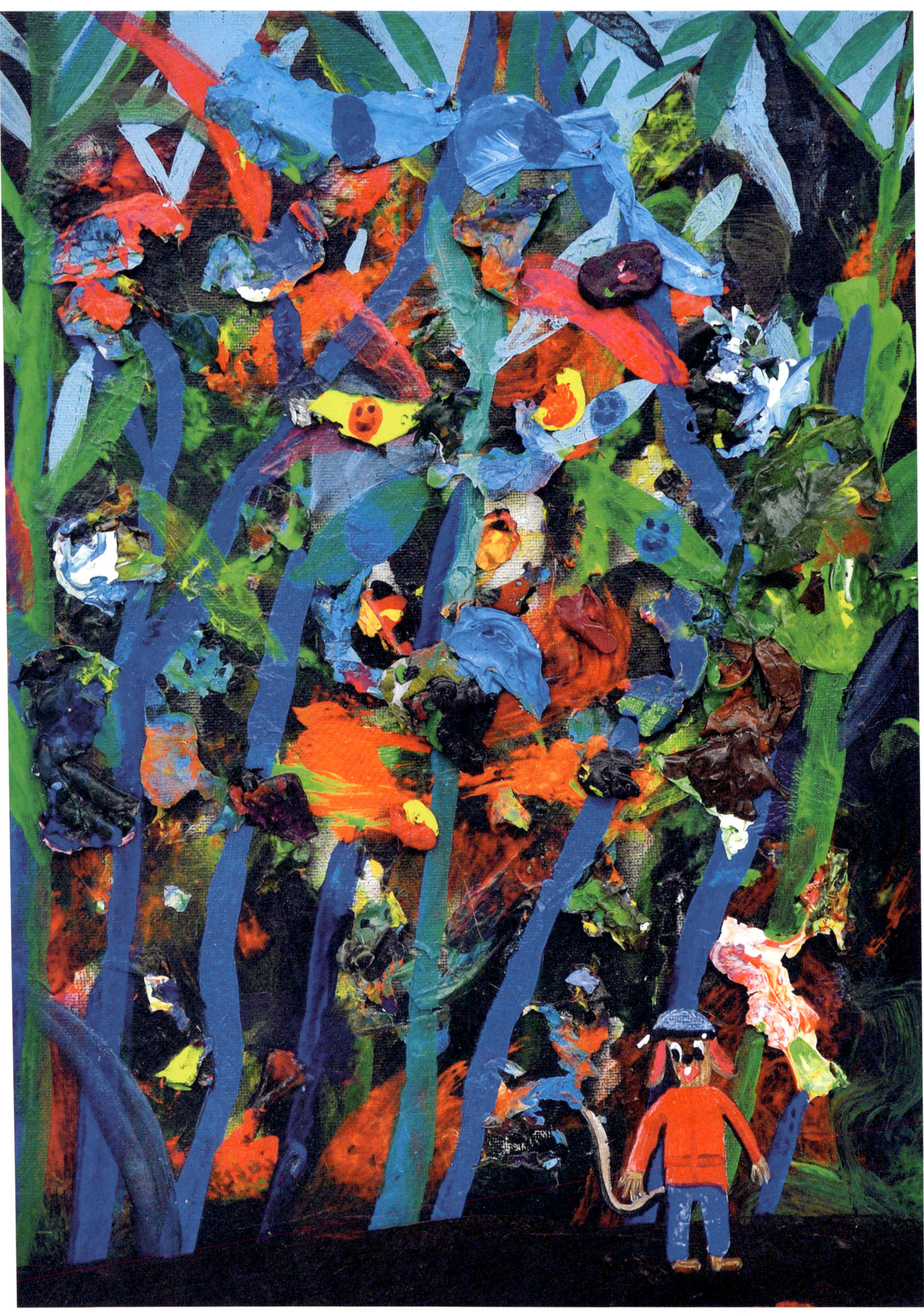

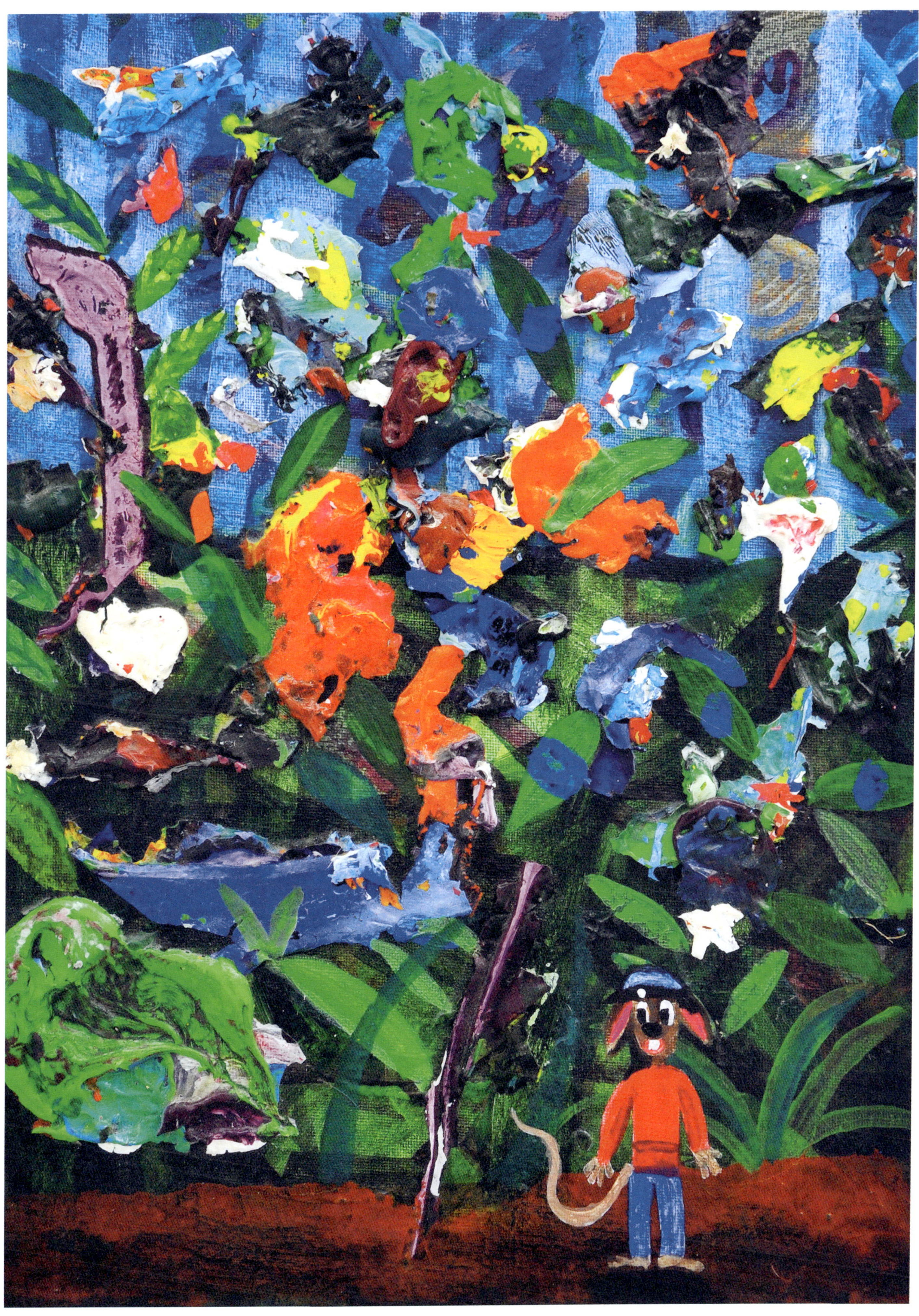

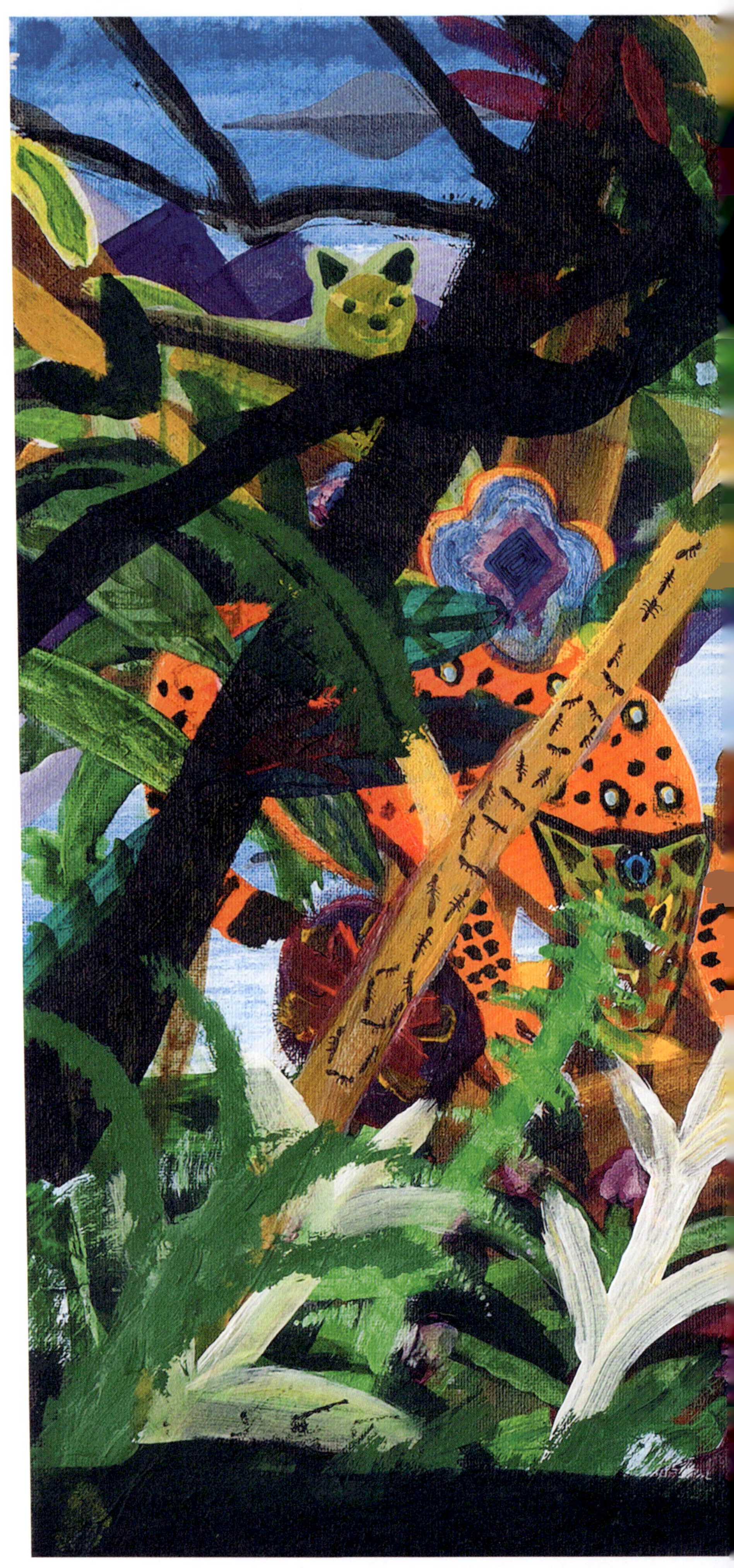

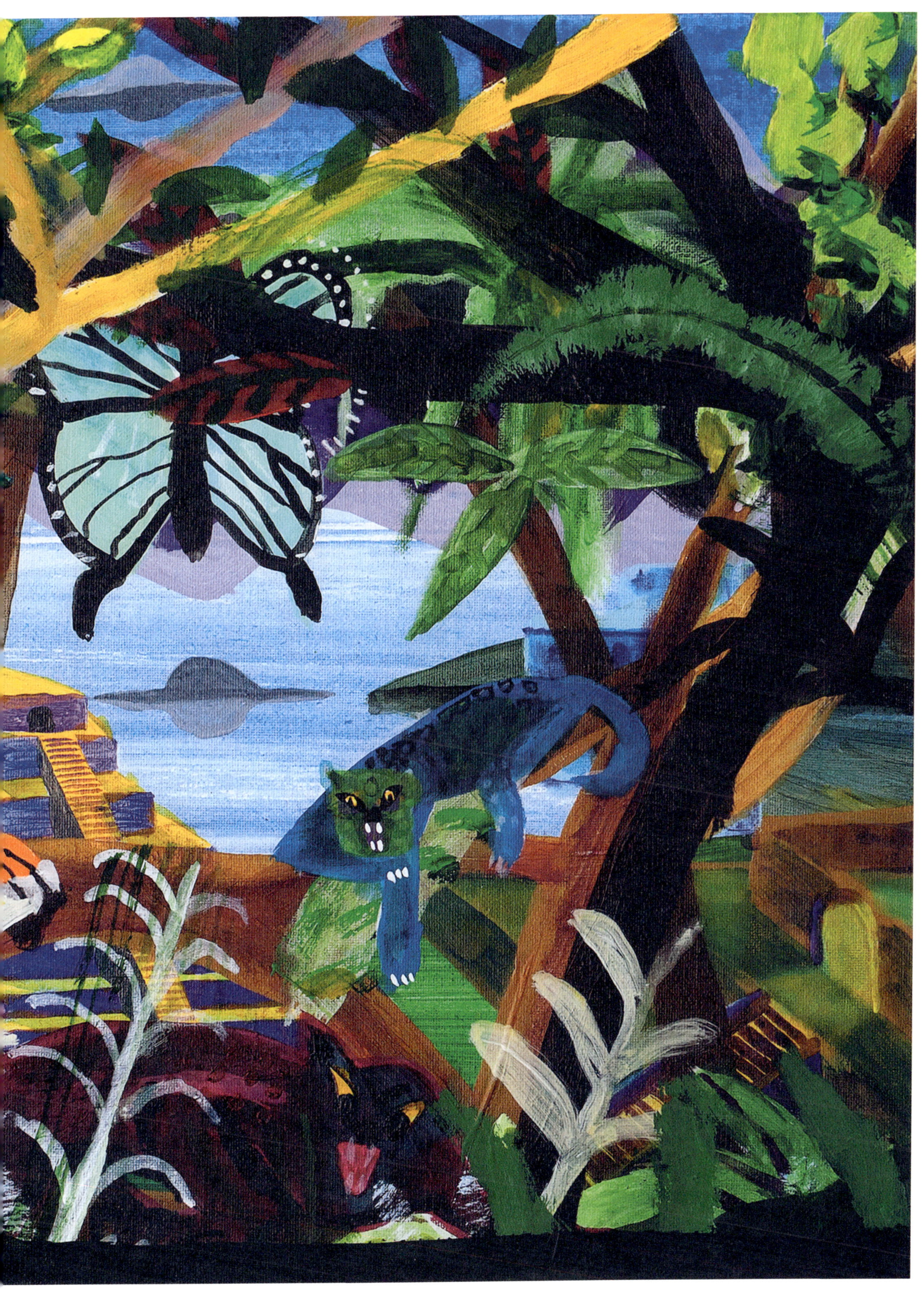

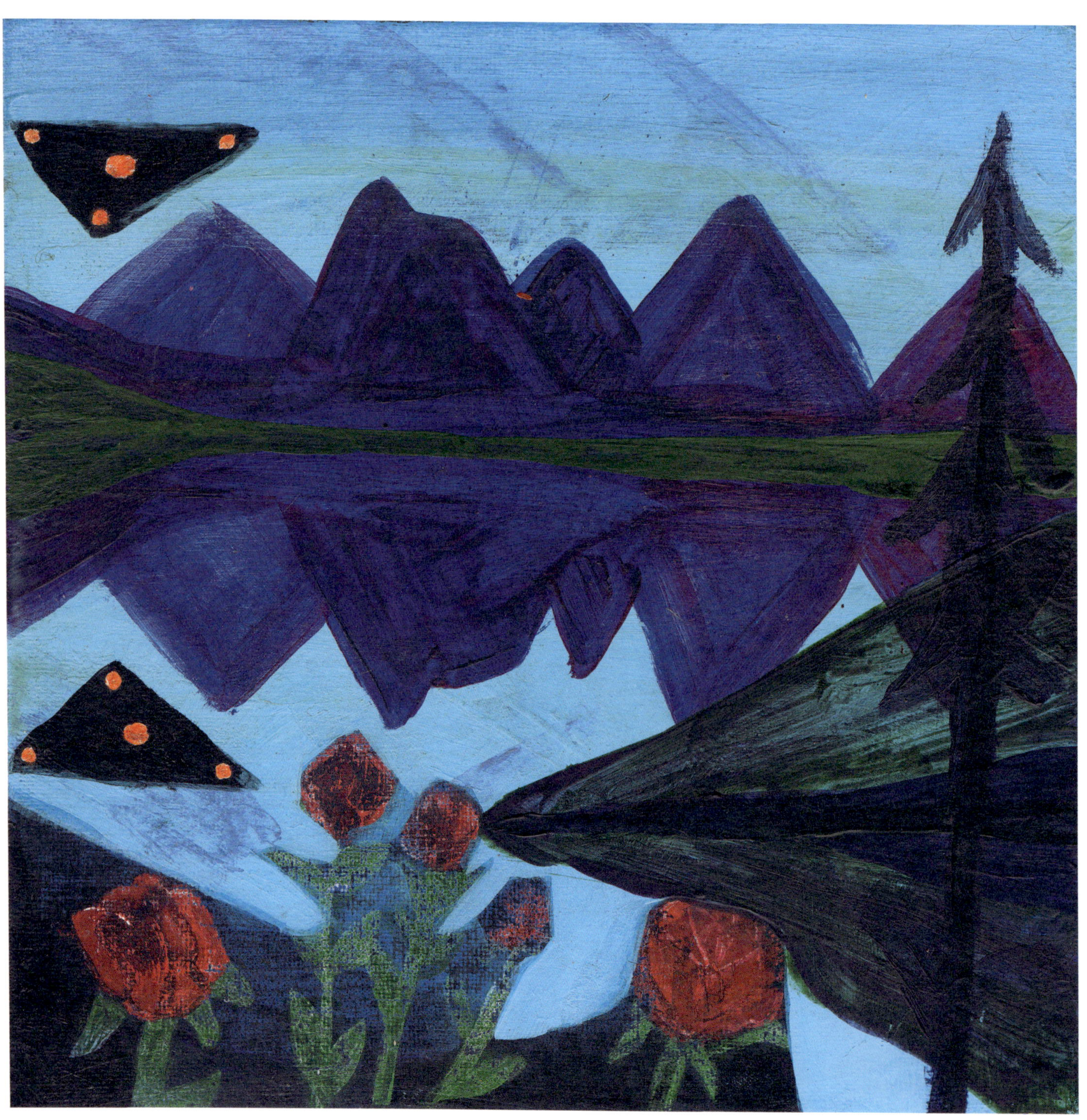

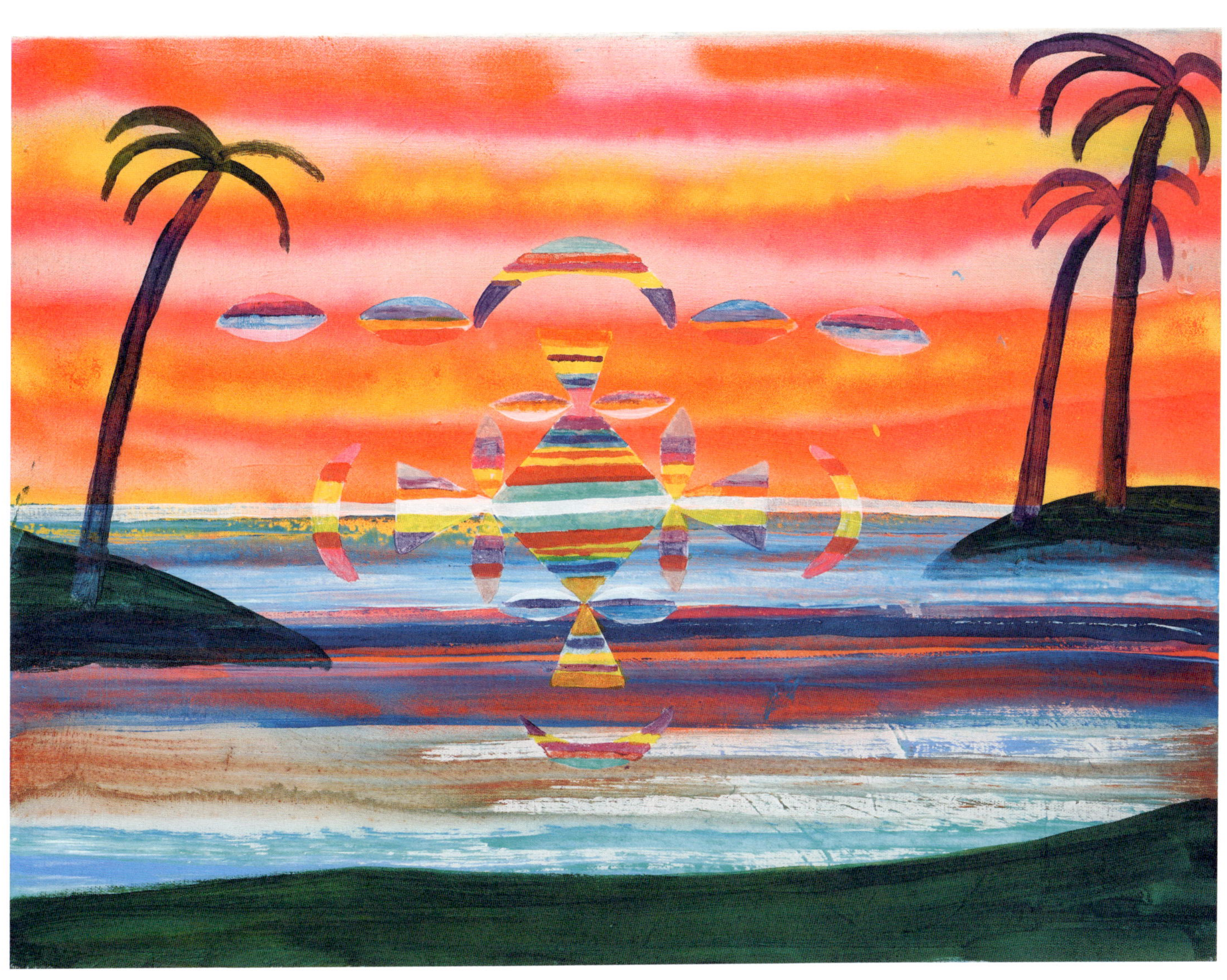

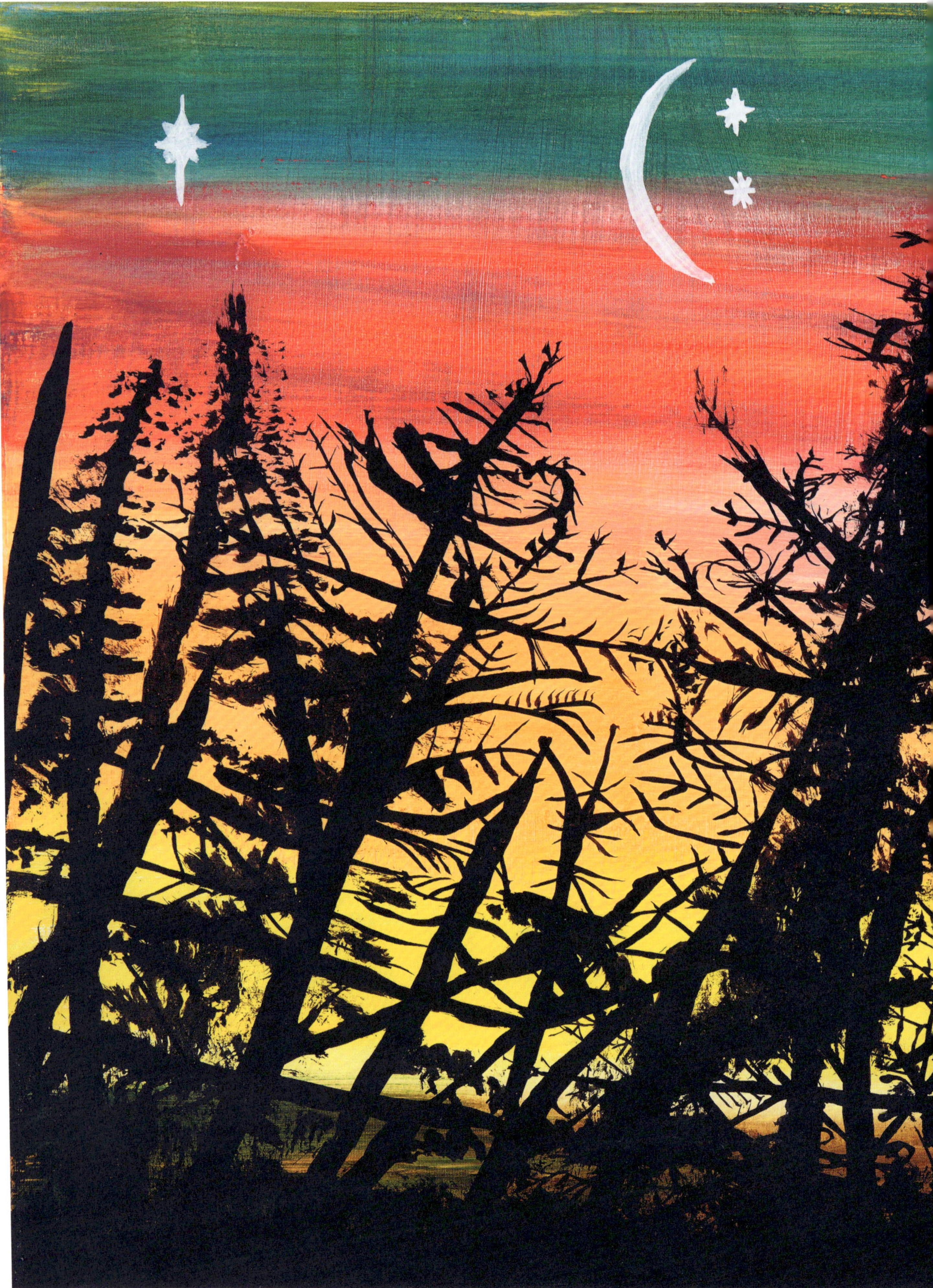

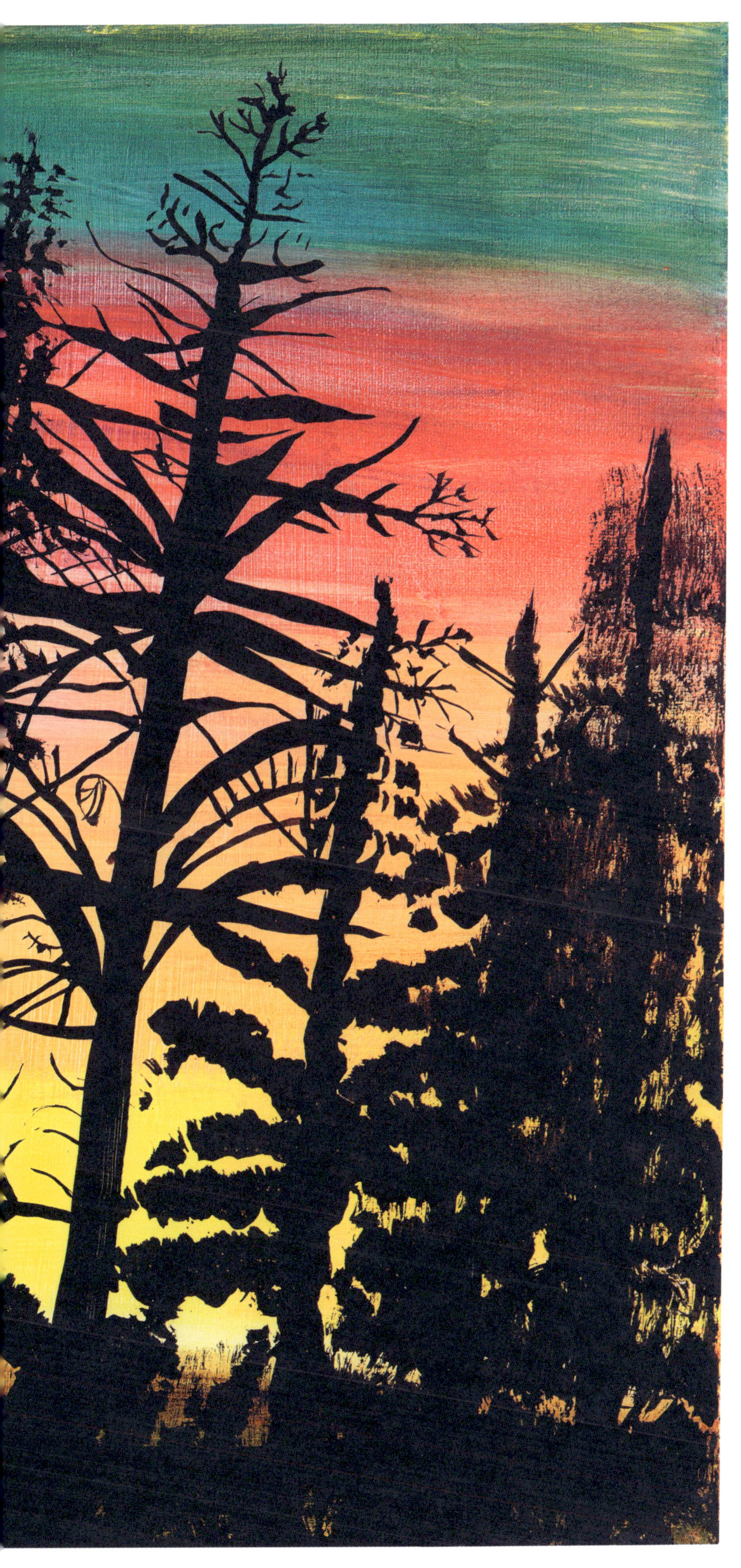

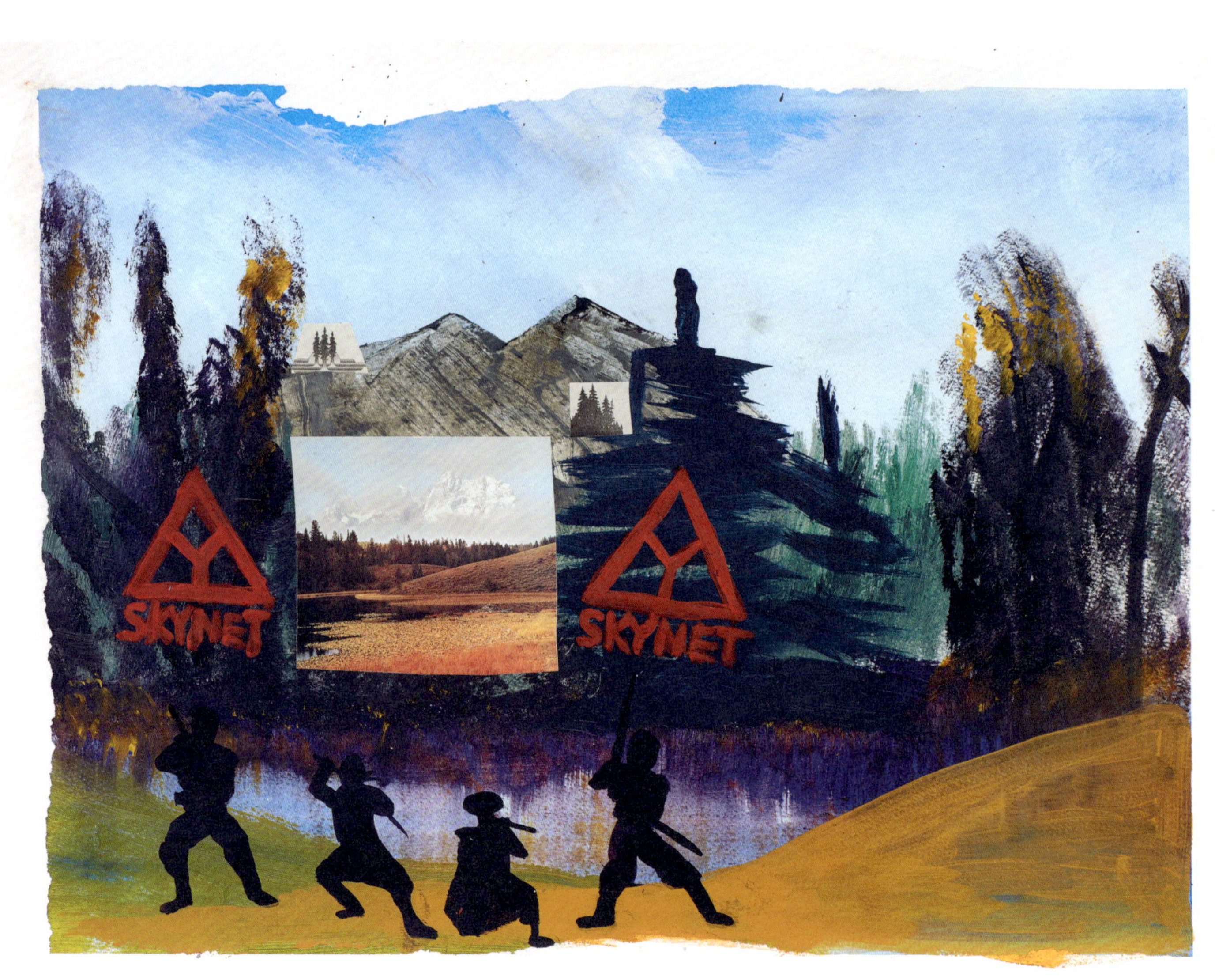

SKYNET
SKYNET

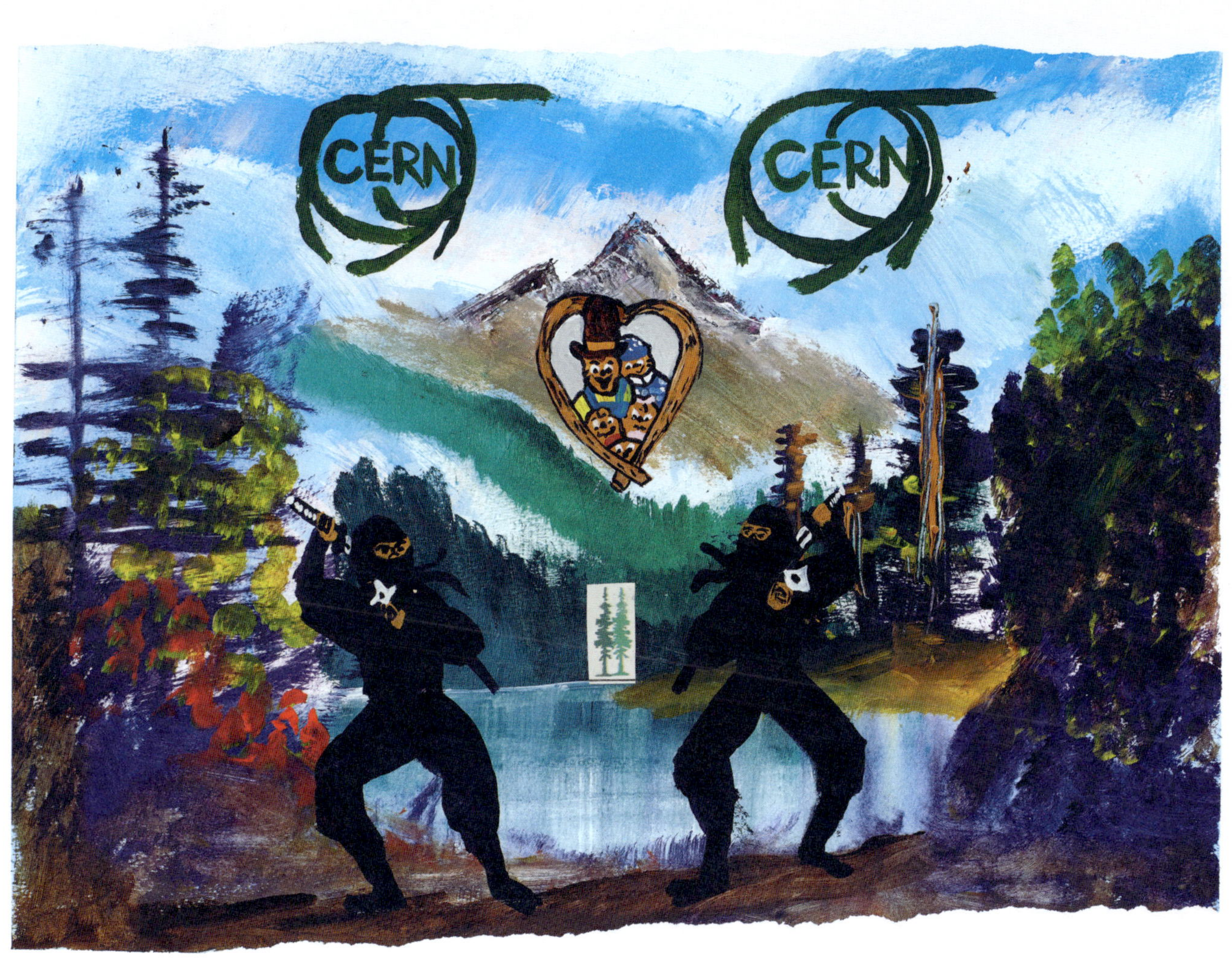
CERN
CERN

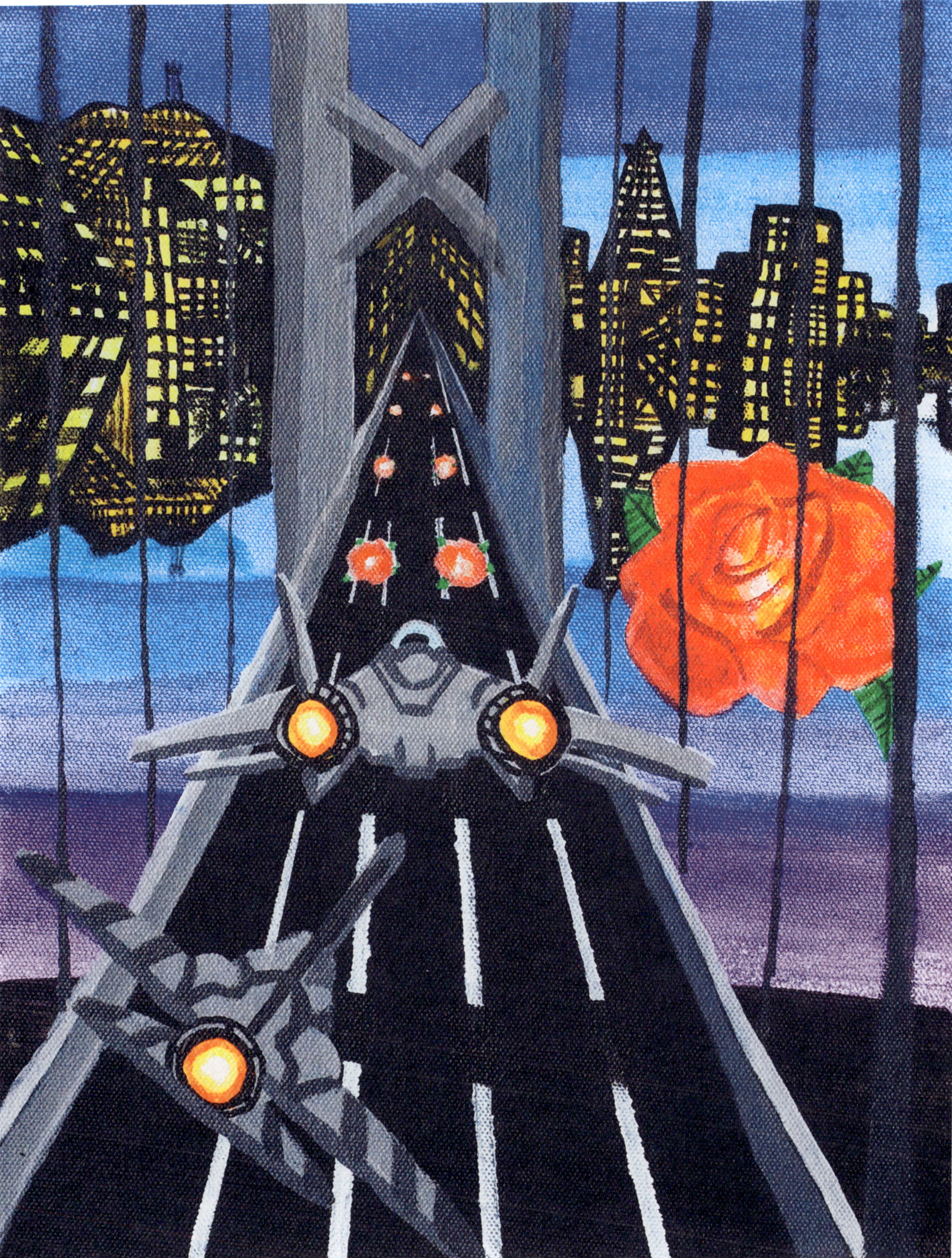

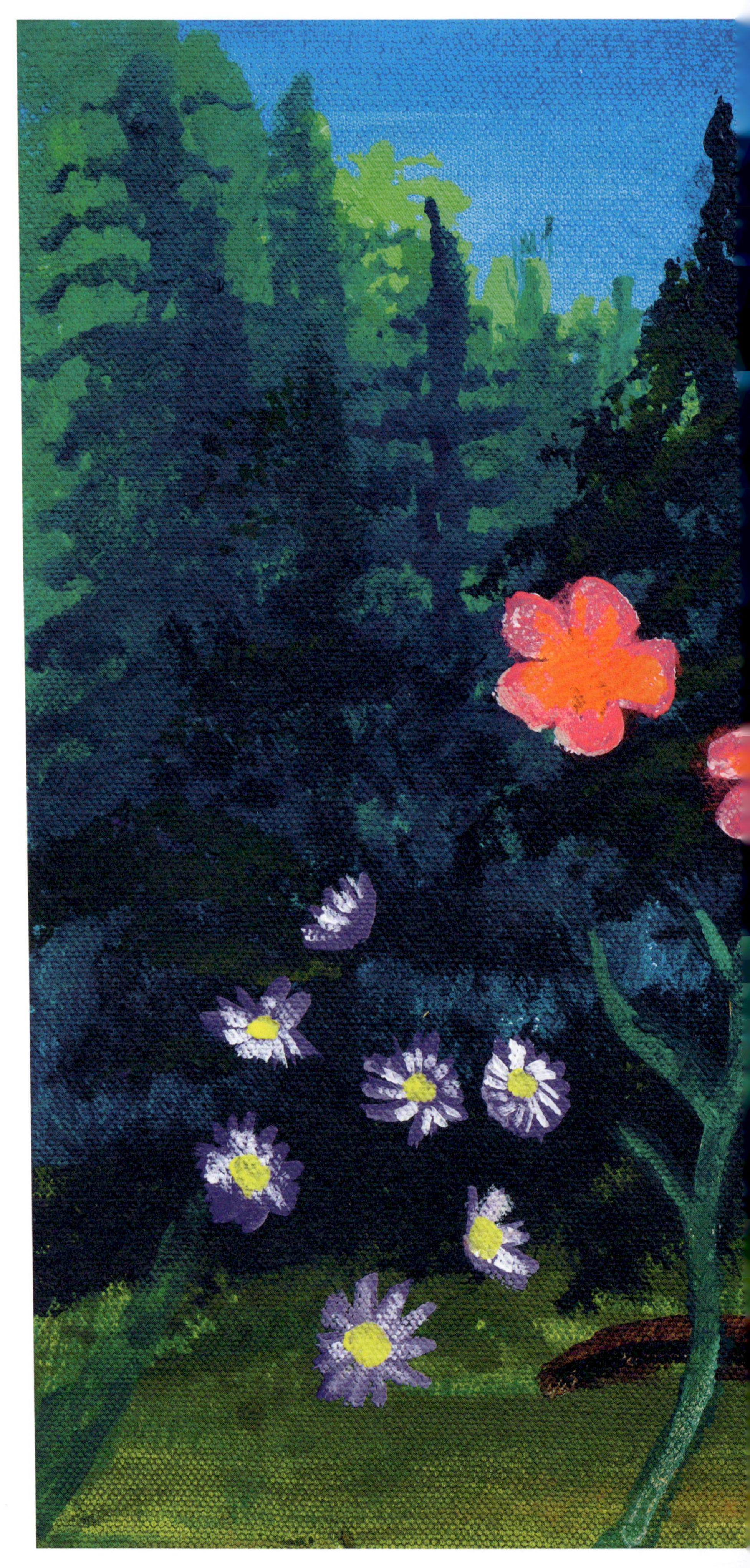

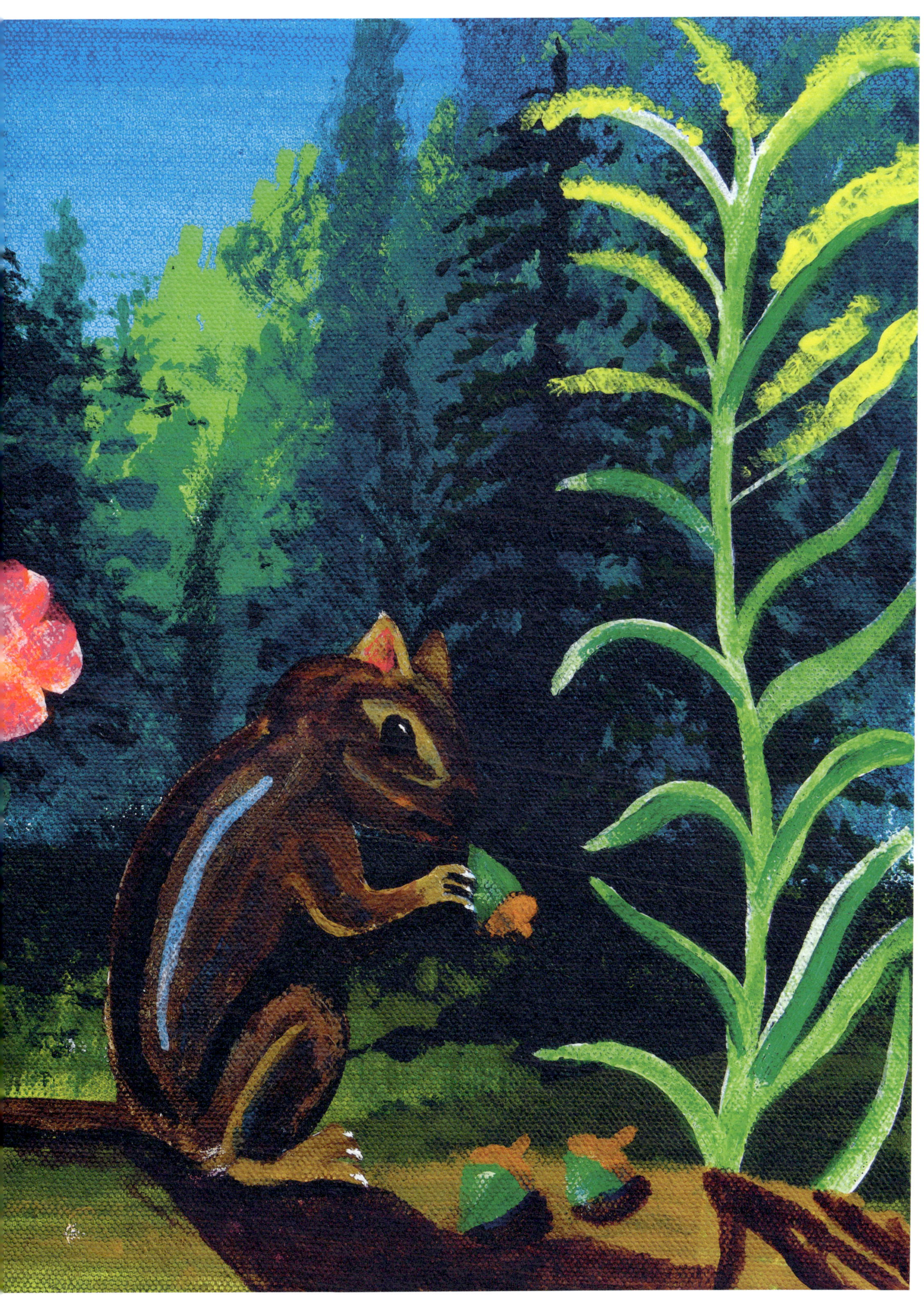

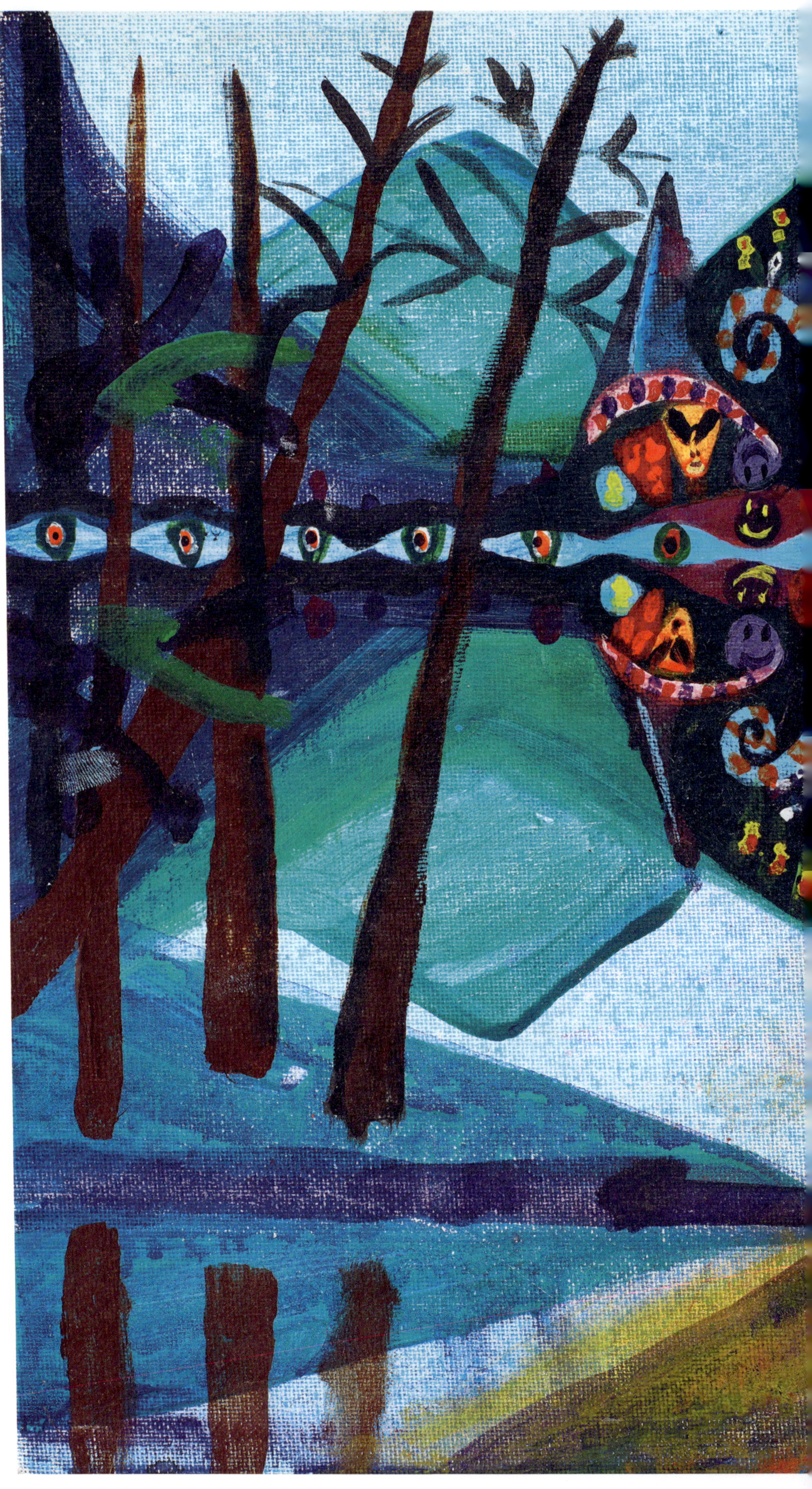

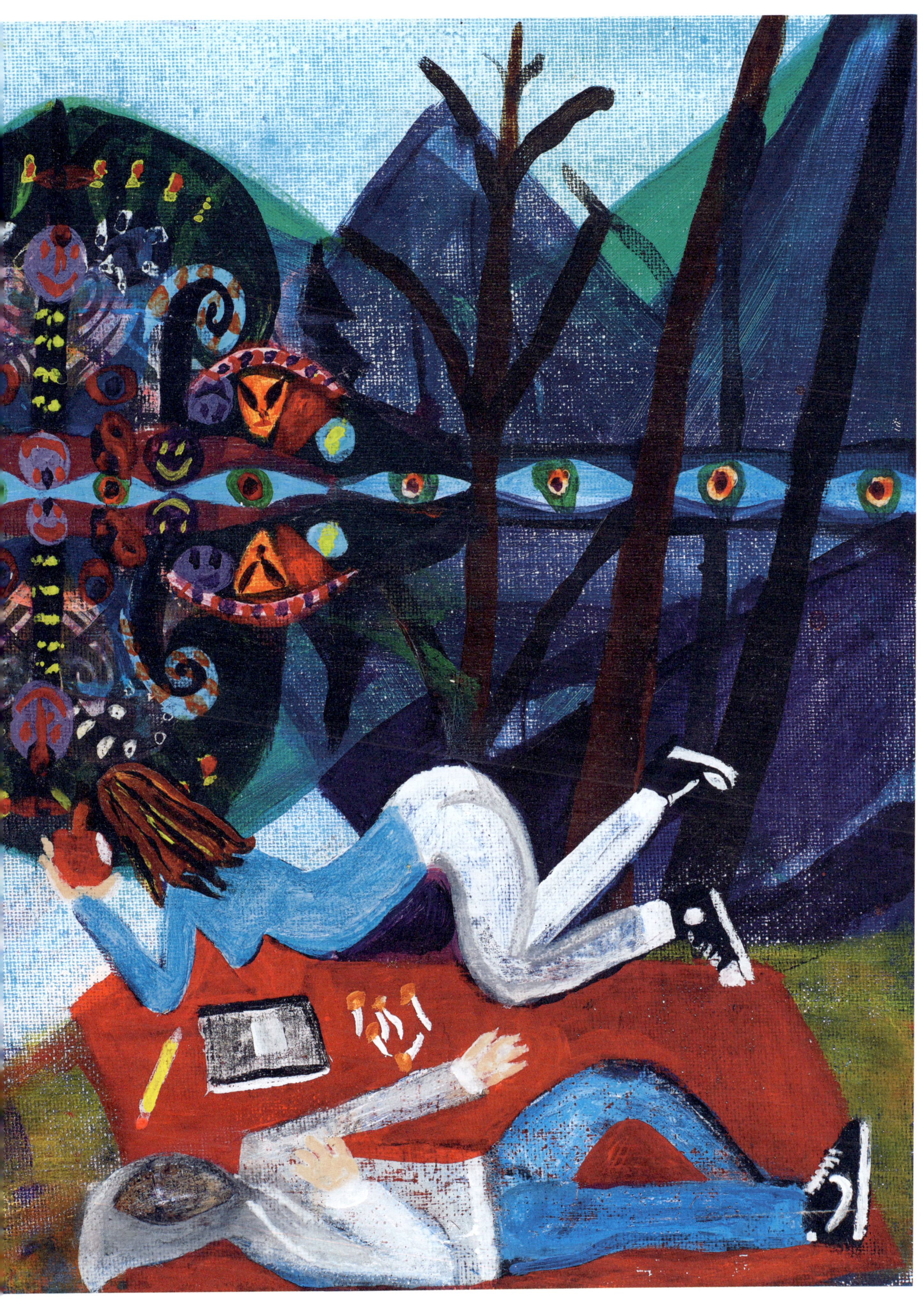

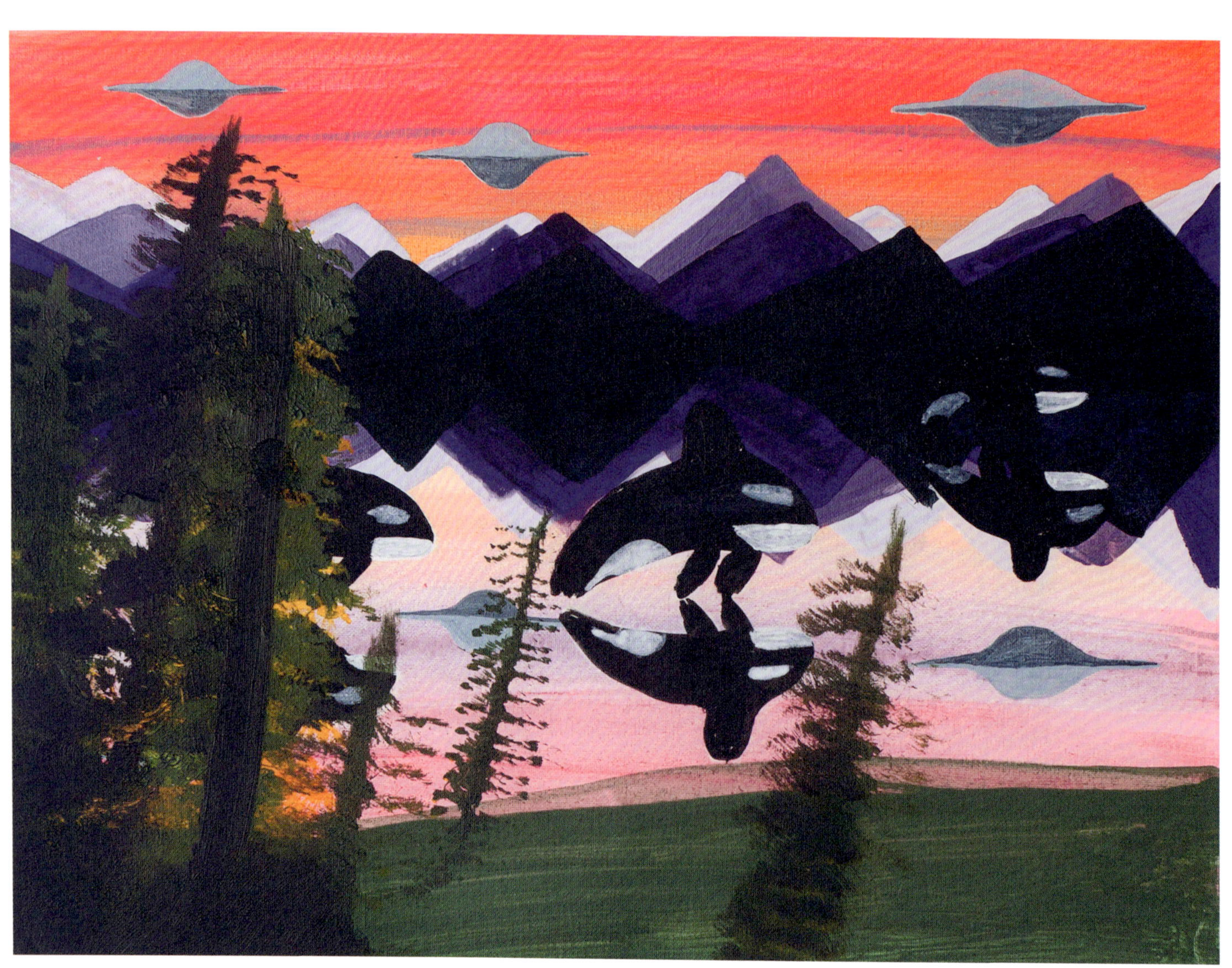

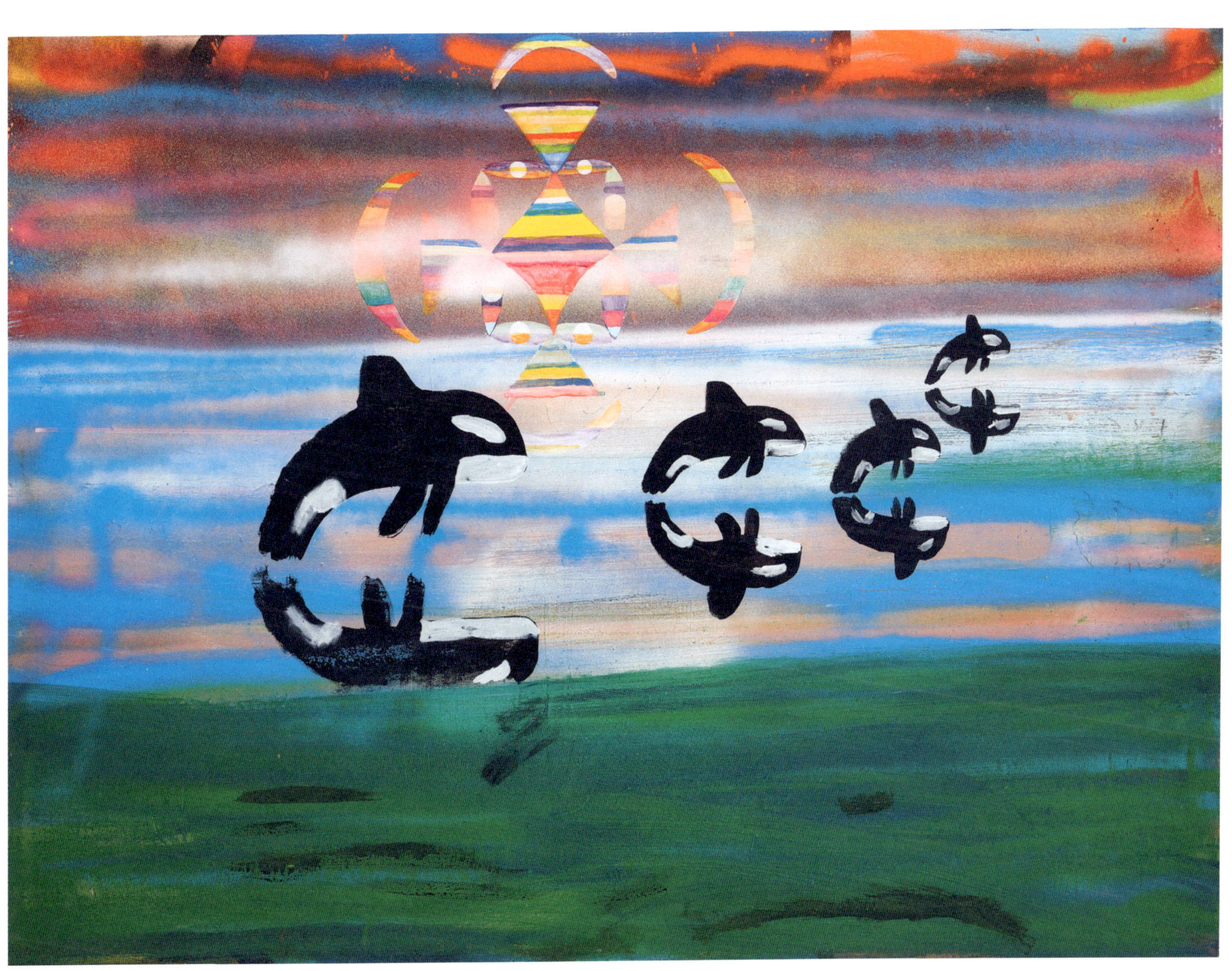

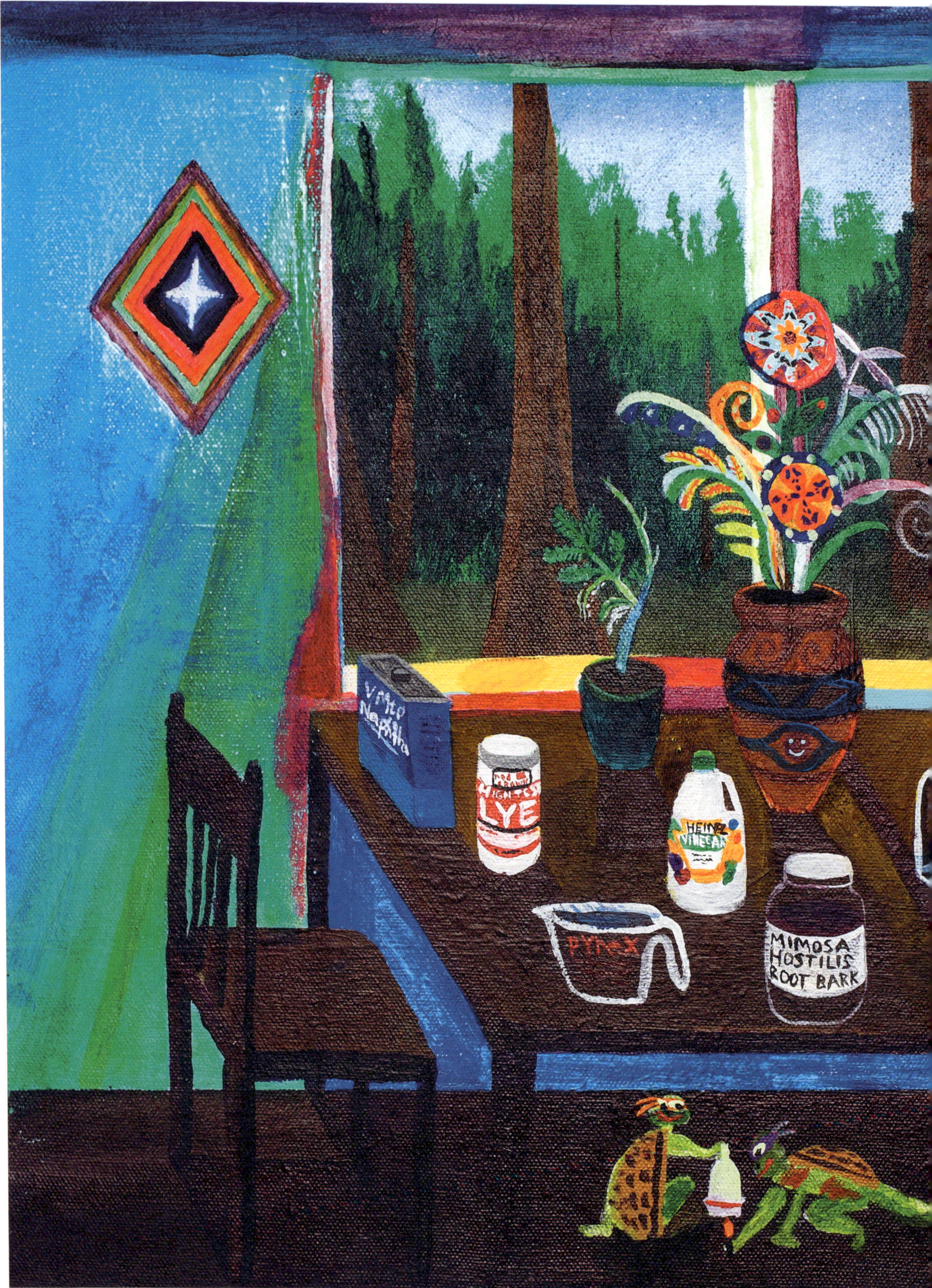

Vrito Naptha
RED DEVIL HIGH TEST LYE
HEINZ VINEGAR
PYREX
MIMOSA HOSTILIS ROOT BARK

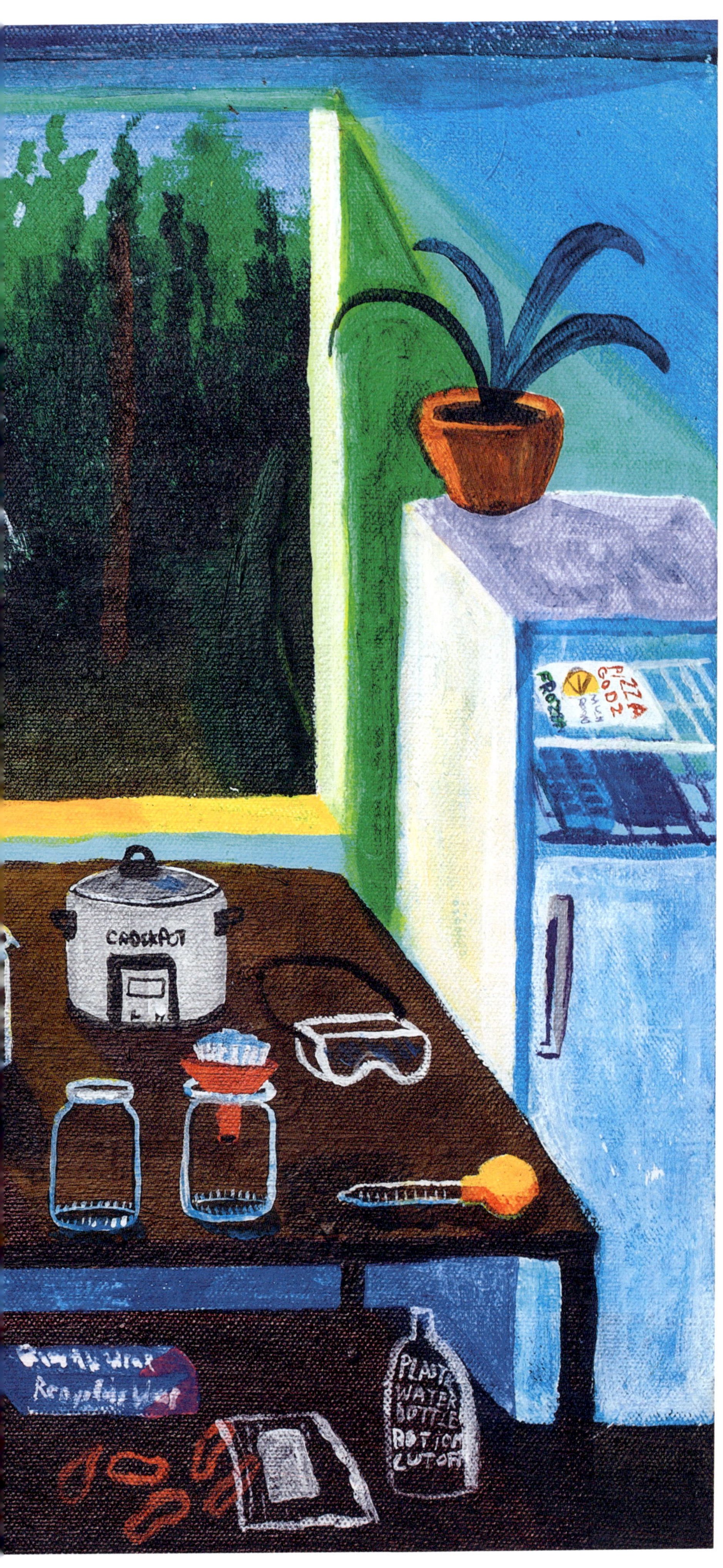

CROCKPOT
PIZZA GODZ
MUCH GOOD
FROZEN
PLASTIC WATER BOTTLE BOTTOM CUTOFF

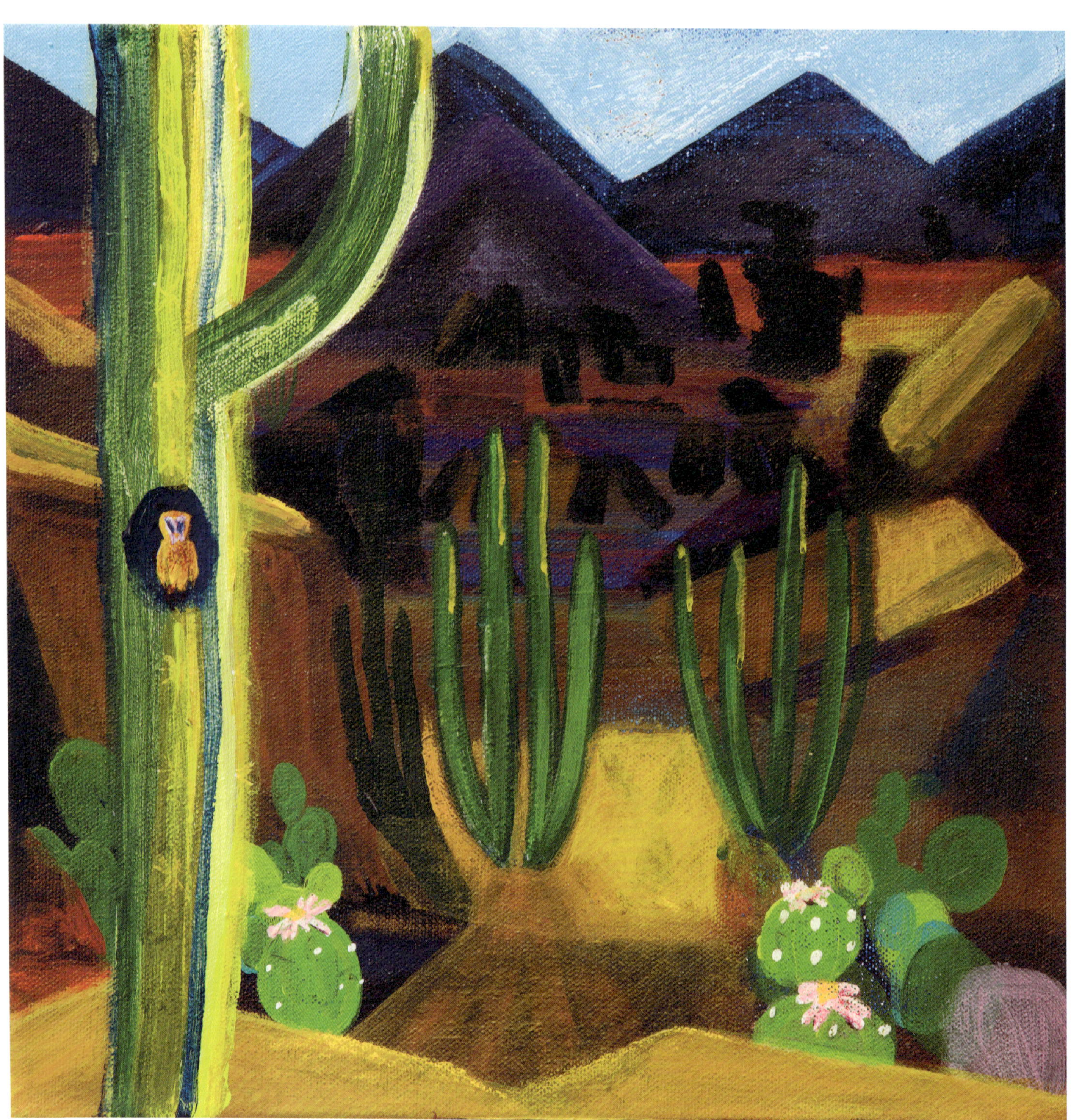

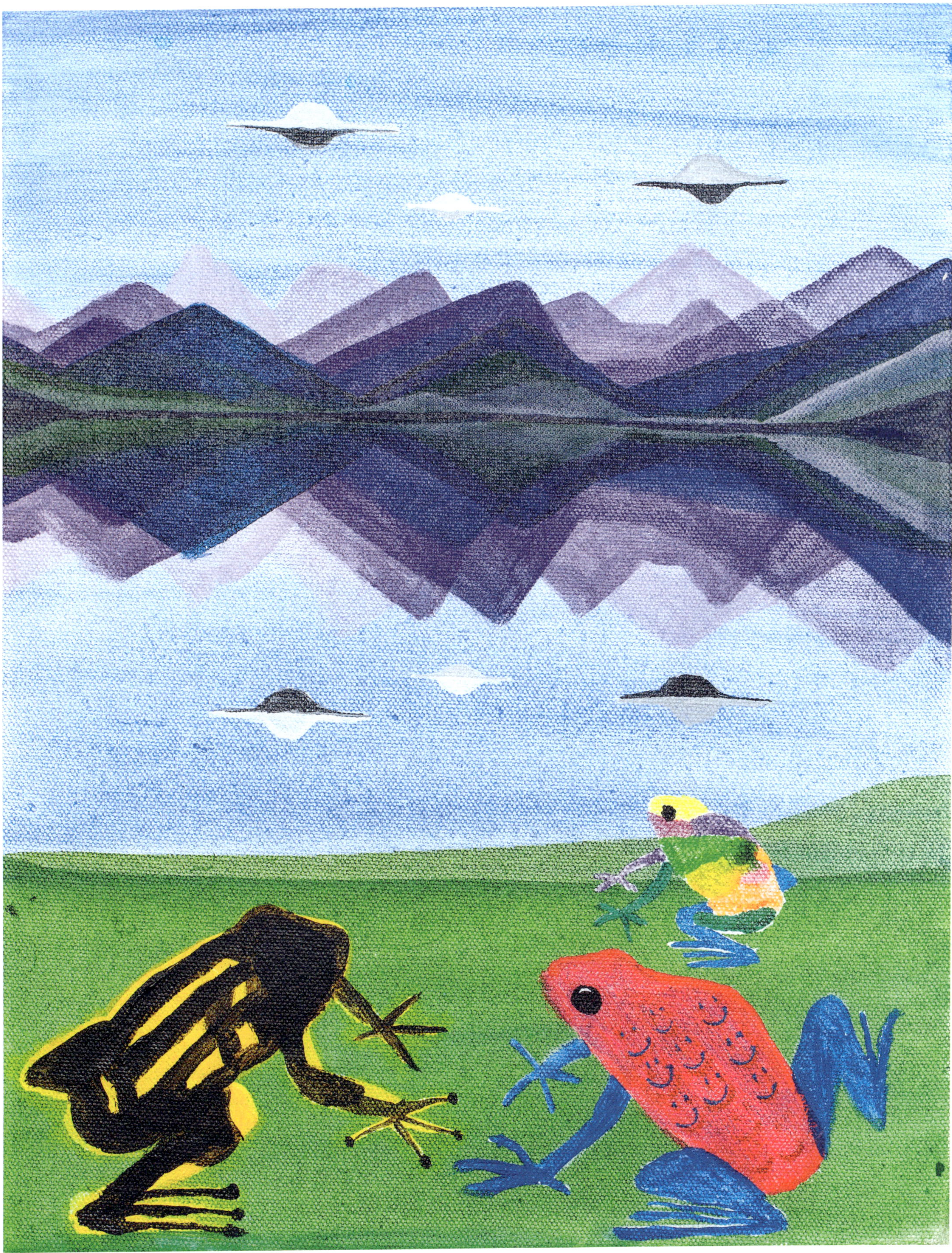

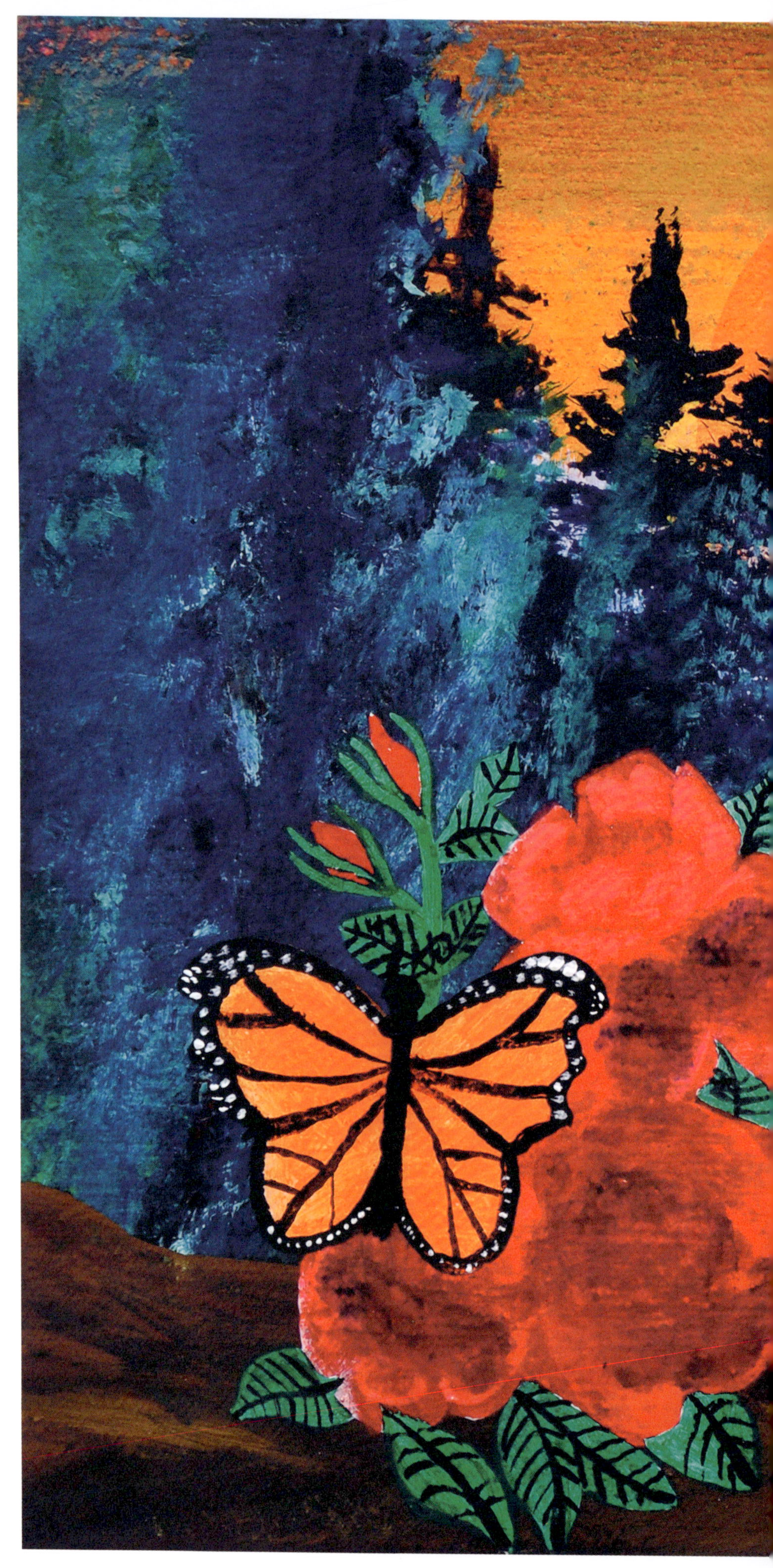

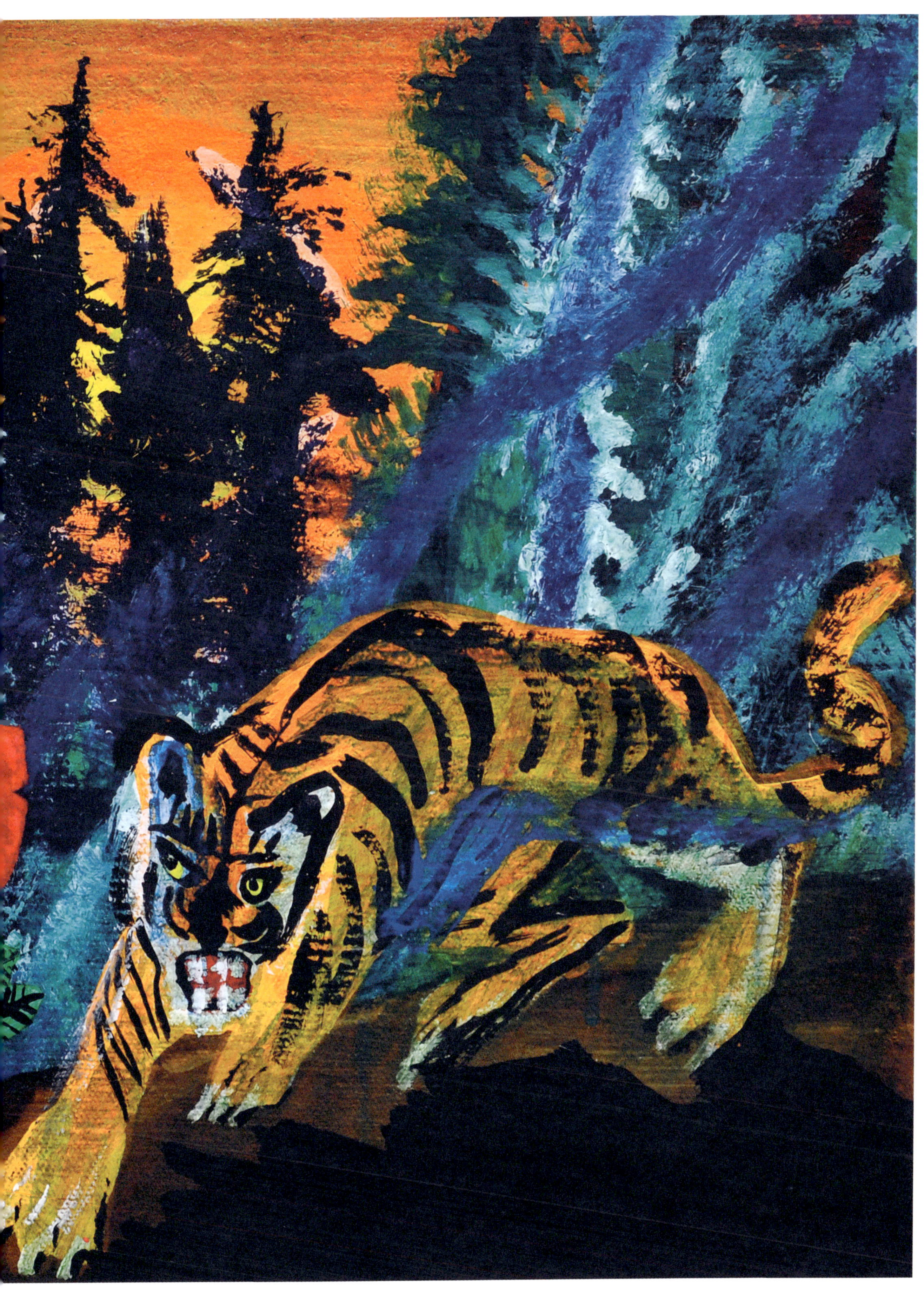

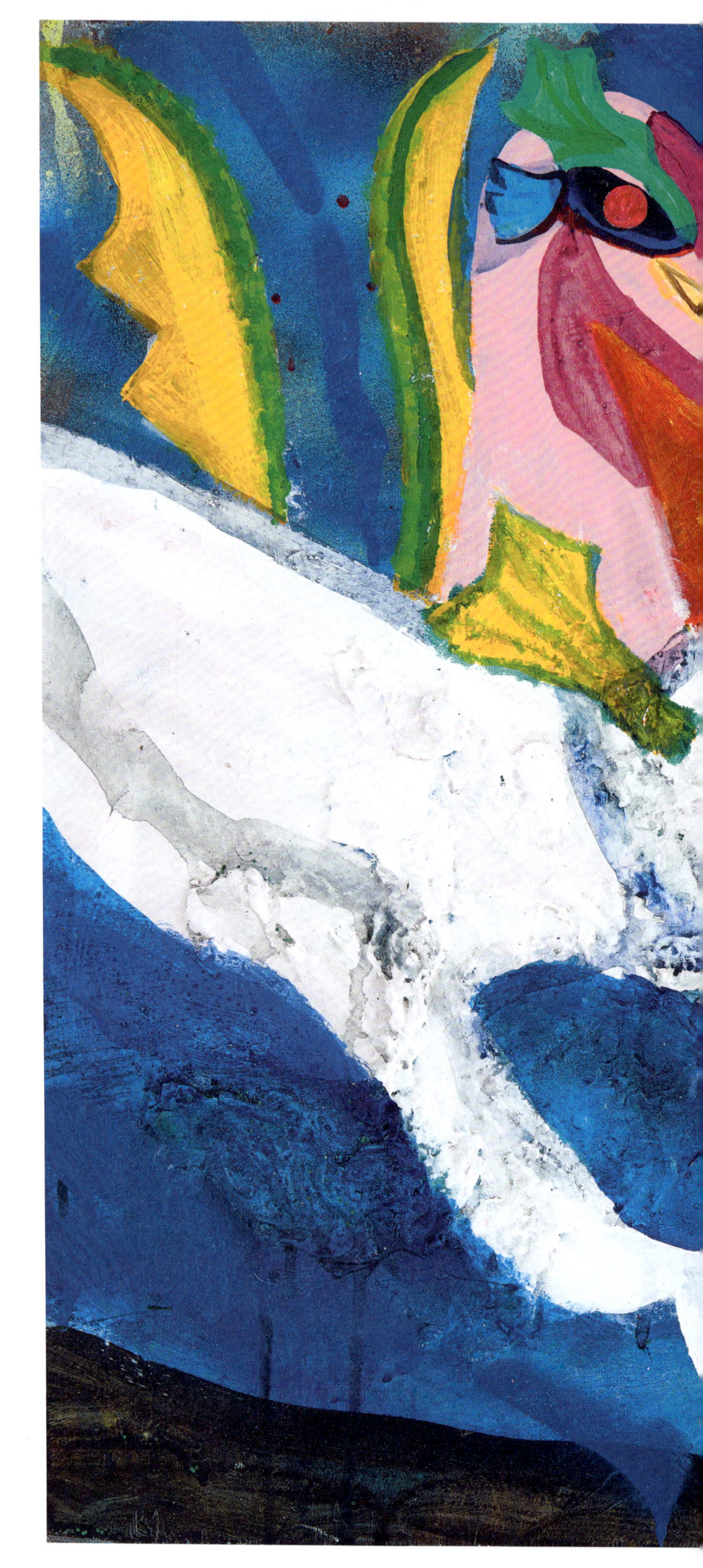

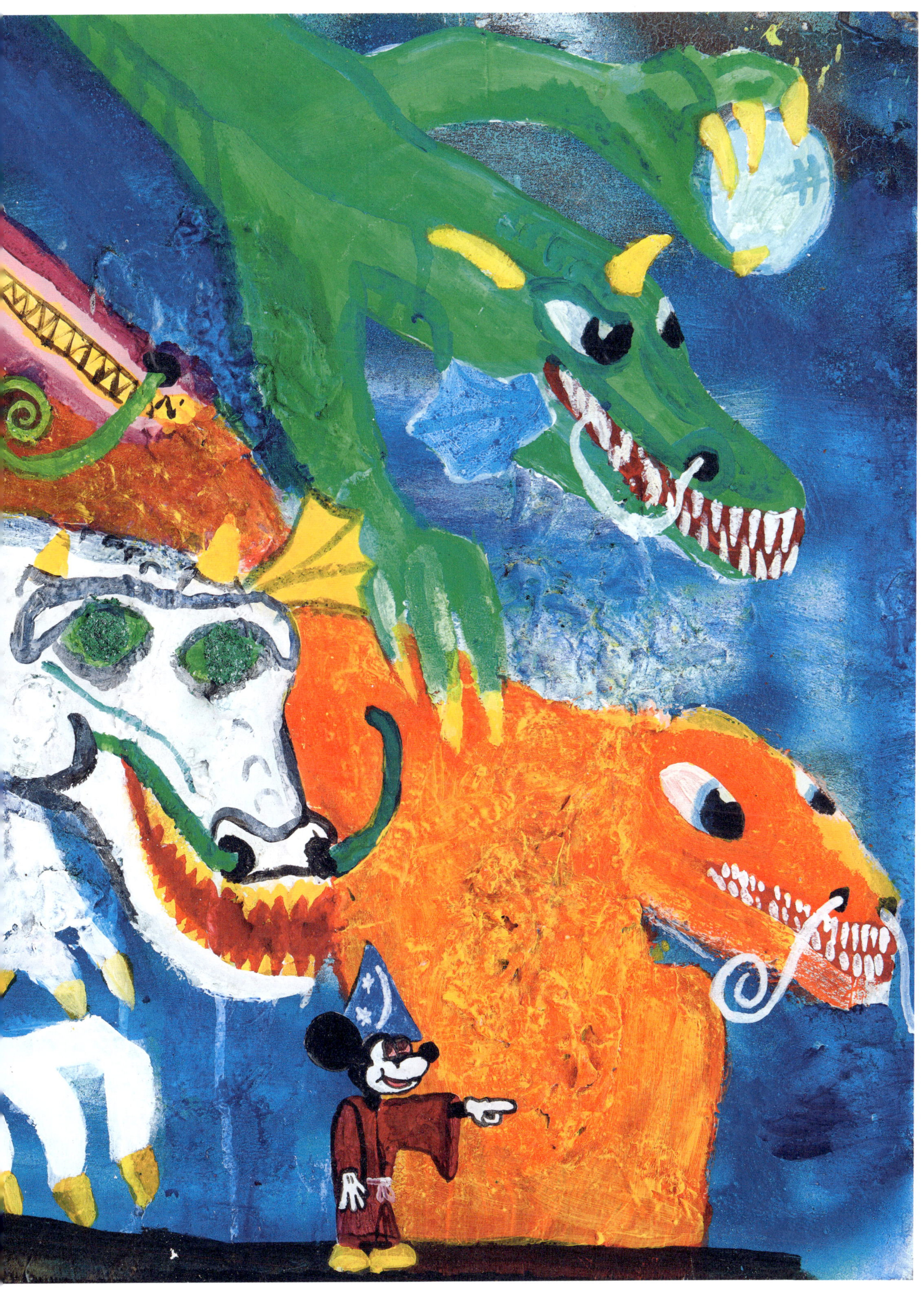

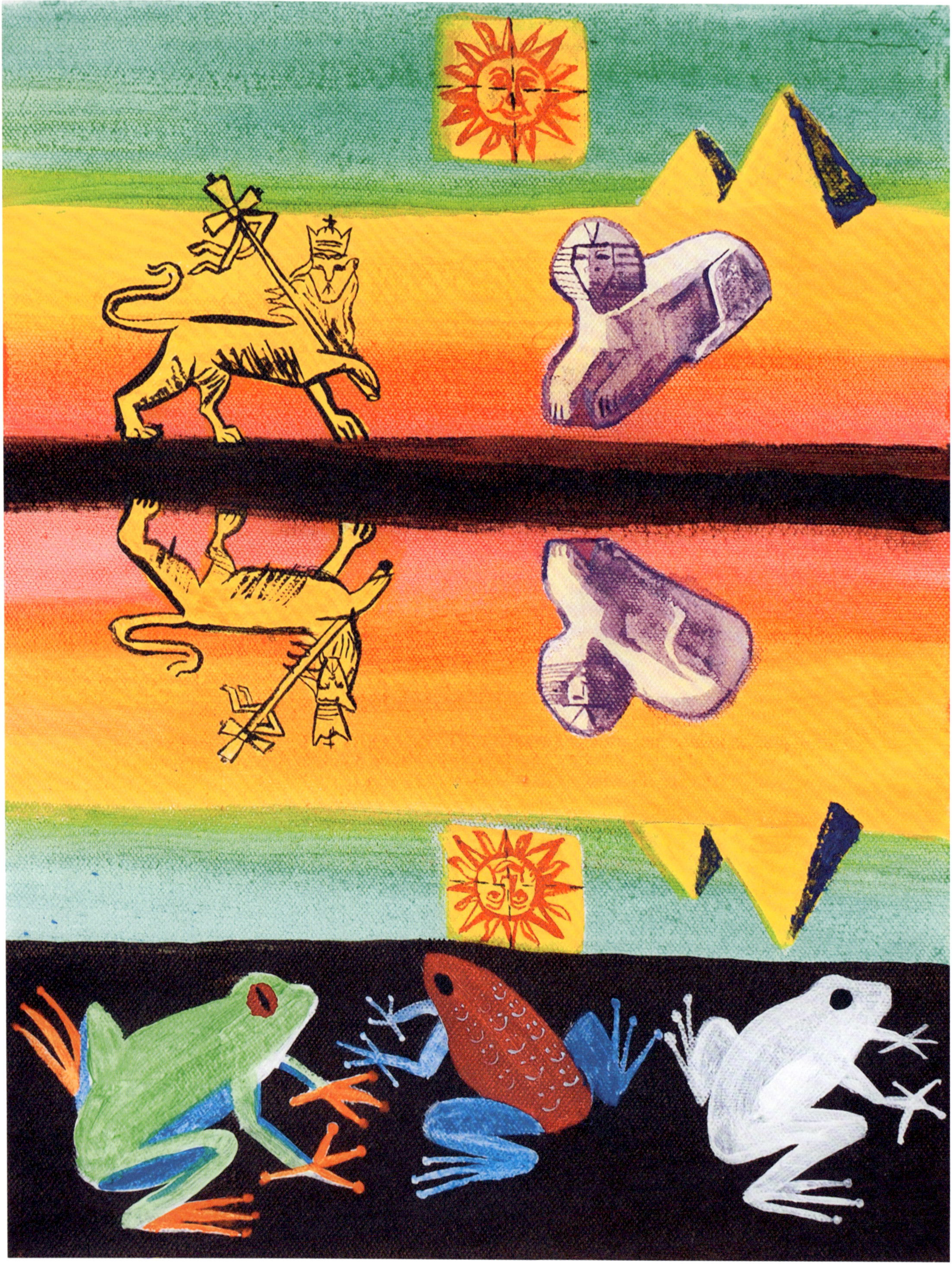

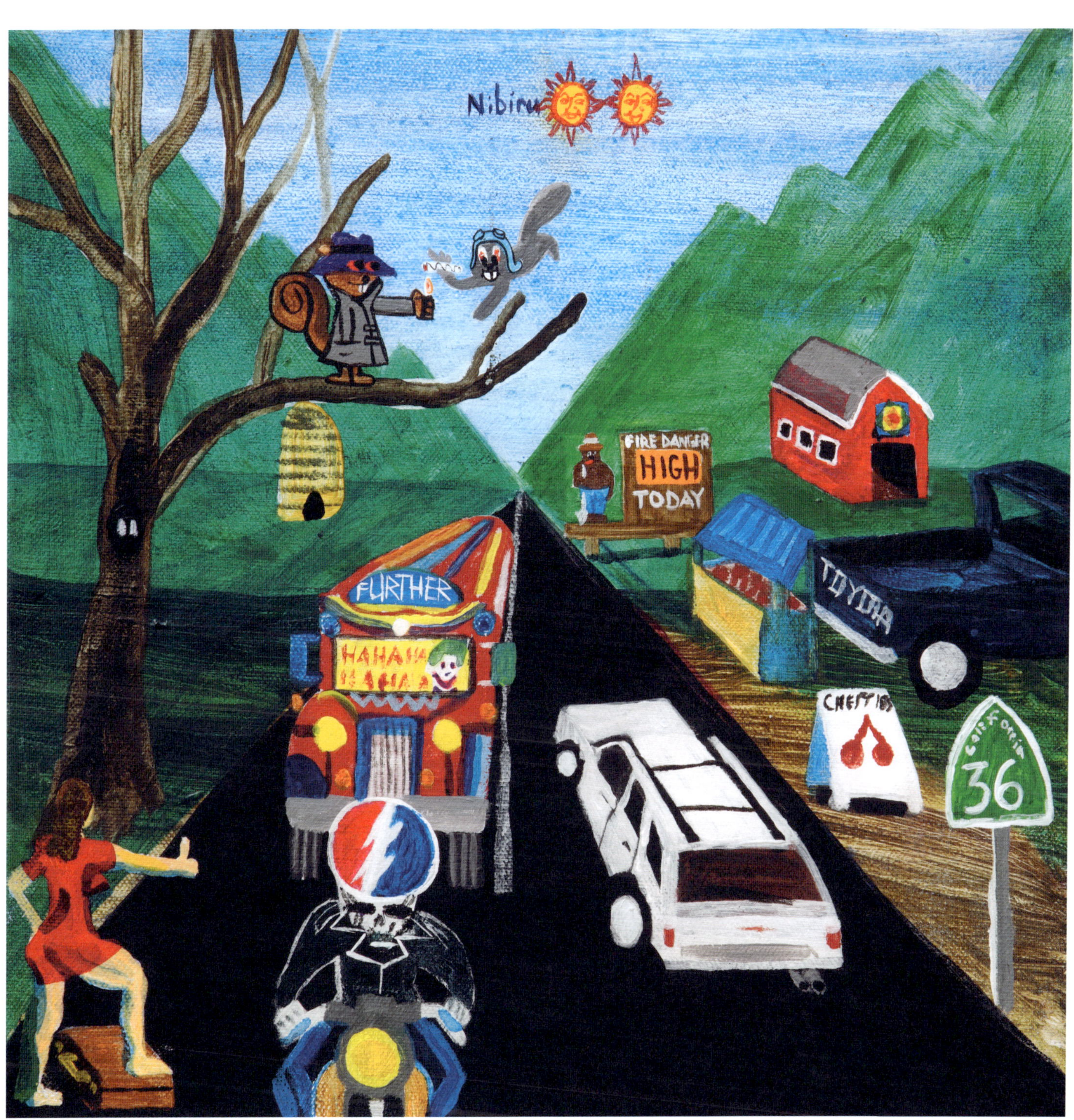

Nibiru
FURTHER
HAHAHA HAHAHA
FIRE DANGER
HIGH
TODAY
TOYOTA
CHERRIES
CALIFORNIA
36

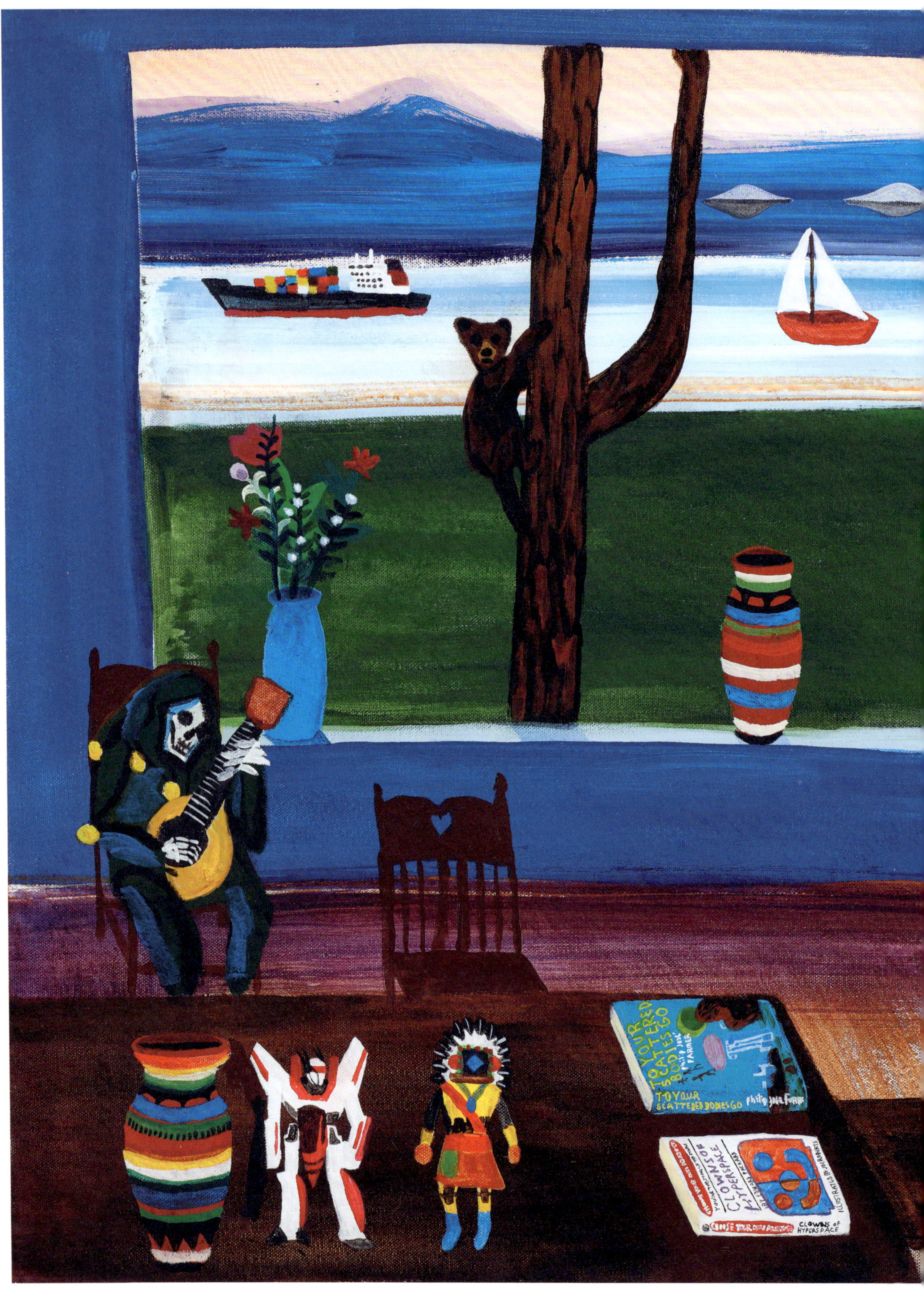

TO YOUR SCATTERED BODIES GO
Philip José FARMER
TO YOUR SCATTERED BODIES GO Philip José Farmer
YOU'RE THE STAR OF THE STORY
CLOWNS OF HYPERSPACE
BY EDWARD PACKARD
ILLUSTRATED BY JOE ROBERTS
CHOOSE YOUR OWN ADVENTURE
CLOWNS OF HYPERSPACE

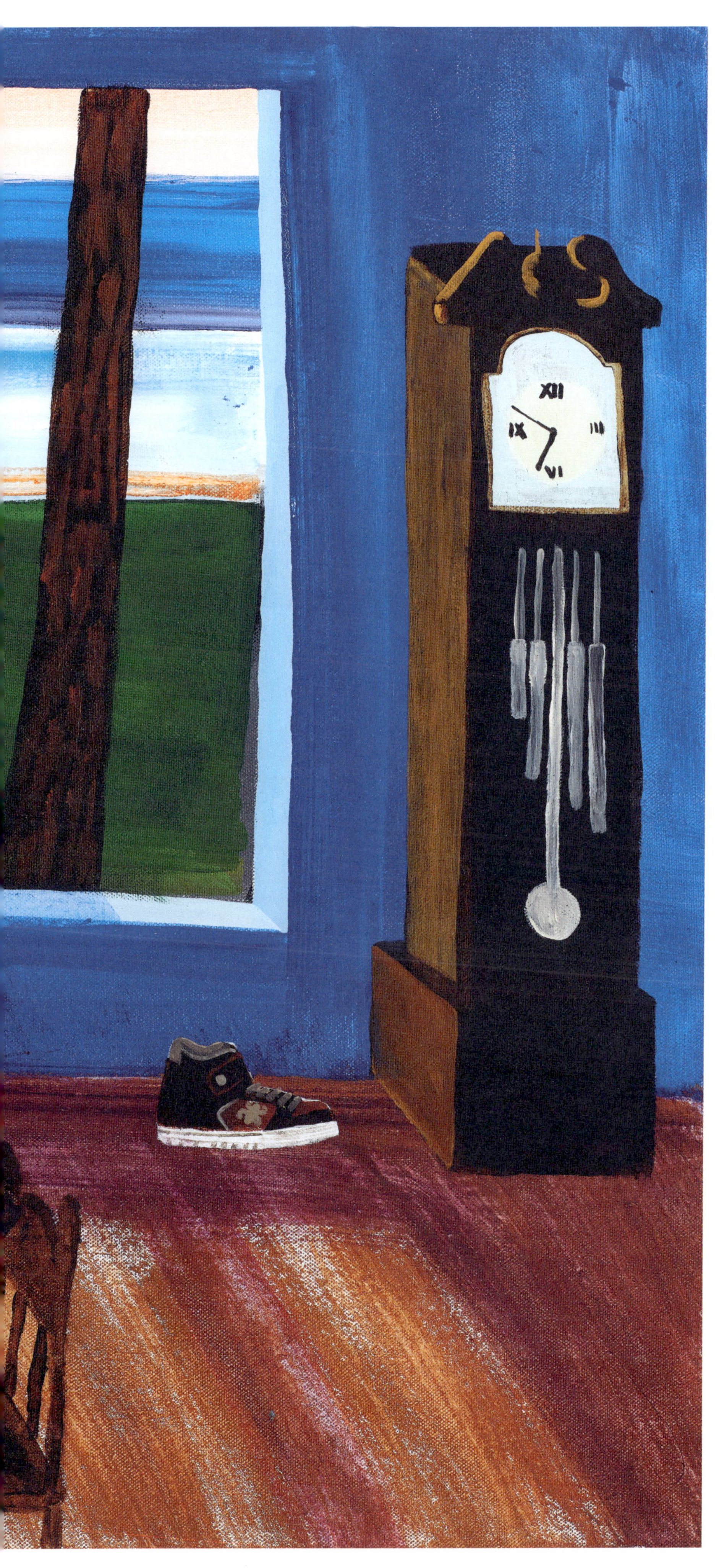

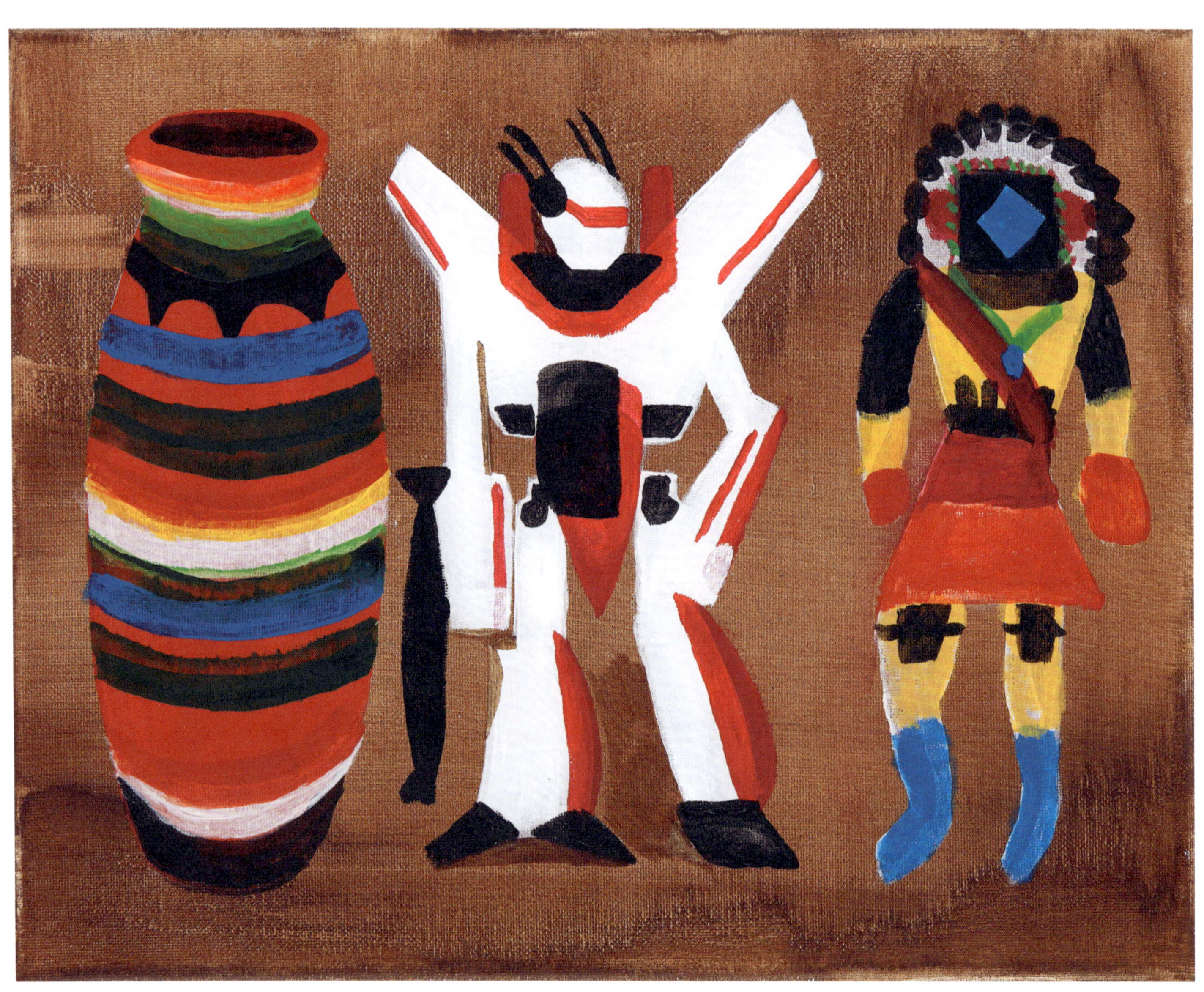

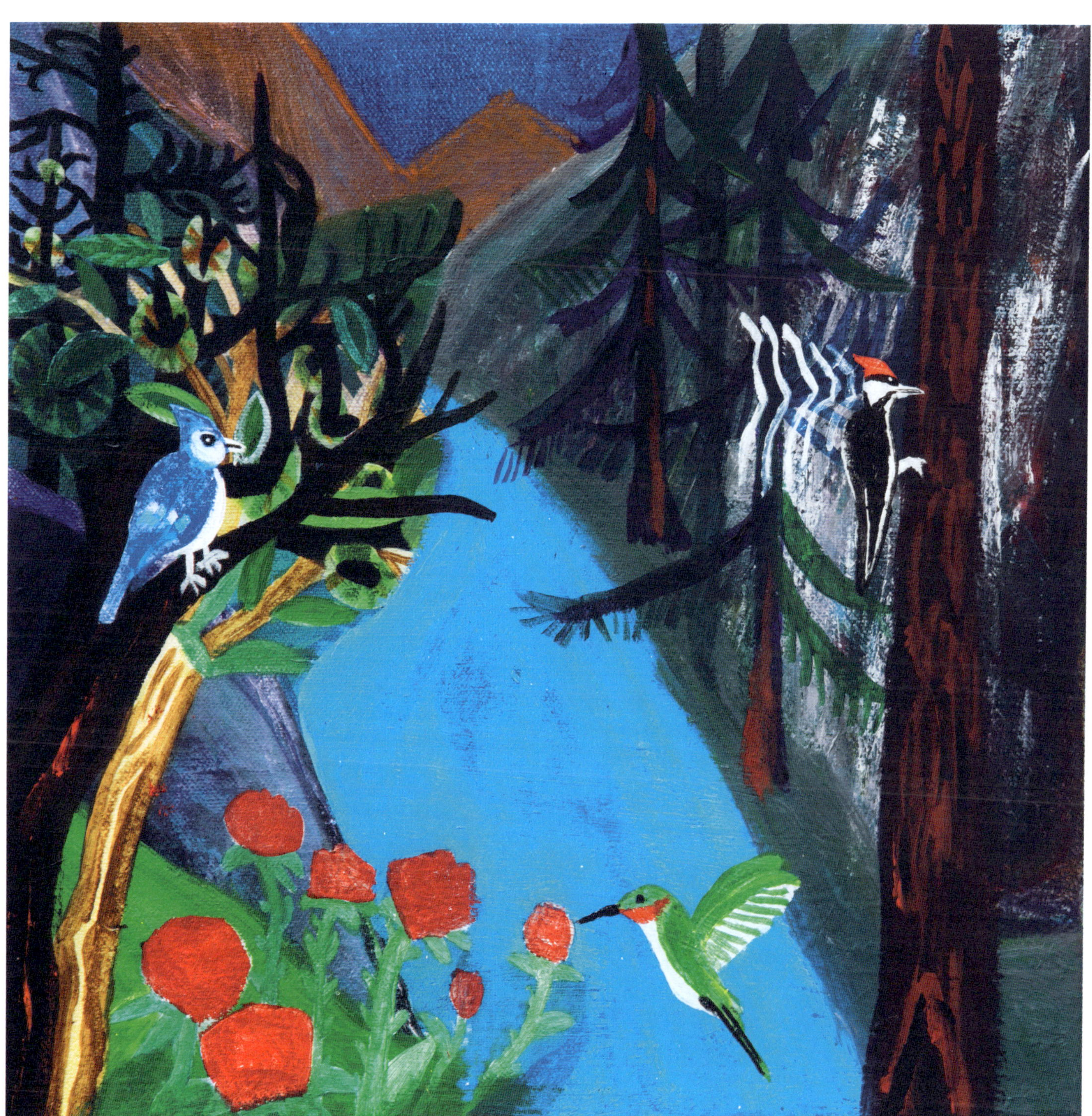

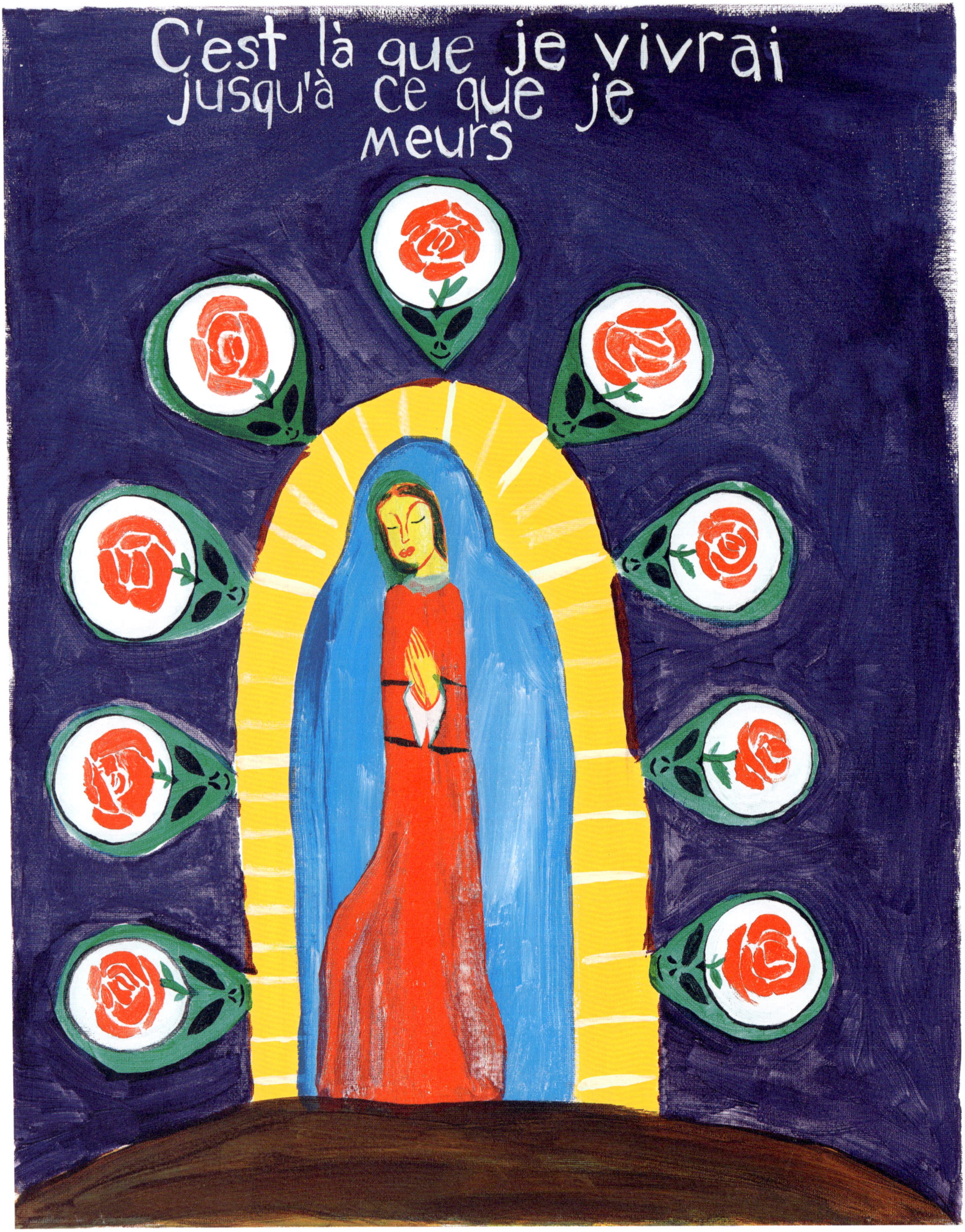

C'est là que je vivrai
jusqu'à ce que je
meurs

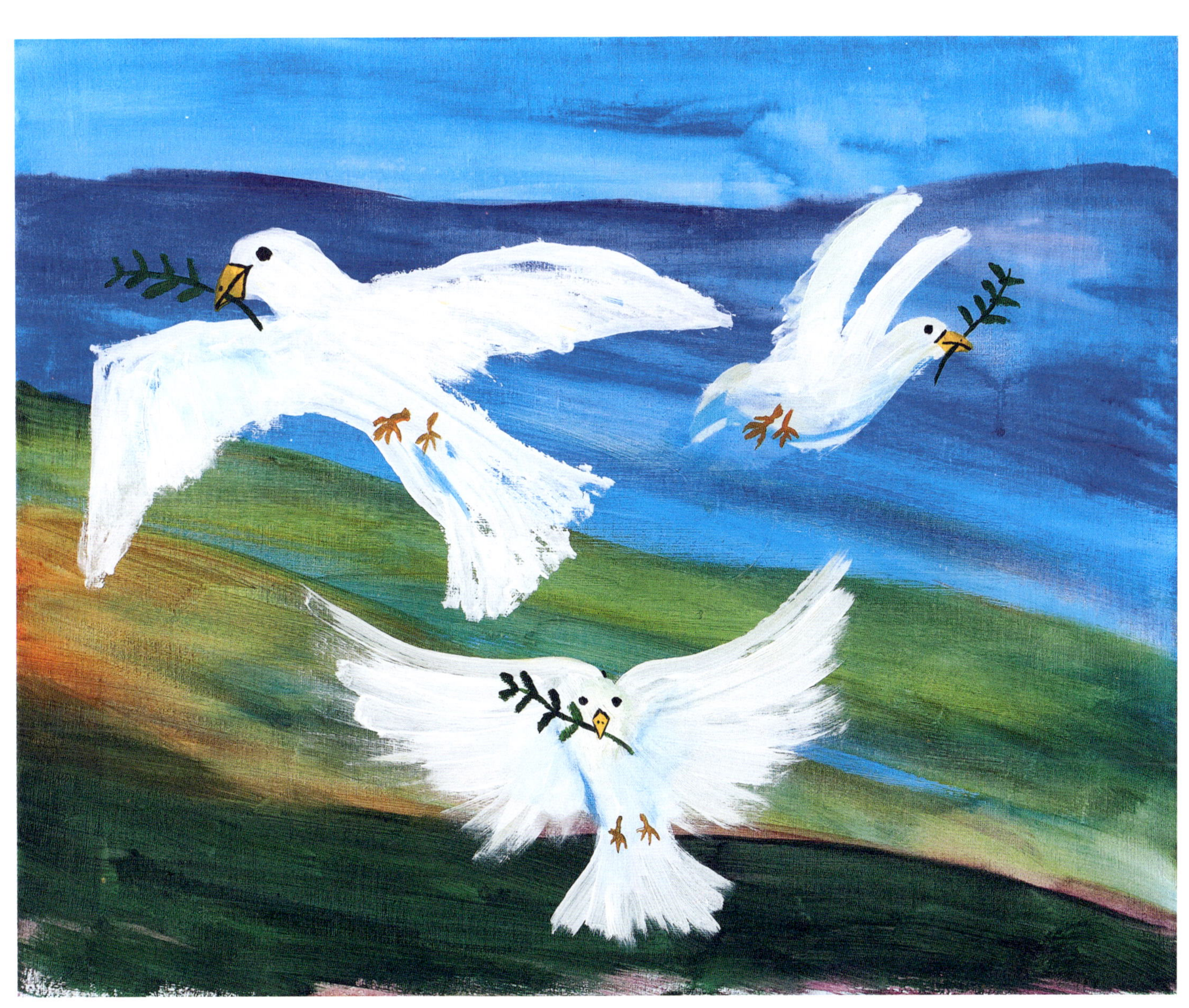

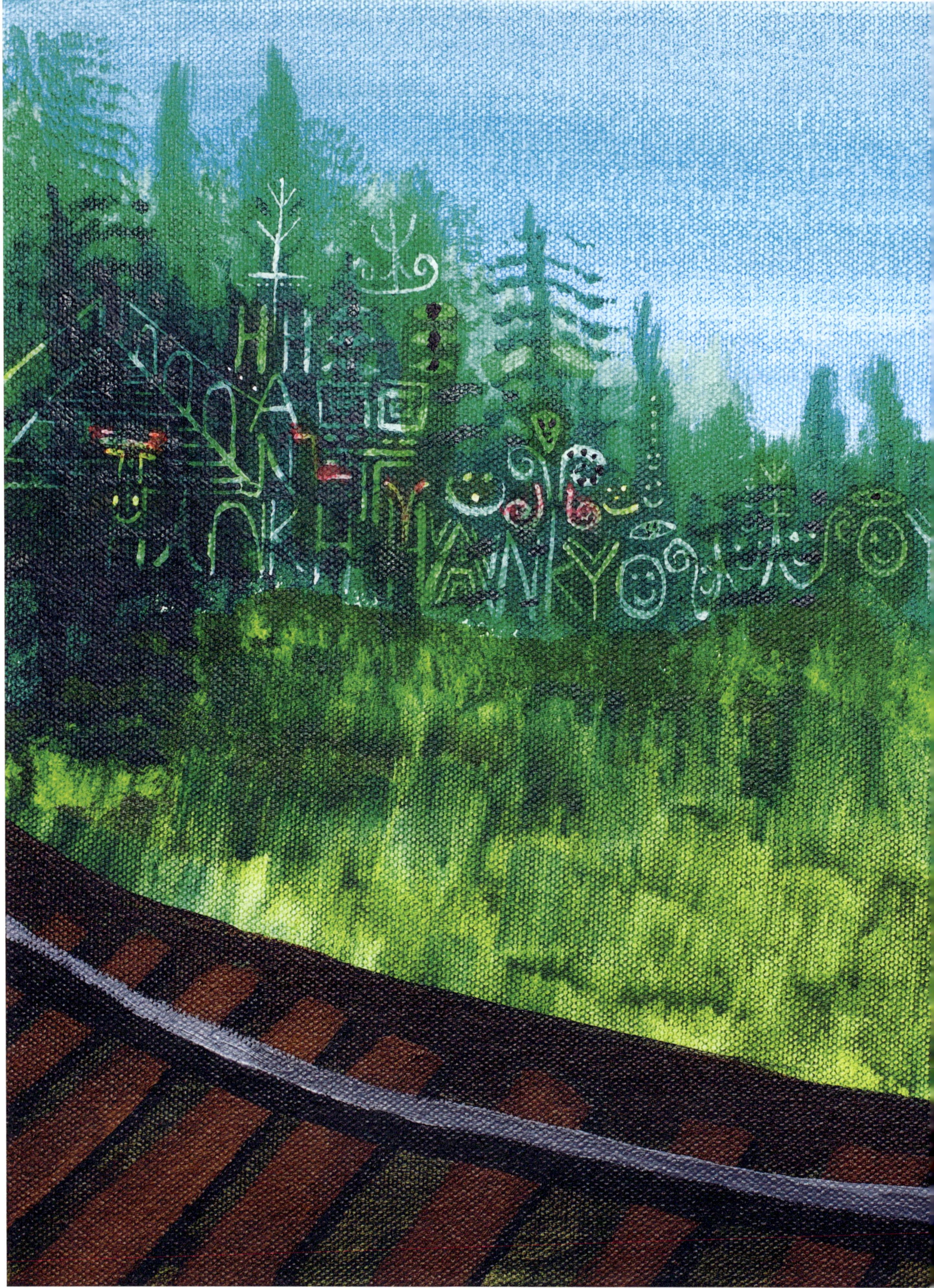

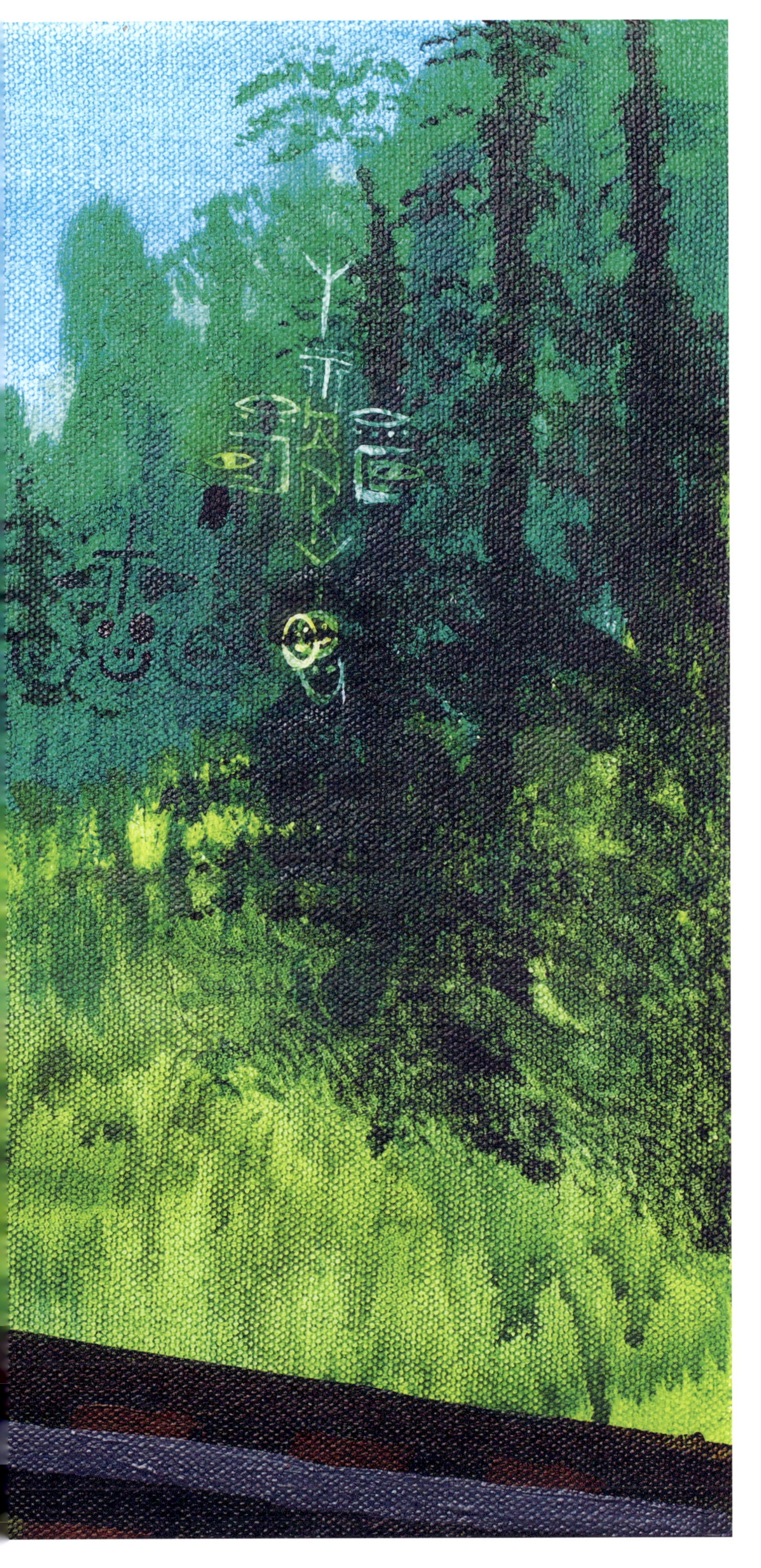

"The true artist helps the world by revealing mystic truths."
    —Bruce Nauman

So you grew up in Wisconsin, correct? Did you enjoy that?

Yeah, I didn't know any better, you know? It wasn't till I was a teenager that
I was like, "I've got to get out of here." But I think it was a good thing to
leave, because now, after not living there for twenty years, I can appreciate
what it was... It's so different from where I am now.

*Were you in a rush to get out of childhood and those surroundings, or did you
enjoy your childhood?*

I think it's only when you become an adult that you realize how special it was
to be a kid. When you're in it, you can't really see it—at least I couldn't.
I wanted to get a life. I was out of the house by seventeen. I wanted to be on
my own schedule; I had the earliest curfew out of all my friends, so they would
keep me out super late, because they thought it was funny to watch me get yelled
at when I got dropped off. And it probably was funny, but it sucked for me.

Were your parents supportive otherwise?

Oh yeah, they were super cool... super hippies. Like, my dad was a Deadhead and
my mom was a mathematician. I remember when I was a kid, my dad had a shirt with
a picture of Ronald Reagan with his finger way up his nose, and it said "Pick a
winner"... I still don't really get it. But I think it was some really hippie
shit. He would say, "I'm not a hippie, I'm a Yippie," and I would be like, "OK,
I don't really know what that means," but now I'm just starting to understand
what that means by reading old books and stuff.

Just curious, do you know how old your parents were when they had you?

They were twenty-three.

Do you ever think about how crazy that is?

Yeah, I thought about that when I was twenty-three, when I was homeless, eat-
ing ramen noodles and skateboarding. I'm old now, but when I think about being
twenty-three, I think I was kind of a dipshit—actually not "kind of a dipshit,"
definitely a dipshit. And in twenty years, when I look back to being forty-one,
I'm sure I'll be thinking to myself, "Well, you know, you were kind of a dipshit,
dude." Hopefully not as much of a dipshit as I used to be, but still a dipshit.
I once heard this thing, that the older you get, the more you realize that everyone is just sort of freestyling it and no one really knows what's going on, and
that kind of makes sense to me, you know?

*For sure. Was there anyone else in your family that encouraged making art, or the
act of being creative?*

I got along with my grandfather really well, and he made art fun. He wasn't really
an artist to start—he worked in a factory, and then he went to World War II, and
then went back to a factory job until he retired. I think he tried to take some
classes at the college near his house and they were full, so what my grandmother
says is that he liked looking at girls so he took a figure-drawing class... he was
kind of, like, that old dude at the college. So when I would go to visit him for
the weekend, he would bring me to school with him. I would watch him weld things
and he would give me clay to play with and show me how to draw. He opened me up
to the whole thing. I didn't realize that that was what he was doing but now,
looking back at it, I know I was lucky that I was around this person who was
around all this cool shit.

And when you would go back to school after those weekends with your grandfather, was there any kind of encouragement there?

No, school sucked. I hated it. I was just drawing Transformers and shit. I didn't really like school—I don't really feel like I had the greatest education, but I do have to say that at one point in high school, I got involved in an art program where they let us go to the Milwaukee Art Museum for half the day; that was, like, the class. We would go down to the museum, and they had these different instructors that actually worked at the museum, and they would teach us about the art. I took it for one year and I learned so much in that one year... that was, like, the most I learned, other than reading *Huck Finn*. I was like, "OK, that made sense for the school to do that." The rest of high school... well, I don't remember math, I sucked at that shit. Well, I don't really remember if I sucked at it, but it was not interesting. Like, the way it was presented, I was like, "I don't care..." But now I'm interested in math—it's, like, the perfect language to describe reality.

When you took those field trips to the museum as a kid, do you remember a certain artist or artwork that stood out to you?

There was that guy who made the realistic sculptures of people...

Duane Hanson?

Yes. They had a janitor [sculpture], so I would always go and trip out on him... that was one of my favorites, which is weird cause my art is nothing like that. There was also Stanley Landsman's *Walk-In Infinity Chamber*. Those two works always stuck with me. In high school, I spent two weeks drawing probably the most realistic drawing I had ever made up to that point—with just pencil—of a Frederic Remington sculpture of a cowboy on a horse, which is weird, but I spent two weeks staring at that thing and drawing it as best I could. Learning about line weight and stuff like that...

And had you already started skateboarding by this time?

I started skateboarding in fourth grade with my friend's sister. She skated and she taught me how to skate, but I didn't really get it—we would just ride down a hill on a plastic board. And then my parents moved to a new neighborhood, and I remember my dad taking me to what he thought was a comic book store, cause there were Batman T-shirts in the window, but it actually turned out to be a skate shop. By the sixth grade I was super into it, and I remember wanting a real skateboard, like a wide skateboard. I had a skinny plastic board but I wanted a big wooden skateboard. For Christmas the next year, I got a purple Tony Hawk Mini with Gullwing Street Shadow IIIs and red Slime Ball wheels.

I feel like for a young person, their first skateboard is equivalent to buying your first house. It's your first major investment at the time, and it represents who you are. Maybe it's not your dream skateboard, but it has to define you in some way. The board, trucks, and wheels all have to be right, which is where I believe the beginning of one's personal style and self-discovery starts. Back then, if you saw someone wearing Vans sneakers, chances are they skateboarded...

Yeah, now everyone skateboards anyway, so it doesn't matter, but back then you were part of something that no one else was part of, so that's cool. I don't think I wanted to play soccer anymore after discovering skateboarding. I was like, "I'm not that good anyway."

Another interesting thing about skateboarding back then is that there was no racism or class system—it was as if everyone was at the bottom of society if you were a skateboarder, no matter where you were from, what you had, or even if you were any good or not. It was just you and a crew, if you were lucky enough to have enough friends to call a crew. Were you a solitary skater or did you have a crew that you would roll around with?

I kind of skated by myself. That was my shit. There was a school down the street
from my house and I would just hang out and skate this little bank—that was the
best. Now, it's like, I still love skateboarding, but I don't want anyone to
see me doing it. And I live in a city, so there isn't really a chance for me to
just skate by myself, but back then I didn't care, or no one was looking, so it
didn't matter.

When did you leave Milwaukee?

In 1997, two years after I graduated high school. I went to San Francisco and
never left. I went to skate, but as I got out here I realized that people were
killing it so much harder than me and I was never going to be that good. I don't
even know what I was thinking, but I just thought it looked way more fun to
skate in San Francisco than in Milwaukee. But then I got here and I was like,
"Oh, the people skating out here aren't kidding around," and I would never be
on that level.

Was there a lot of shit-talking and vibing going on in SF at the time?

I think it was a real wake-up call for me to realize that not everyone who skateboarded was going to be my friend, and I'm alright with that now, but when I first
moved here I was like, "Wow." I still remember all the people who were cool, and
I remember the guys who were dicks, which sucked because I used to look up to
them, but then you meet them in real life and they turn out to be dicks.

*Which is weird because professional skateboarders are only famous within skate-
boarding; they're not like other athletes.*

And you can meet the people you looked up to... it's not like a basketball
player. Like, you'll never find yourself playing basketball with a famous basketball player, but if you skate you can end up at the same skate spot with someone
you looked up to.

Did you have any fan-outs or freak-outs when you first arrived in San Francisco?

To me it was such a different place... it was a city. People don't really think of
San Francisco as a city-city, but where I came from it was a city. There was tons
of graffiti going on, which I was super interested in, and I met a lot of my friends
here. It was, like, Brad [Staba], Brian [Anderson], Tony [Cox], and myself. I was,
like, super blown away, like, "These guys are actually cool people." So yeah, I
don't know if I fanned out—I fanned out on the city. I was happy to be here, and
I didn't want to leave.

*Were you checking the art scene at the same time? Skateboarding and the art scene
in San Francisco seemed to kind of go hand and hand at the time.*

Oh yeah. I realized I wasn't going to kill at skating, like, the minute I got
here, like, I was not that dude. So I applied to the art school here and I got
in, and I went there for a year and a half and then I quit. I knew that that
wasn't exactly for me either because, while it was cool, I couldn't really afford
it. Also, I was like, "You don't have to go to school to make shit—you can just
make shit."

*Did you feel like the art school was trying to push you in a certain kind of
direction or teach you "how" to make art?*

I wish I had taken better advantage of the resources I had at my fingertips, but
at that point in my life I still wanted to skateboard every day, and I was starting to experiment with drugs and shit, and was like, "Oh, this is this whole
other world that I'm fascinated by." There was a lot of that in San Francisco at
that time—that was, like, a whole wormhole for me too. I wish I had taken more
advantage of having access to a printing press and forced myself to learn things
like that, you know? But I didn't do that, I just went to school, smoked weed
on the roof, tripped out after school with people... and then realized I didn't
really want to be in school.

Oh yeah, there were two—I can't remember their names right now, but they were into what I was doing, and of course, I was like, "If you are paying attention to me, then I will pay attention to you," which I guess is a good teacher. Because I would go to their classes; other classes, I would find ways to not go. You know, I was falling into debt and working at a smoothie place, and all I really wanted to do was hang out with my friends and skateboard. I don't really think I have the best discipline towards making art, like other people who, like, make a painting every day... I was drawing and writing every day or some shit like that, but I wasn't trying to be head of the class.

What about other artists in and around the Bay Area? Were you drawn to any specific scene or artist that was happening at that time?

When I first moved to SF, there was the Mission School group of artists that were super heavy. I was super into that stuff, and this was happening right outside my door, like I would walk outside my door and see a Barry McGee tag or Chris Johanson tags. Lo and behold, I realize there is an art gallery under my house that I didn't even know about, and they're having shows, and I walk out my door and Ed Templeton is there and shit. I'm like, "Whoa, that's a skater and he makes art—there's a whole world here."

Would you say that the Mission School was one of the last great movements in SF before the influx of money?

I don't know, man, but those were the people I looked up to who were making things I wanted to see. They came out of the same kind of world that involved skateboarding and graffiti, so I felt that connection and wanted to be part of that, but I was too young and still figuring shit out.

So do you remember when you started putting your work out into the world? Like your earliest group shows or maybe your first solo show?

People would ask me to be involved in stuff, like, a piece in a show here, a piece in a show there. But none of them were very serious. I think the first time I really had an art show it was in a gallery called Lake Gallery, which was connected to a store that sold equipment to grow weed... a hydroponic store. Mat O'Brien worked there, it was cool, and I had my friend's band play there—they were called Blasted Canyon; I don't think they're around anymore—but it was fun, it was a good night. That was my first art show. My second art show was with Erik Foss's Fuse Gallery with Derrick Snodgrass—it was a two-person show. And then my third show was at your gallery, Home Alone 2, but before all that I think I had a piece in a skate-boarder art show at a hair salon here, and I remember that Brian Anderson bought my piece. He was the first person who bought my art, and I was like, "Shit, one of my favorite skateboarders just bought my piece." That made me feel like I was doing OK.

Was it a feeling of being respected by one of the people you looked up to, or being considered a peer instead of a fan? That is a pretty heavy feeling.

Oh yeah, I was so stoked, I was like, "It's Brian Anderson!" And now he's, like, one of my good friends. It's funny how it all worked out.

Do you still find it uncomfortable to go to openings and put not only your art but yourself out there?

Yeah, I still feel uncomfortable at openings, so I tend to probably drink too much alcohol just to fit in... and it's weird to sell art—it's a trip. Yeah, it's weird, but I feel lucky that people are interested enough to spend money on some shit I made smoking weed.

So now that you have had a few shows and are about to release your second book, do you feel more comfortable/confident being in the art world and being a part of the contemporary art conversation?

I don't know if I feel more confident. I still am scared to show people the new stuff I have been working on, but I don't want to be stuck doing the same shit all the time... I have these big fears when I see other artists making the same shit they made ten years ago. I don't want to get caught up in that.

That being said, how do you think your practice has evolved?

Well, like, my first show with you at Home Alone 2, that show was kind of easy to make, because I was already making that kind of work. But then my second show with you, at Viewing Room, that was actually kind of hard for me, and I don't know if it was a good show or not. But I kind of taught myself how to paint for that show, and I'm not saying I'm a great painter or anything like that, but I taught myself how to do things I didn't know how to do. Now I'm trying to step off of that and still grow.

So now with a few shows and two books under your belt, are you still hesitant to play the art-world game... aka, market yourself? Do you find the real world strange enough that you don't want to even begin to think about the art world in terms of where you want to be, what it means to be happy and/or successful as an artist?

I don't know. I don't really know how to navigate the art world so well, but at the same time I think that I figured out something within it where people will buy my stuff. I just like making stuff, so I'm still going to do it and don't really plan on ever not doing it. Yeah, it is a marketing world and I'm horrible at that, but I feel lucky that I have friends that are digging my stuff and buy it.

And how do you approach giving away work as opposed to selling it? Because in the uptight art world that's a big no-no, but I've always championed it. Well, not giving it away, but trading... I honestly think money can corrupt what an artist is doing and can drive wedges between friendships because of status and competitiveness, especially in the age of the Internet, where the information is there if you want it.

I'd rather give something away than sell it. If someone really wants something of mine then they don't need to give me anything for it—if they're my friend they've already given me so much.

How do you feel the economy and atmosphere in San Francisco are changing the artistic landscape and output? Is it a losing battle? Because it is not cheap anymore, that's for sure.

No, it's not cheap, but I'm lucky enough to have fairly cheap rent. I am not a person who buys stuff, so I am happy that I can have rent money, money to eat food, and I am just starting to make enough money that I can travel, which is something I never got to do when I was younger and I love it—even though I've only been to Argentina and Mexico, and I'm like, "Wow, I can't wait to go somewhere else." I love it. Traveling is probably the funnest thing I've ever done in my life. Suddenly I've realized that I've never really traveled, but I've taken a lot of drug trips, so I am starting to understand the idea of a trip. Like, "Oh yeah, I get it... it's a trip." Like, I went to Mexico and I got sick and I had a hard time, but when I got back, I was like, "That was the shit, that was so fun, I can't believe how much fun that was," but I was miserable the whole time, but I was so stoked that it happened.

So speaking of trips, let's talk for a sec about your relationship to LSD and DMT, because outside of those two drugs I wouldn't consider you much of a druggy. Are you comfortable talking about that?

Oh yeah, I'm cool talking about drugs. I've taken a lot of acid and I appreciate it, but I don't really feel the need for me to do it like I used to anymore. I went through a phase where I ate a lot of acid and I feel I learned a lot of things from it. Same with DMT. Again, I was lucky enough to be hooked up with a decent amount of DMT at one point and I smoked my way through it. I feel lucky— I don't have anything negative to say about those two drugs at all.

Say at some point you do get priced out of San Francisco—is there somewhere else you'd like to live?

Well, honestly, I think in northern California, near Humboldt, maybe Arcata. I'd like that; I really like it up there. When I first moved to California, one of the first things that blew my mind was the first time I saw an actual redwood tree. I was like, "Wow, this is some prehistoric shit." And that feeling has never left me. I was just up in Humboldt a couple of weeks ago, and even though I came home and found ticks all over me and shit, I still thought that place rules. I can't be upset up there, and there's less people. When I was younger, I wanted to be around people all the time, but now that I'm getting older, it kind of doesn't matter to me. I'm kind of a weirdo anyway and prefer to talk to myself. It's nice up there, the trees are pretty, the air is fresh and I can feel it.

Do you feel like there's something bigger than ourselves out there?

I'm kind of obsessed with what happens when we're done here, and I think that it's kind of normal for everyone to wonder what happens when we die. Maybe because I did a certain amount of psychedelics I have tapped into that more than some people, but I don't think it's a bad thing. It's scary for sure but that's part of it. Part of our deal. We get to be here, and then we get to not be here, and that makes me feel like, "Well, since you're here, you should make the most of your time here." You do what's best for you, and on top of that you try to be a good person with everyone you come in contact with. I'm cool with that.

What would you like to happen to your body once you've passed away? I can't imagine you'd like any type of celebration or ceremony like a funeral with a headstone and all that.

I don't know man, I don't think I'd want a headstone... Maybe if they could plant a tree in my stomach and have that grow out of my body because of the nutrients or whatever. Because we are not our bodies—like, I don't feel of my body... Sure, we're stuck in our bodies, but I am not my body, you know?

THIS IS NOT ABOUT DRUGS
THIS IS NOT ABOUT DRUGS
THIS IS NOT ABOUT DRUGS
THIS IS NOT ABOUT DRUGS
THE LAST TIME
WE MET WE BOTH
FORGOT ABOUT THE
AND NOT AGAIN
REMEMBERED
LAST TIME
WE BOTH FORGOT
GOOD TO SEE YOU

THANK YOU THANK YOU THANK YOU THANK YOU
MEGAN GAGE · KEVIN · LINDA ROBERTS · MICHAEL ROBERTS
ALLEGRA ROBERTS · MELINDA ROBERTS · CHRIS LEE · WM
JESSE POLLOCK · LEO FITZ PATRICK · HAMILTON MORRIS
MARK IOSIFESCU · BRYAN CIPOLLA · DENNIS MCGRATH
ANDRÉS SANTO DOMINGO · KEITH ABRAHAMSSON · LSD
TONY COX · WILL WELCH · MAT MCGRATH · DMT
RYAN GARSHELL · DONOVAN QUINN · CHRIS HAFNER
BRIAN ANDERSON · BRAD STABA · ERIK FOSS · RON MORELLI
TIM COHEN · MAT OBRIEN · MYLA DALBESIO · PETE LENORD
STEVE VASY · MARJORIE VASY · STEPHANI DALBESIO · CLYDE
FRED GUERRERO · DAVID SOUTHCOMBE · NEAL SHAW · WIZARD
AARON POLANSKY · LUCUS JORDAN · DAVE SADLER · ADAM KIEDROWSKI
LANE · ERIC BERZONIK · EASE · SEVE · DESA · NEUS · SEB · 2FER
POOH BEAR · FRANK LATINA · BRIAN WEBB · TOM NOBEL
TERESE REYES · GREG GARDNER · CHAD COLLINS · BEN CHASNY
ROGER GASTMAN · ANDRES GUERRERO · KEN GOTO · TIM DALY
DAVE BONK · DARREN YOUNG · BOB LINDER · JEANINE FENTON
WEST RUBINSTEIN · GABE ROSNER · KAWS · DAN WOLFE
LEAH MARTIN · KEVIN WITTIG · SHAYDE SARTIN · BIGANT ·
TINO RAZO · VANESSA VANWALRAVEN · DAN JOHNSON · MATT BEACH
FAYTHE LEVINE · HEATHER WOJNER · JOHN MCGUIRE · NITE OWL
SCOTT OGDEN · JONNINE STANDISH · JOHN MOTTA · ELLIOT
ALICIA MCCARTHY · JOE GRILLO · FOREST · TAHITI PEHRSON
NATE LOWMAN · JEREMY SHOCKLEY · TONY VITELLO ·
STEVE REE · DERRICK SNODGRASS · THEO KENNEDY · ARCHIE MCKAY
TOM KENNEDY · ZACH MEXICO · TODD JORDAN · JERRY HSU
HUNTER MURAIRA · JACK HANLEY · JOHN DWYER · YASHA WALLIN
RICHARD TOOMER · DAN SMITH · PETER SUTHERLAND · BRIAN PENROD
BRIAN DEGRAW · STEPHEN MCCLINTOCK · ANDREW SCHOULTZ
GRACE SRINIVASIAH · CHLOE MARATTA · CASEY WHALEN
ANDY CABIC · NATHAN BURAZER · AARON HANSEN
LUCY PATINO · MAXINE ELM · BRETT WILDE · MUSHROOMS